THE LAWYER'S GUIDE TO
Microsoft®
WORD 2007

Ben M. Schorr

ABA Law Practice Management Section
MARKETING • MANAGEMENT • TECHNOLOGY • FINANCE

Library of Congress Cataloging-in-Publication Data
The Lawyer's Guide to Microsoft Word 2007. Ben M. Schorr: Library of Congress Cataloging-in-Publication Data is on file.

10 Digit ISBN: 1-60442-761-2
13 Digit ISBN: 978-1-60442-761-5

12 11 10 09   5 4 3 2 1

Discounts are available for books ordered in bulk. Special consideration is given to state bars, CLE programs, and other bar-related organizations. Inquire at Book Publishing, American Bar Association, 321 N. Clark Street, Chicago, Illinois 60654.

www.ababooks.org

Dedication

To my parents Morris and Sharon Schorr. You've always been there for me when I needed it and helped make me the man I am today.

Contents

Chapter 5
Stuff Lawyers Use   85

Chapter 6
Collaboration   97

Chapter 7
Working with Data   **125**

Chapter 8
Automating Word   **137**

Chapter 9
Managing and Maintaining Word 2007   **151**

Chapter 10
Troubleshooting   **177**

Chapter 11
Mistakes Lawyers Make with Microsoft Word   **187**

Chapter 12
Tricks to Impress Your Law School Classmates With   199

Chapter 13
Keyboard Shortcuts   213

Acknowledgments

I'd like to give some special recognition to the following people:

At Microsoft, Jensen Harris, Jamie Sloan, Ed Hickey, and the Microsoft Word team in Redmond for being terrific, accessible, and giving so much of their time to help me understand how the product works.

Diane Sherman and Rhonda Steinhoff for their great feedback.

Beth Melton, Stephanie Krieger, and Shauna Kelly . . . great ladies who've forgotten more about Microsoft Word than most people will ever know.

John, Kim and Justin Steffey for keeping me laughing on those rare times I wasn't nose down trying to get this written.

My business partner, Matti Raihala, and the rest of the Roland Schorr and Tower team for keeping things running smoothly so I could spend all this time banging out yet another book.

Sharon Nelson and John Simek for their support and friendship. Sharon's unending faith and enthusiasm and John's steady whipcracking are what got me to finish this book and only be six months late.

And last, but most definitely not least, to my beautiful Carrie Rae, who came along at exactly the right time and brought with her hope and happiness. Thank you for giving me a new reason to achieve.

About the Author

Ben M. Schorr is a technologist and Chief Executive Officer for Roland Schorr & Tower, a professional consulting firm headquartered in Honolulu, Hawaii. In that capacity he consults with a wide variety of organizations including many law firms. He is frequently sought as a writer, teacher, and speaker for groups as diverse as the Hawaii Visitor and Convention Bureau and the American Bar Association. More than eleven years ago Microsoft named Mr. Schorr as an MVP in their Outlook product group, and he has been supporting Outlook, Exchange, and most recently OneNote ever since. Prior to cofounding Roland Schorr, he was the Director of Information Services for Damon Key Leong Kupchak Hastert, a large Honolulu law firm, for almost eight years.

Mr. Schorr was a contributing author for *Using Microsoft Office 2000* by Que Publishing and has been a technical editor or contributor on a number of other books over the years. For several years, he was half of the "Ask the Exchange Pros" team for Windows Server System magazine. He is the author of *The Lawyer's Guide to Microsoft Outlook 2007*, published by the American Bar Association (2008).

In October of 2005, Mr. Schorr was named by the Pacific Technology Foundation as one of the Top 50 Technology Leaders in Hawaii. He is a member of the Institute of Electrical and Electronics Engineers' (IEEE) Computer Society, the American Bar Association, and the United States Naval Institute. In his free time, Mr. Schorr enjoys coaching football, running marathons, reading, playing softball, and kayaking in the ocean, and he has completed the Tinman triathlon three times. His dog is not impressed. You can reach him at bens@rolandschorr.com.

Introduction 1

Microsoft Word is one of the most venerable elements of the Microsoft Office suite—there are few applications more fundamental than putting words on paper.

As always, I began this project by asking myself the key question:

What is my message? What do I want the readers to get out of this book and how can I make it truly compelling and useful?

OK, so maybe that's three questions. Anyhow, the answers to these questions are something I spent a lot of time thinking about and considering. The answer is pretty clear: Most lawyers use Word and few of them get everything they can from it. With this book, I want to help you get the most out of Microsoft Word in order to make you more effective, more efficient, and more successful. I'm hoping you find this book to be useful, powerful, and maybe even a little enjoyable. I'm also hoping this book finds its way into the hands of legal assistants and paralegals—each of whom also spend a great deal of their time in Microsoft Word and will hopefully get some benefit from reading this.

To accomplish my goals, I'm going to tell you about Word through my eyes. Through the eyes of a 10-year veteran of Microsoft Word who is also a 20-year veteran of law office technology. I'm hoping that you'll keep turning the pages because every new page will bring a series of moments. "Gee whiz" moments, "Holy cow!" moments, and

"Light Bulb" moments. Hopefully, you'll put this book down repeatedly as you rush to your computer to try that new trick. If this book ends up on your desk with a colorful array of sticky notes protruding from the pages, I'll know I've succeeded.

What's So Special About Word Processing?

We all use Word and it seems like typing, saving and printing are relatively simple tasks. So, why do you need a book to explain how to do it? Because the documents we create are complex and important—your law practice depends, to some degree, upon the quality of the documents you produce and the efficiency with which you can produce them. In this book, I'm going to try and help you do it more productively, more efficiently, and more enjoyably. And since this is a book aimed at lawyers and law firms, I'm going to skim over the features I don't think are very useful to lawyers and try to focus more on those tools that you actually use. For example, I don't think most lawyers care much about SmartArt, so I won't waste a lot of time on it in here. I could easily write 700 pages on Microsoft Word 2007 if I tried to cover every feature and option in depth. I'll save your time (and mine) and try to keep my emphasis on those features and capabilities that will matter to law firms. If you really want a large comprehensive work on Microsoft Word 2007, there are some excellent general books on the market—anything with Beth Melton or Stephanie Krieger's name on it is undoubtedly worth reading if that's what you're after.

Those Who Love Software or the Law Should Not Watch Either Being Made

I thought an exploration of how the Office 2007 suite was made would be enlightening here. The story really begins with Office 2003. When you installed Office 2003 a funny little icon was added to the system tray (down on the task bar, next to the clock) where it sat, mysteriously staring at you. Eventually you clicked on it and when you did a dialog box was presented that offered to let you opt-in to something called the "Customer Experience Improvement Program." The Customer Experience Improvement Program (CEIP) sends a lot of non-identifiable data back to

> **"** Designing Microsoft Office is like ordering pizza for 400 million people.
> —*Steven Sinofsky, Microsoft* **"**

Microsoft about how you actually use their software. Don't worry, it doesn't send any actual documents or e-mail addresses or anything like that. Instead it's primarily concerned with *how* you use the software—what buttons you click, how many documents

> ▼
>
> The most commonly clicked toolbar button in Microsoft Word 2003, and it's not even close, is "Paste." Followed, in order by "Save," "Copy," "Undo," and "Bold."

you have open, how many subfolders you create, and how long you spend in each program (that's how we know that Outlook stays open longer than any other Office application). The reason for this data (known internally at Microsoft as "SQM" or "Service Quality Monitoring" data) is entirely focused on making the next version of Microsoft Office by gathering historical usage data.

Prior to the CEIP, boxes of dry erase markers were used in brainstorming sessions. Huge quantities of Chinese food were consumed behind one-way mirrors in the usability labs, and survey after survey after survey were analyzed all in the name of trying to figure out how users actually used the products. The results of all of that work became Office XP, the immediate predecessor to Office 2003. Clearly a better way was needed and the CEIP is it. Microsoft receives a mind boggling volume of data from the CEIP. In fact, as of April 2006 they had received more than 1.3 billion sessions of Office 2003 usage. That data taught a lot of interesting, useful, and surprising lessons and was of tremendous help in designing Microsoft Office 2007. As a result, Office 2007 is the first version of Office that was really built with volumes of direct feedback from real end-users in real-life situations.

Those results can be seen in several areas. Most notably in the user interface (UI), where the old "File, Edit, View" menu structure has been replaced with what is called "The Ribbon." (See Figure 1.1.) When you first fire up Outlook 2007 (not Word 2007) you're going to wonder what I'm talking about because the File, Edit, View menu is still clearly in evidence. Click the button to start a new Outlook Mail item, then you'll see what I mean. The ribbon is intended to be a more discoverable interface where every feature in the product is easy to find and use and was developed using CEIP data. CEIP data was also used to find out what desirable features—features that users asked for—were rarely used, indicating that they were too hard to find.

FIGURE 1.1

An indicator that a new UI for Office was needed after four of the top 10 requests received from Word 2003 users were for features already in the product. People just didn't know how to find them! According to Jensen Harris, Group Program Manager for the Microsoft Office User Experience Team (which means he's the lead dog on the team that designed the new UI), features like adding a watermark to Word documents were so hard to find that a lot of users asked how to do it or didn't realize you could. With Office 2007, the feature is prominently located on the "Page Layout" tab and Jensen has had a lot of users comment on what a "great new feature" that is.

And Now, by Popular Demand . . .

Since you've probably already bought Word 2007 (seeing as how you're reading a book on it), I'm not going to try and sell you on why you should go get it. Let me just briefly highlight some of the key new features of Word 2007 that lawyers are going to love. I'll explain them in more detail later in the book, but here's the teaser. . .

1. The Ribbon
2. Live Gallery Preview
3. The Floating Toolbar
4. New File Format: Open XML
5. New Compare Documents
6. Metadata Checking and Cleanup
7. Digital Signatures
8. Save to PDF natively (sort of)
9. Building Blocks

There are a lot more new features that will really excite your consultant or IT person but might be a tad esoteric for you. I'll mention them throughout the book, but mostly I want to focus on the features and tools that you're really going to use and care about in your daily practice.

So, let's get right into it. Chapter 2—A Quick Tour.

A Quick Tour 2

Word 2007 is quite a bit different from previous versions of Word in that it features the new Fluent interface, which is most prominently evident in the "Ribbon" at the top of the screen. (See Figure 2.1.) This may be a bit of a shock to users who are used to the old "File | Edit | View" menu structure. So while this chapter is titled "A Quick Tour," the tour may not be all that quick after all. You may want to settle in with the refreshing beverage of your choice as we dig into the new interface. We're not going to spend a lot of time explaining the features here—the idea is that you come out of this chapter feeling comfortable with the interface and feeling like you know where to find everything you need. In subsequent chapters, we'll go into how you use what you need.

FIGURE 2.1

The first element I want to talk about is the Office button located at the top left.

When you first install Office 2007, this button will pulse at you slowly until you click it. That's the Office team's way of getting you to click on it so that you can see what's located beneath it. So let's not disappoint them. . .

> ▼
> The Office Button is sometimes humorously referred to as the "Pizza Button."

The Office Button

When you click on the Office button, the Word menu will open. This is vaguely similar to what you used to find when you clicked the File menu in Word. Most notably the buttons to create a new document, open an existing document, save or save as the current document, print and so forth are all on this menu.

Additionally, you'll find the "Most Recently Used" (MRU) list under the Office button as you can see in Figure 2.2. Want to see more (or fewer) documents on that list? I'll tell you how in Chapter 9.

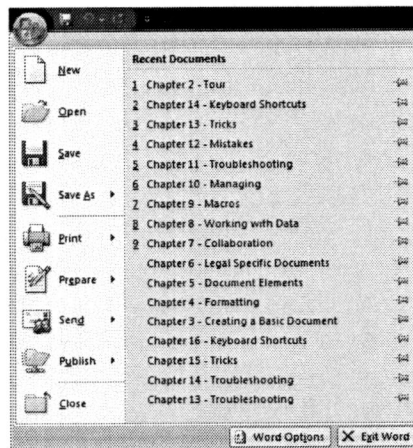

FIGURE 2.2

Quick Access Toolbar

On the Word 2007 title bar you'll find the Quick Access Toolbar (QAT), which was added as a concession to those who wanted to retain some customizability to the interface. You can add or remove commands that you use often from the QAT. In Figure 2.3, you might notice that I've added the "Insert Text Box" button to the QAT. To add something to the QAT, click the downward chevron button immediately to the right of the QAT. You can add a few standard elements (like "Save") to the QAT or click the "More Commands" option to select from a list of every command or macro in the program. With some time and patience, you

FIGURE 2.3

can actually build out the QAT to be a powerful personalized toolbar of commands.

There are two other commands on the Customize Quick Access Toolbar menu (see Figure 2.4) that you will want to get to know:

1. Show Below the Ribbon. This will, not surprisingly, move the Quick Access Toolbar to a line of its own at the bottom of the ribbon. This gives you a lot more space to work with, if you're adding a lot of commands to the QAT, and also reduces the distance you have to move your mouse to get to the QAT by an inch or two. Word 2007, you'll find, has made a few efforts to reduce the amount of mileage you put on your mouse to reach your commonly used commands.

2. Minimize the Ribbon. One of the first things people say when they first see the ribbon is "Wow, that takes up a lot of screen." Well, if you're one of those users who would like to reclaim some of your screen real estate, then you can minimize the ribbon to a single line (much like the old menus), which tucks it nicely out of the way. You can also minimize (or restore) the ribbon by right-clicking any empty area on the ribbon or QAT and selecting "Minimize the Ribbon" on the resultant context menu.

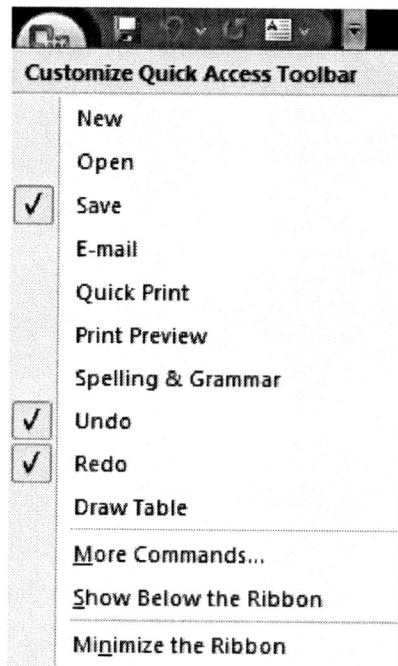

FIGURE 2.4

The Ribbon

The most noticeable difference in Word 2007 is the Ribbon (see Figure 2.5). The Ribbon is the name for the new interface at the top of the screen where all of the program commands are found.

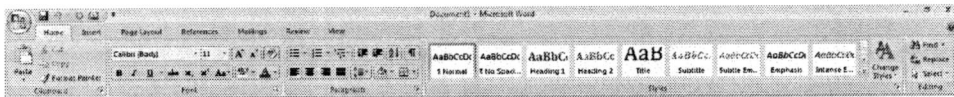

FIGURE 2.5

The key elements of the Ribbon are the Office Quick Access Toolbar and a series of Ribbon tabs that contain various commands. The Ribbon is far less customizable or variable than the old menu structure was. It will change a bit if certain document elements are selected on screen, but otherwise it will, by design, remain basically the same. An example of when it will change a bit is when you add a table to your document. In that case, a couple of extra tabs, related to tables, will be added to the Ribbon. (We'll talk more about Tables in Chapter 4.) The tabs on the ribbon are made up of groups, which collect the commands.

Some of the groups have a tiny "button" to the right of the group name that is called a Dialog Launcher. Clicking that dialog launcher opens a larger dialog box containing more commands for working with that family of commands. We'll spend time with the dialog launchers as we go thru the book.

One thing to keep in mind with the Ribbon is that it will adapt a bit depending upon the size of your Window and your screen resolution. If you don't have Word running full-screen and you drag and drop the Word window wider and narrower, you'll notice that the Ribbon changes a bit as you go so that the various groups compress and expand to fit the available space.

> 66
> I don't know the key to success, but the key to failure is trying to please everybody.
> —*Bill Cosby*
> 99

To be fair, not all users like the Ribbon. Some have such a long history with the old menu structure that the change to the Ribbon is uncomfortable. Some have long-engrained habits that they'll have to break and some simply don't like it. It is a significant change from the old way. On balance, however, most users do seem to like it, at least eventually. I've heard from a number of users who didn't care for it initially, but after spending some time with it have grown to appreciate it.

So, let's introduce you to the ribbon and see if you don't hit it off. . .

The Home Tab

The Home tab (seen on the previous page in Figure 2.5) on the Ribbon is the default tab and contains the most commonly used editing commands.

Clipboard

At the far left side, you can see the clipboard commands such as "Paste," which we've learned was the most commonly clicked on toolbar button in Word 2003.

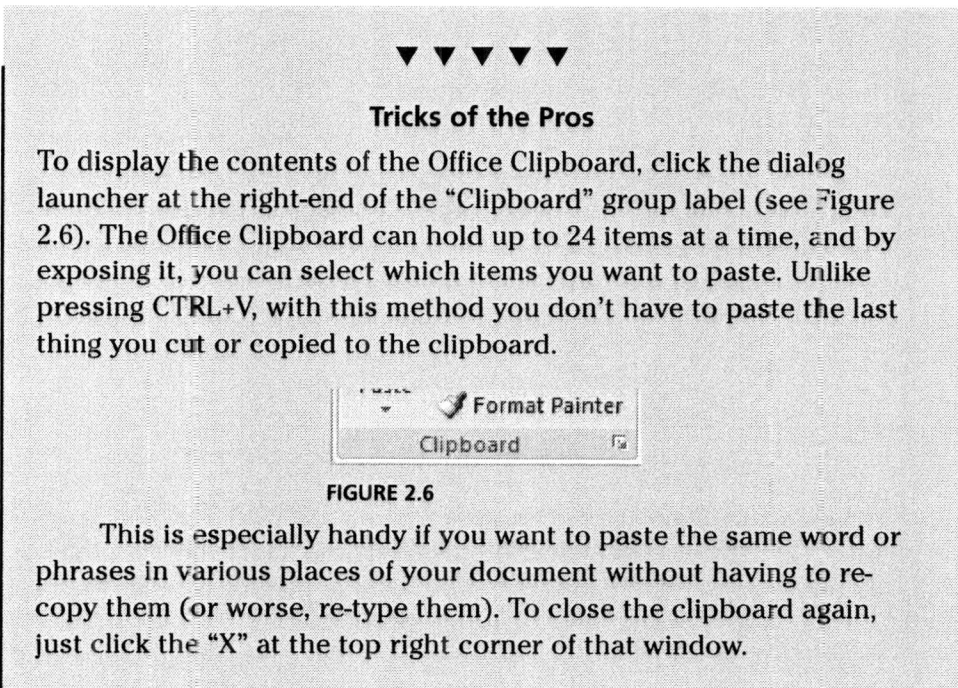

▼ ▼ ▼ ▼ ▼

Tricks of the Pros

To display the contents of the Office Clipboard, click the dialog launcher at the right-end of the "Clipboard" group label (see Figure 2.6). The Office Clipboard can hold up to 24 items at a time, and by exposing it, you can select which items you want to paste. Unlike pressing CTRL+V, with this method you don't have to paste the last thing you cut or copied to the clipboard.

FIGURE 2.6

This is especially handy if you want to paste the same word or phrases in various places of your document without having to re-copy them (or worse, re-type them). To close the clipboard again, just click the "X" at the top right corner of that window.

Font

Next to the Clipboard group you'll find the set of Font commands that include the font (such as "Times New Roman"), font size, font color, highlighting, change case, and others.

The fonts listed in your document (Times New Roman, Arial, etc.) depend entirely upon the fonts supported by your current printer. Change the default printer for the document or system and the list of fonts may change slightly—though most modern printers support a fairly common set of fonts.

One feature I find very useful is the "Change Case" feature. Occasionally I'll type something, especially a section heading, which I want to have in "Capitalize the First Letter of Each Word" format. In the past, you might have had to retype the sentence or at least the first letter of each word. Now just select the sentence, click the Change Case button and select that option. Word takes care of the rest. This is one of those great "new features" that has been in Word forever, but many users are just now discovering thanks to the Ribbon.

Paragraph

Next to the Font group you'll find the Paragraph group that contains buttons for bullets, numbering, justification, fill color, line spacing, borders, sorting, and other features. We'll talk more about most of these options in Chapter 4.

Notice that the Paragraph group does have a dialog launcher at the bottom right corner. Clicking it will fire up the Paragraph dialog box you see in Figure 2.7. In that dialog box, you can do some tricky things with indentation, line and page breaks (notice the tabs at the top of the dialog?), line spacing, and more.

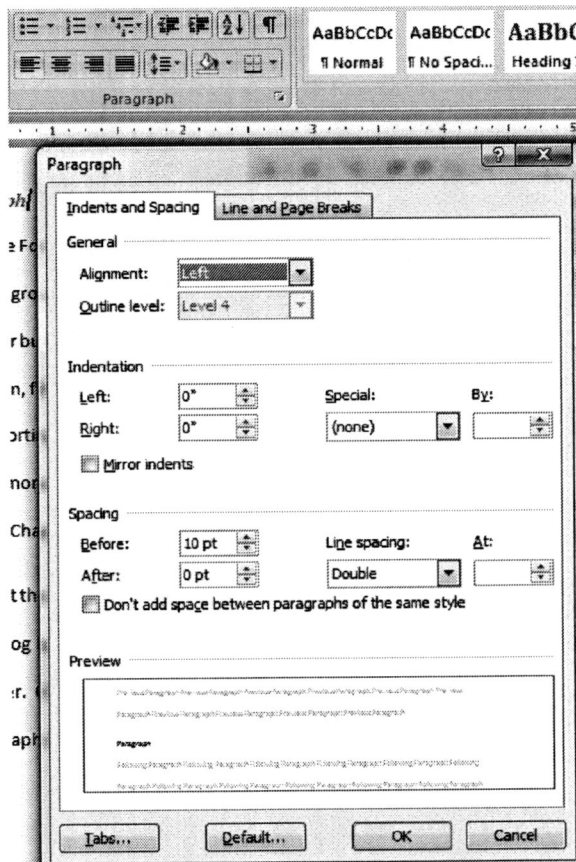

FIGURE 2.7

I want to call your attention to is the Tabs button, which launches the dialog box you see in Figure 2.8 below. This lets you customize your tab stops quite easily. You can create/customize tab stops on the ruler, but I've found that some people have trouble getting the tabs just the way they want them using only the ruler, so this dialog box may be a little more intuitive for you. We'll talk about this in more detail in Chapter 4.

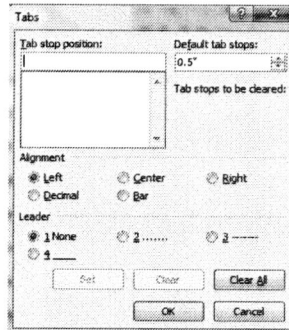

FIGURE 2.8

Styles

The next group in the Home tab contains the Styles Galleries, which lets you apply a style to selected text. It's also easy to modify or create new styles from this part of the Ribbon. Like most of the things on the Home tab, we'll be spending some time with Styles in Chapter 4. This is a nice example, however, of the new Galleries feature in Word 2007 that gives you WYSIWYWGIYCT (What You See Is What You Will Get If You Click This) capabilities. Despite my doubts that the acronym will catch on, the feature certainly will. If you select some text in your document, then simply hover your mouse over one of the elements in the gallery, such as "Heading 3" for example, the text changes temporarily to show you what it will look like if you click. That eliminates the trial and error of the old days; now you can quickly "try" a bunch of different formats.

Editing

Finally, the curiously named "Editing" group contains three buttons: Find, Replace, and Select. Find and Replace both do essentially similar things: pop up the Find & Replace dialog box. The only difference is which tab it opens to. I've clicked "Find" to get to what you see in Figure 2.9, but clicking "Replace" would open the same dialog box and take you to the Replace tab. Find and replace are pretty handy tools when you're working with large documents. "Find" lets you search your document for instances of specific text—a witness name, for example. "Replace" lets you replace

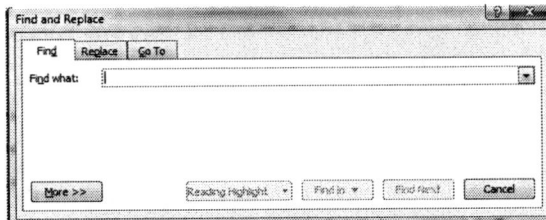

FIGURE 2.9

something with something else—if you just realized you've been misspelling your client's name throughout the entire document, it's fast and easy to change the 37 instances of "Smith" to "Smyth."

The Select tool is one of the most underused tools in Word and, honestly, for good reason. Of its three capabilities, two of them are much easier to do other ways. Select All is most easily done by just pressing CTRL+A on the keyboard. Select Object is awkward to do with the Select tool; easier just by clicking on the object with your mouse.

The one option in the Select tool that I find marginally useful is the ability to select all text with a similar formatting. Of course, if you're using Styles (as you should be) then you don't really need to do that with the Select tool either. Moving on . . .

The Insert Tab

Next up is the Insert tab (see Figure 2.10 below).

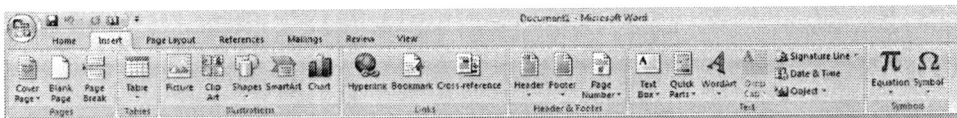

FIGURE 2.10

Pages

The first group you'll find on the Insert tab is the Pages group, which includes the Cover Page gallery that lets you select from a number of pre-created cover page templates or allows you to create your own cover page to save to the gallery.

The second and third buttons in the Pages group are the Blank Page and Page Break buttons, which insert a blank page into your document at the current cursor location. Those of you who've used older versions of Word are probably thinking "Wait, doesn't CTRL+Enter do the same thing?" Yes, it does.

Tables

The next group over on the Insert tab is the little group that could. It has only one button, but it's one button that you will want to remember the location of and that's Table. To use it, click the button to open the Insert Table tool and then just drag your mouse from top left to bottom right to create a table that matches your needs. Everything from 1 x 1 (which you may also know as a "Text Box") to 10 x 8—it's a quick and easy way to create a table that's just the size you need. If you need more, there are ways to do that, which we'll talk about in more detail in Chapter 4.

FIGURE 2.11

Illustrations

The Illustrations group gives you a handful of tools to insert all sorts of pretty pictures. From actual pictures (photos, scans, or other graphics files) to clip art, shapes, SmartArt, or charts.

The Picture tool is pretty self-explanatory. You click it and a dialog box opens that lets you browse your storage devices (hard drives, flash drives, inserted SD cards, CDs, DVDs . . .) for one or more pictures that you might want to insert into your document. This can be handy if you want to include photos of certain exhibits, properties, or pieces of evidence in your document.

ClipArt is basically eye candy—small graphics that just add some color and visual elements to a document. They're great in presentations and probably have a role in marketing materials, but you're not going to use them in your legal documents, so we won't spend a lot of time on them in this book. When you click the Clip Art button, you'll get the search tool you see in Figure 2.12 on the next page. You can search for clip art, photographs, and other media based on keywords, then when you find one you like either double-click it or drag and drop it to insert it in your document. If you use a *lot* of clip art, you can manage "collections" of clip art, download more clipart from the web (including Office Online), and even create your own. Again, handy for the brochures and occasional PowerPoint presentation, but not something lawyers use in Word that often. So, we'll leave it there.

FIGURE 2.12

Unlike the fluffy ClipArt, SmartArt and Charts are both tools that might be useful to you in client communications or to illustrate concrete ideas and principles.

SmartArt lets you create custom graphics like cycle and process diagrams. Not only does it work in Word 2007 but also Excel and PowerPoint as well. I'll give an example of using SmartArt in Chapter 12.

The Chart tool lets you embed a wide variety of charts and graphs into your documents to illustrate comparative data. For instance, showing revenue over time or to graphically show relative ownership in a disputed piece of real estate. If the interface for the tool looks like Excel, that's because it is Excel. And you can embed or link to Excel workbooks and/or charts in your Word documents too. We'll talk about that in Chapter 7.

Links

The next group on the Insert tab is the Links group. This is a deceptively useful set of tools—the first is the Hyperlink tool that lets you insert a hyperlink into your document (see Figure 2.13 below). Most people think

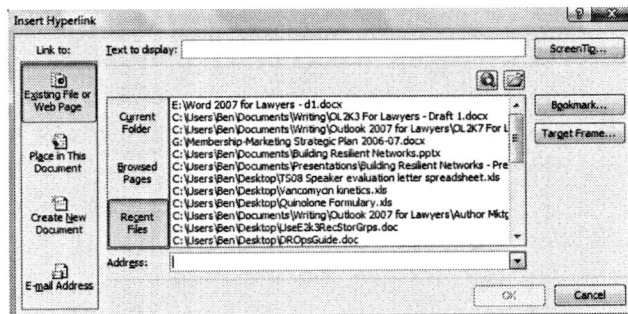

FIGURE 2.13

of this as inserting web links, (i.e., http://www.officeforlawyers.com) but you could also use this to insert a hyperlink to an internal source like a file on your intranet or a link to something else, like a link to a note in OneNote. This feature does make your documents highly interactive, but of course you have to keep the ultimate form of the document in mind. If this is a document that is intended to be printed, then it doesn't do you any good to insert lots of links—they won't translate to paper in any meaningful way.

Also, remember who your audience is . . . if this document is going to stay electronic but be transmitted outside your organization, then it does you no good to create hyperlinks to documents inside your internal systems—the recipients probably won't be able to access those links from their location. This is a mistake I see made a *lot* by the way. I often receive documents from clients that contain dead hyperlinks . . . because the link points at a location on a private network that I can't access.

The next tool in the Links group is one that I use a lot. As you can imagine, I write a lot of long documents (like 200 page books) and I don't usually write them in a single sitting (no matter how many Frappacinos I drink), so I frequently have to save my place and come back to it later. I also don't tend to write books sequentially. Right now I'm writing Chapter 2, but I've already written most of Chapter 12 (it's a good one but wait for it). I can't just press [END] and go to the bottom of the document to pick up where I left off. To make matters even slightly more difficult, I also tend to write multiple chapters at once. Obviously, here I am in Chapter 2, but I've also written some of several other chapters. So how do I quickly get back to where I left off in a particular chapter? Bookmarks.

The Insert Bookmark tool (seen below in Figure 2.14) lets you create a new bookmark at your current location, delete an existing bookmark, or go to a bookmark you've already defined in the document. As you can see in Figure 2.14, I currently have four bookmarks defined. You can have as many as you'd like and sort them either by name or by location. A location sort will place them in the order they appear in the document from

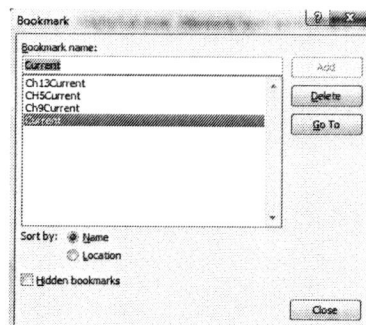

FIGURE 2.14

page 1 forward. The way it works is pretty simple, you click in a spot or select a block of text and then go to the Insert tab of the Ribbon and choose Bookmark (or you can press CTRL+SHIFT+F5 if you're mouse-averse). The Bookmark dialog box will appear and you can type a name for your new bookmark. You can't use spaces or many of the punctuation characters (like hyphens) in your bookmark name but you can use under-scores ("_") to separate words.

Notice the checkbox for Hidden bookmarks? Those are a special case, generally, Word uses them for a variety of purposes—usually with-out you realizing it. One example is the Table of Contents. When you add a Table of Contents to your document and flag an item for inclusion, Word puts a hidden bookmark at that spot so that the hyperlink from the Table of Contents can take you back there when you click it.

The third item in the Links group is the Cross-Reference tool. This lets you build links between text and figures, pages, tables, and so forth. If the table or figure is moved, the cross-reference can be "automatically" updated. I am a little disappointed to have to put "automatically" in quotes, but the reality is that it doesn't quite get automatically updated—you have to initiate the update by pressing F9. To update ALL cross-refer-ences, use CTRL+A to select the entire document, then press F9.

Header & Footer

Next to Links you'll find the Header and Footer group. One of the more straightforward groups, this is where you can add a Header or a . . . wait for it . . . Footer. A header is the section at the top of a page that fre-quently might include the name of the firm, the name of the case, or other title information. The footer is the section at the bottom of each page that might include the date, page number, or other information.

The Header and Footer group contains good examples of one of the new features of Word 2007 known as the galleries. Figure 2.15 shows what happens when you click the drop arrow under Header. You're presented with a fairly long gallery of predefined headers you can choose from—and if you don't like any of the predefined ones, you can just choose "Blank" and then edit it to create your own header. Footer works in much the same way. Clicking the drop arrow opens a large gallery of predefined footers. We'll talk more about Headers and Footers in Chapter 4.

The third feature in the Header & Footer group is Page Number which, when clicked, gives you a number of galleries to view in the follow-ing four different categories:

- Top of Page creates a header for you that contains the page num-ber in a variety of formats.
- Bottom of Page creates a footer that contains the page number.

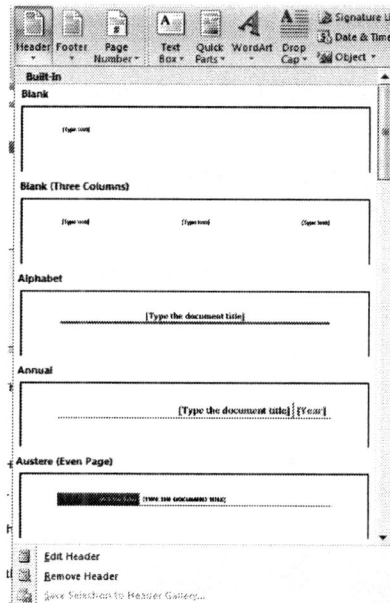

FIGURE 2.15

- Page Margin creates a page number on the left or right side of the page—depending upon the option you choose.
- Current Position will let you insert the page number right where you are on the page.

We'll cover page numbering more in Chapter 4.

Text

The next group you'll find is the Text group. This contains a number of items you can add to your document such as Text Boxes (graphical boxes that contain text), Quick Parts, and others. WordArt lets you create text with very stylish graphics. Drop caps are a stylish way to open a paragraph and are especially useful in newsletters and other marketing materials. Figure 2.16 shows the WordArt gallery.

FIGURE 2.16

QuickParts are where you'll find the Building Blocks Organizer, a *very* useful tool that we'll talk about more extensively in Chapter 8. The other things you'll find in QuickParts are Document Property and Field, which let you automatically populate a document with information like the Author name or various formulas.

There are three more options in the Text group, the first two of which are very useful to lawyers.

Signature Line lets you save and insert a standard signature line for use on letters, contracts and other documents. It can also insert a digital signature for use in electronic documents.

Date and Time is a feature you'll likely use often; it inserts the current date and/or time in a variety of formats (as you can see in Figure 2.17).

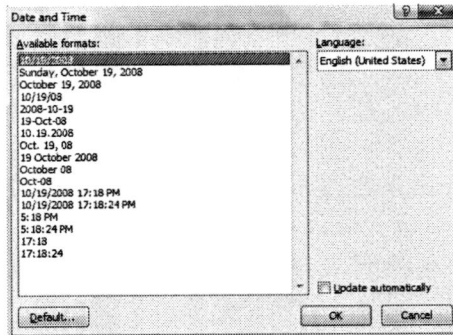

FIGURE 2.17

One option you have with Date and Time is the "Update Automatically" option. If you check this box, Word will automatically update the date and time to the current date/time. This is handy if you're creating a template and want the date to always be today's date. But be careful . . . if you're creating a letter where you want the original date to be persistent, you should leave this unchecked.

The Object feature on the Text group has two options in it, both of which can be very useful for lawyers. The first option is to insert an object and that's how you embed items from other applications, as you can see in Figure 2.18. What you're going to see in this window will vary a bit depending upon what applications you have installed. We'll look at some uses of this feature in Chapter 7 and it might make an appearance in Chapter 12 as well. You can either create a new item from that application or you can insert an item from an existing file.

The other option you'll find if you click the arrow next to the Object button is "Text from File." This is a deceptively helpful feature that will insert all of the text from an existing file. Let's say you have a document on

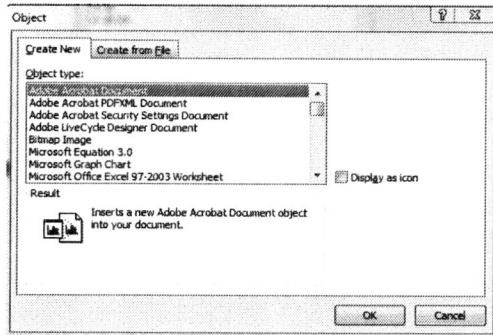

FIGURE 2.18

your hard drive and you want to incorporate all of that text into your document, but you don't want to have to retype it or open that document separately, and do a Copy/Paste. Use Object | Text from File and Word will just insert all of the text from the file you select at the current insertion point. It's a great way to reuse content from other documents. You may know this feature as "Insert File" from previous versions of Word.

Symbols

The last group on the Insert tab is the Symbols group, which contains two commands. The equation button actually launches a gallery that lets you select from a wide selection of items like Pythagorean Theorem, Quadratic Equation, and others. Probably not something lawyers are going to use very often, to be honest, but if you have a kid over the age of 13 they may find it useful in doing their homework. The second command in the group, Symbol, is more useful to lawyers, however. Δ, § and © are among the law-useful symbols you'll find under this command. Note also that if you use a command from the "More Commands" list it, will be added to the initial gallery of symbols so you don't have to click into More Symbols to find it next time.

The Page Layout Tab

The Page Layout tab contains the features and commands that let you control how your page will appear on the printed page. Most notably, things like page margins, paper type, and themes. (See Figure 2.19.)

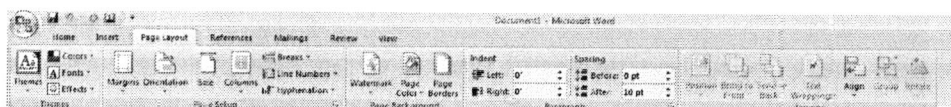

FIGURE 2.19

Themes

The Themes group includes four commands related to the look and feel of your document. The first one is a Themes gallery that lets you select one of many built-in themes, manage the currently applied theme, download additional themes, or even create your own theme.

The next three options are all nicely related to the theme—in fact they are the elements that the theme controls: Colors, Fonts, and Effects. Each of those buttons launches a gallery that lets you set the text colors, available fonts, and graphical effects that will be used in your document.

▼ ▼ ▼ ▼ ▼

What does that mean?

For the most part I think it's pretty rare that lawyers will ever need to tweak those things. The vast majority of your documents are going to be black text on white paper and with a relatively small number of fonts or "effects." The reality is that many of your documents are mandated to a certain look and feel by the court and I don't care how liberal your judge is, he or she probably doesn't want a pink or green font on yellow paper. Accordingly, we're not going to spend much time on Themes in this book.

Page Setup

The Page Setup group contains commands that let you control the basic layout of the page, most notably things like margins, paper size, and columns. (See Figure 2.20.)

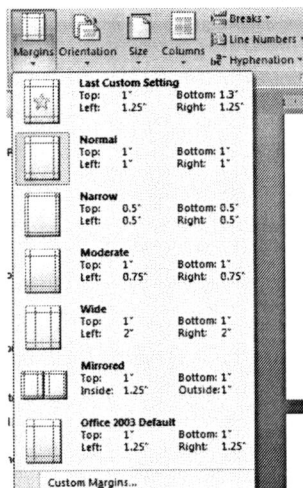

FIGURE 2.20

Margins are a feature that is pretty familiar to folks who work with documents—they control the white space around the edges of your document. Clicking the Margins button opens a gallery of common margins that you can use for your document. If none of those are exactly what you need, you can always click "Custom Margins" at the bottom of the list to create your own. Keep in mind that if this document is going to be printed, your printer almost certainly has an unprintable area. Very few printers can print all the way to the edge of the paper—the vast majority will have some small area, on the sides especially, but also at the top and bottom areas, that it just can't put ink or toner on. So, no matter what you set your margins to in Word, your printer will generally enforce some minimal unprintable area.

Orientation is fairly simple—there are only two choices: Portrait or Landscape. Portrait is the typical vertical alignment, like this book. Landscape is with the page rotated 90 degrees, more like how the typical computer monitor is or an HDTV.

Size lets you set the size of the paper you're going to print on. We're all used to "Letter" (8.5″ x 11″) or "Legal" (8.5″ x 14″) but you can also choose from a variety of other sizes like A4 or Envelope or you can specify a custom paper size.

Columns are a little trickier to work with and we'll talk about those in more depth in Chapter 4. Clicking the Columns button here however, drops down the Columns gallery like you see in Figure 2.21 below. You can choose from five default column settings or you can click "More Columns" to set something custom. Generally speaking, if you need something other than one of the five default column selections, then you might consider using a Table instead of columns, but there may be occasions when you'll want some sort of fancy custom column arrangement.

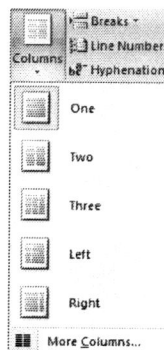

FIGURE 2.21

The Breaks command gives you a number of choices for breaks you can insert. As you can see in Figure 2.22, the gallery is actually pleasantly notated. Not only does it give you a graphical hint of what the command

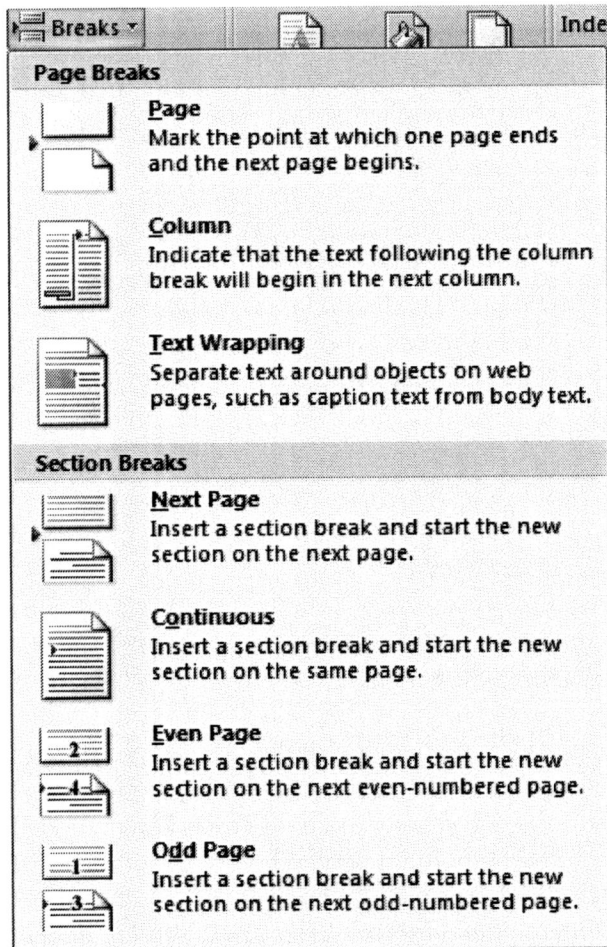

FIGURE 2.22

will do, but there is some explanatory text as well. That's a big improvement over the old File, Edit, View menus that never really told you much about a command's function.

Page breaks are the most common breaks you'll use, and perhaps Column breaks as well. If you're using sections in your documents, and I don't think many lawyers really do, then you have some choices there as well.

Page Background

The Page Background group has three commands that affect what goes around and behind the text in your document. For lawyers, the first one, Watermark, is generally the most useful.

Watermark, which we talk about in more depth in Chapter 12, lets you create a faded bit of text or image that sits behind your text. It is most oft-used, in law firms, to apply words like "DRAFT" or "CONFIDENTIAL" to a printed or digital copy so that the reader is aware of the status of the document.

Page Color lets you change the background color of the document.

▼

Jensen Harris, the lead dog on the User Interface team at Microsoft, has been heard to say that he gets a lot of compliments on the "New" watermark feature in Word 2007. What users don't realize is that watermark has been in Word for years . . . they just never knew where to find that feature before. The Ribbon exposes it readily so now they realize it's there.

This is mostly useful for digital versions of the document. If you want to make a document that is white text on a blue background, for example. As for printed versions, it's usually a lot easier and cheaper to just use the font color you want and print the document on colored paper. Plus, the sort of documents a lawyer would normally print with colored backgrounds are most likely to be brochures or flyers, and if you're printing that kind of quantity of those sorts of documents, you're probably just sending your text to a commercial printing company, rather than relying upon Word's Page Color settings and your own color printer.

Page Borders lets you create graphical "boxes" around the text in your documents.

Paragraph

The Paragraph group contains two related sets of commands for controlling your indent and spacing. As you might suspect, these settings apply on a paragraph by paragraph basis. I'm not going to really get into these here, but we'll discuss them in some depth in Chapter 4. Suffice it to say that these commands on the Ribbon are an example of direct formatting, and you'll generally be better served by the indirect formatting provided by Styles. If this is a subject you're passionate about, you'll have to flip to Chapter 4 to enjoy more about it.

Arrange

The arrange group controls how text and items on a page interrelate. This is especially useful when you have a graphic image, chart, text box, or other item on the page and you want to be able to control exactly where it appears and how the surrounding text will behave.

Many of the commands in this group will only be active if you have an object (like an inserted image) selected.

The Position button opens a gallery (see Figure 2.23) that helps you align the object with your text. You can position it so that the text wraps around your object or so that the object stands by itself on the page. Like all galleries in Word 2007 this demonstrates a powerful feature—if you move your mouse over the various gallery options Word 2007 will display what your document will look like if you were to select that option.

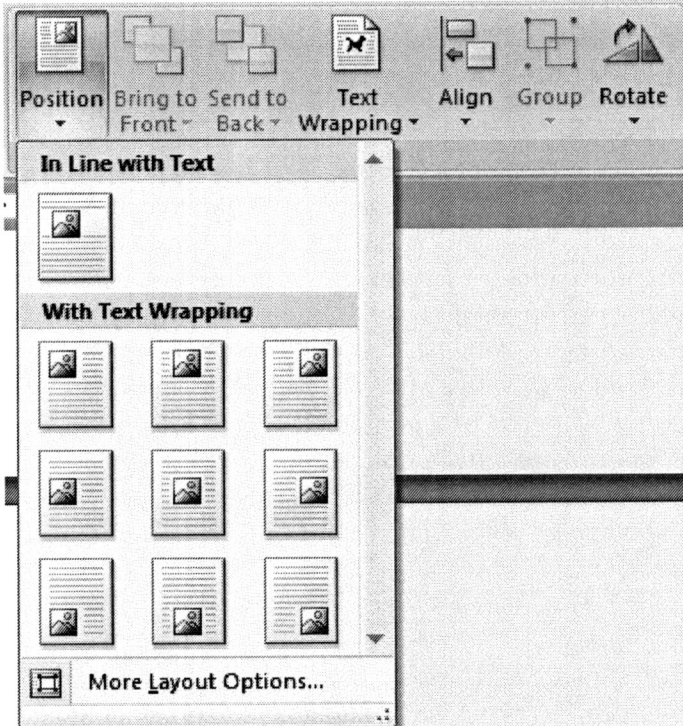

FIGURE 2.23

The next two commands (Bring to Front and Send to Back) demonstrate a surprising capability of Microsoft Word—the ability to have multi-layered documents. There are more options than just having text next to images. You can actually have text in front of (or behind) images or multiple images stacked on top of each other. You can use the Front/Back commands to arrange the images the way you like them. This really isn't a feature lawyers use very often so I'm not going to spend additional space on it in this book.

The References Tab

The References tab on the Ribbon, see in Figure 2.24 on the next page, is one that can be *very* powerful for lawyers creating complex documents

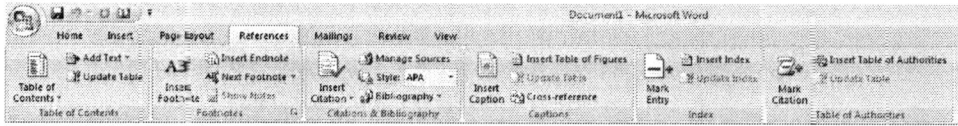

FIGURE 2.24

by helping to automate some of the more challenging and time-consuming tasks.

In Chapter 5, we'll see examples of using many of these features.

Table of Contents

The Table of Contents group contains tools that help you create and maintain a table of contents. In Word, this is primarily accomplished by using the Header styles, but you can also use the Add Text command to add a current bit of text, such as a custom heading to your Table of Contents.

Update Table does just what you think it does, making another pass thru your document and updating the Table of Contents with any new headings that you've added since the last update. Also, it will update any headers that have moved to a different page number and make sure your Table of Contents is always correct.

Footnotes

Lawyers love footnotes. With the Footnotes group, you have some powerful tools for creating and maintaining footnotes and endnotes.

Insert Footnote lets you create a footnote at the bottom of the current page. Insert Endnote creates a note at the end of the document.

The Show Notes feature takes you to the actual notes area. If you're working in a document that has both footnotes *and* endnotes, then Word will politely ask you which one you want to see. (See Figure 2.25.)

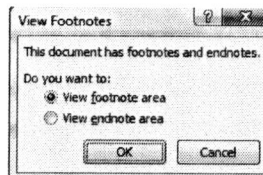

FIGURE 2.25

Citations and Bibliography

The Citations and Bibliography tool has a lot more than meets the eye. At first glance, you may not realize that it helps you maintain a database of sources and insert them, consistently, where and when you need them. The feature is powerful enough and useful enough that we'll devote a little space to it in Chapter 5. For now . . . this is where you find these tools.

Captions

The Captions tool is for images or graphics inserted into a document. It should be really useful, and in some cases it probably is, but to be honest, every time I've tried to use the feature I found it more in my way than helpful. The problem with it is the manner in which the caption is created is so inflexible that you don't have much control over it. Unless you really love the way it chooses to create the captions, you'll spend a lot more time trying to fix it than if you'd just created the captions manually.

If you do decide to use the captions, I'd advise not applying them until you're nearly done with the document. If you caption images and then re-order the images (or insert one), the caption numbering can sometimes stay in the original order . . . meaning that your "Figure 3-6" may end up after "Figure 3-7," which is confusing to everybody. Applying the captions last will give you a better chance to get them right.

Index

The Index group does for indexes (typically found at the end of your document) what the Table of Contents group does for Tables of Contents (typically found at the beginning). This is a really useful set of tools that lets you create and maintain an Index. You can mark any term or phrase as an entry for the Index and Word will automatically add it. Best of all, if that text should move to a different page through subsequent editing, simply clicking "Update Index" will correct the page numbers associated with the terms in the index.

Table of Authorities

Lastly, Table of Authorities employs commands essentially similar to the Table of Contents and Index groups to create and maintain a Table of Authorities. Using this tool is actually pretty easy. When you create a citation in your document that you want to add to the Table of Authorities, you just highlight that text and then click the "Mark Citation" button on the Ribbon. Once you've gone through and marked your citation, just go to the place in the document where you want to place your Table of Authorities and click the "Insert Table of Authorities" button. The table will be nicely created for you.

If you later want to add some more citations to the Table of Authorities, just mark them as the others and then click the "Update Table" button.

The Mailings Tab

The Mailings tab on the Ribbon (see Figure 2.26 below) is primarily concerned with helping you create mail merges; very handy for doing large "personalized' mailings, but it also contains the commands for creating envelopes or mailing labels.

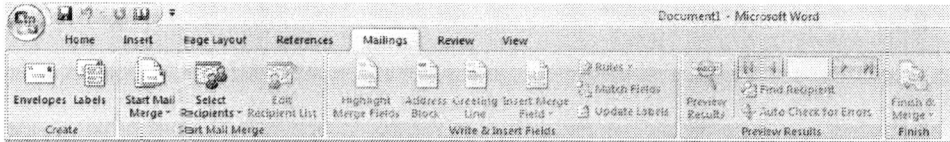

FIGURE 2.26

Create

A feature I've always used in Word is the ability to create and print envelopes using Word. We'll talk about it more in-depth in Chapter 12.

Creating mailing labels is a fairly similar process—clicking the command on the ribbon launches the "Envelopes and Labels" dialog box to the Labels tab. You'll notice right away that it offers you a large field to type the address you want to appear on the label. Less obvious is the tiny "Address Book" icon just above the address field (it looks vaguely like an open book) and you can see it next to the "Use return address" checkbox in Figure 2.27 below. Clicking the address book icon will let you access your Outlook address books, especially your Contacts folder, so that you can select one or more addresses from those lists to print on the labels. Yes, that's really handy.

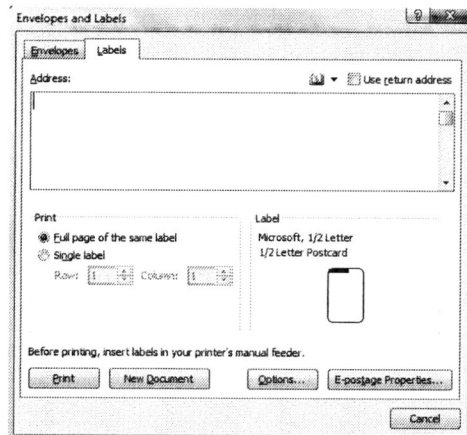

FIGURE 2.27

▼ ▼ ▼ ▼ ▼

Tricks of the Pros

One of my client firms uses this tool to print a whole page of mailing labels when they open a new file for a client. They know there will be a number of mailings and deliveries to this client, so after adding the client to Outlook, they come into this tool and print a full page of labels, which they then put in the paper file. Anytime they need to send something to the client they can just peel the next label off the sheet and they're ready to go. If they run out of labels, it's trivial to just print up a new sheet.

Start Mail Merge

Start Mail Merge is the button you'll click to initiate the mail merge. It has a whole collection of options that let you specify what kind of document you're going to merge to. I won't spend much time on it here because we will go into detail further in Chapter 7.

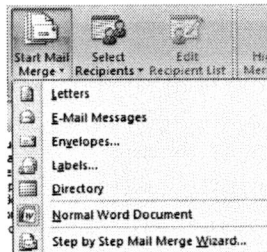

FIGURE 2.28

Write and Insert Fields

The Write and Insert Fields group contains the tools you'll use to build your merge documents. This is another group we'll spend a lot more time with in Chapter 7. One of the features I do want to point out here, though, is the "Rules" command. This lets you take your mail merges to a whole new level by letting you add some logic to your mail merge that you never really had before. For example: if you know the address of the property in question, you may be able to use a rule to automatically insert the address of the relevant courthouse.

Preview Results

Preview Results is an underappreciated set of tools—these let you see what your merge results are going to be without having to waste paper to do it. Click "Preview Results" to get a test merge on-screen. Then you can use the forward and back arrows to scroll thru your merge set and make sure everything looks right before you commit to printing or sending it.

Finish

The Finish group seems a little silly because it contains only a single command: Finish & Merge. This is the command you'll use when you're confident that your merge is ready to go. Clicking this button will perform the final mail merge of your data and template and create the finished documents for printing, e-mailing or whatnot.

Tip

If you have Adobe Acrobat installed you'll get a "Merge to Adobe PDF" (see Figure 2.29) group and button on the right end of the Ribbon. It's just a handy way to create a set of merge files as PDFs instead.

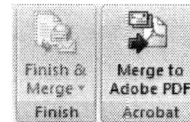

FIGURE 2.29

The Review Tab

The Review tab contains a number of tools you'll use to collaborate with other parties on documents as well as to review and finalize a work in progress. You can see the tab in Figure 2.30 below.

FIGURE 2.30

We'll dig into many of these features in Chapter 6, but let's introduce you to them here.

Proofing

The proofing group contains some tools that you can use to check and finalize a document before sending it out. The spelling and grammar tools are largely active as you type—we've all seen the red squiggly lines that appear beneath text that Word believes is misspelled.

The Research tool is a *very* handy piece of your toolkit for making sure that you're using exactly the words you want to use—it helps you check the definitions of words or phrases as well as find alternatives that might be better. See Chapter 12 for a lot more coverage of the function Research.

The Thesaurus can help you to find exactly the word you want—showing you synonyms (and antonyms) of the word you select so that you might decide to use a something else.

Translate is one of those features that you won't use often, but when you do need it, you'll be happy to have it. Word 2007 has the ability to help you translate text from more than a dozen different languages or into more than a dozen different languages. Is that pretty cool in our very international world? Creo que si.

> 66
> Never use a big word when a diminutive one will do.
> 99

▼ ▼ ▼ ▼ ▼

CAUTION! (CUIDADO! AVERTIR!)

The Word translator is not perfect and should not be used as a substitute for a capable human translator. If you use it to translate anything important, you should be sure to have that text proofread by a person who is fluent in the language you're translating to or from.

The translation screen tip, which is turned off by default, allows you to highlight a piece of text in your document. Then Word will pop up a screen tip that shows you information about the word and its translation in one of four languages. (See Figure 2.31.)

Translation ScreenTip
- Arabic (Saudi Arabia)
- English (United States)
- French (France)
- ✔ Spanish (Spain, International Sort)
- Turn Off Translation ScreenTip

FIGURE 2.31

The Set Language command lets you specify that a particular piece of text was written in a particular language and that the spell checker should treat it accordingly. Word does a pretty good job of automatically detecting what language text is in, but there may be times when you'll need to give it a hand and tell it what language you've used.

The Word Count tool shows you how many words, sentences, paragraphs, etcetera that you have in your document, but this isn't the best way

▼

Anybody notice that one of the language choices is Hawaiian?

to get to this tool. Keep reading; later in this chapter we're going to talk about the Status Bar, which you'll find is a really powerful tool.

Comments

If you're going to review a document, you'll almost certainly want to include comments. You won't believe the number of comments my editors will be inserting in this manuscript before they send it back to me! Comments can be colorful and those colors are automatically assigned to each reviewer through a magical algorhythm involving page count, margin size, and the phase of Jupiter . . . ok, I'll be honest, I can't find anybody who knows exactly what the algorhythm is and it really doesn't matter. The bottom line is that you can't readily control what color you're assigned without manually assigning everybody's colors.

The comments (you can see one in Figure 2.32) are identified not just by color but by the intials of the reviewer ("BMS" in my case) followed by a number indicating which comment (sequentially) that is. My next comment, predictably enough, would be "BMS2." You can't easily control the colors but you can easily control the initials. Click the Office Button, then Word Options and on the Popular group you'll find a place to specify the user's initials. You'll want to change the initials if you inherited the machine from another user or if another user you collaborate with frequently shares the same initials you do.

Comment [BMS1]: Surely you didn't mean to say that?!

FIGURE 2.32

There is a little hidden shortcut for getting to the Popular group to change your initials from here. The next group over is "Tracking," we'll be talking about it in a moment, and under the Track Changes button is the "Change User Name" option. Click that and you can change the initials.

Tip

Be VERY careful with comments. This is one of those document elements that can get you into trouble if you're not careful. Before you finalize any document and prepare it to be sent out of the firm, even to the client, be sure that there are no comments in the document that you wouldn't want to see on the front page of the *New York Times*.

Other than being able to add or delete comments, there are also buttons here that will help you navigate to the previous or next comments in the document.

Tracking

The tracking group is one of the most important groups on the Ribbon, especially for lawyers. This is one place where you can control track changes and adjust how (or even if) Word displays those changes.

The Track Changes button lets you turn tracked changes on or off, and the options you'll find under the drop-arrow on that button lets you have more control over how track changes behaves. Clicking the "Change Tracking Options" command will get you the Track Changes Options dialog box. (See Figure 2.33.) We'll get into this more deeply in Chapter 6. The Change User Name command opens the Word Options dialog box where you can set the username and user initials. You can get to the same thing by hitting the Office Button and clicking "Word Options"—one fewer click if you're not already on the Review tab of the Ribbon.

The Balloons button gives you some options for how (or if) you want Word to use Balloons to show the revisions. You can see an example of a balloon in Figure 2.32, even though that's a comment balloon it looks basically the same. For the next version of Word, I'm suggesting Microsoft let us make balloon animals! The primary function of the Balloons button is to let you control if you want your tracked changes to appear inline or off to the side (AKA "in balloons"). Generally speaking, I tend to prefer inline

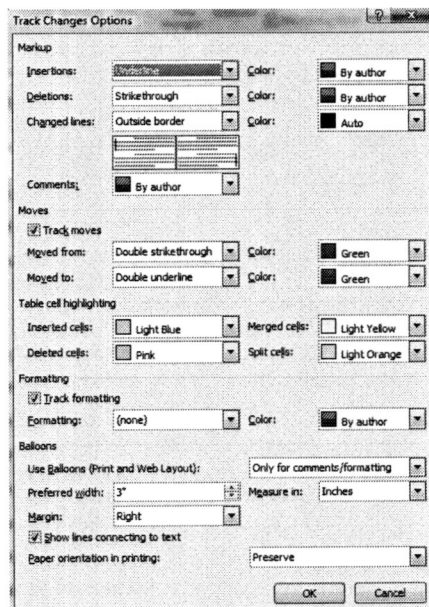

FIGURE 2.33

unless there are so many changes that it makes the document difficult to read. Since this is just a display setting, there's no harm in leaving it set to "Inline" and then switching to balloons later if the inline starts to annoy you. Or vice-versa.

The next two options in the Tracking group are very important so you may want to read this section twice. In fact, I recommend buying a second copy of this book and opening them side-by-side just to get the full effect. The first is the "Display for Review" drop list which you can see in Figure 2.34. We'll explain it in more depth in Chapter 6 and I'll mention it again in Chapter 13. More than a mere shameless attempt to reuse content in order to inflate my page count this really is an important discussion about a feature of Word that lawyers *need* to be aware of. Yes, really. It's no less than the way you display, or hide, markup and metadata in the document.

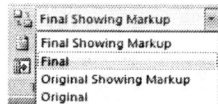

FIGURE 2.34

The next option, Show Markup, is equally important because it controls what kinds of markup the "Final/Original Showing Markup" views will reveal. Figure 2.35, shows what you'll see there. Of particular interest to us are comments, insertions, and deletions.

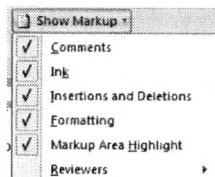

FIGURE 2.35

Changes

The Changes group (see Figure 2.36) contains tools that you'll use to specify what you want to do with changes made to the document. You use this in conjunction with Track Changes. Accept and Reject will accept or reject (of course) the currently selected change and then move on to the next change. Note that the Accept and Reject drop-down menus include

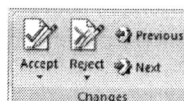

FIGURE 2.36

the ability to accept or reject *all* of the changes in the document in one shot. That can be really handy—especially if you're finalizing and you know that you want to accept all the changes. Accepting the changes, then turning off track changes, then running the Metadata checker is a good way to finish your document before you send it off.

Generally, when I'm reviewing a document, I will reject the changes I don't want and leave the other changes alone until I'm done with the review. Once I've completed my review, and I may take multiple passes at it, I assume that all of the remaining, un-rejected, changes are changes I want to accept, so I'll simply Accept All to the remaining changes and go from there.

If you don't want to accept or reject the currently selected change, just click Previous or Next and it will leave the current change unresolved. I don't think I need to explain those beyond that, do I?

Compare

Compare is another feature that lawyers use a *lot*. We'll demo this a bit in Chapter 6, but these tools have been significantly improved in Word 2007. The compare feature lets you put two documents side-by-side and it will show you the differences, what we used to call "Redline" but now seems just as often to be called "Blackline." Whatever color you like to call it, that's what this tool does—shows you the two documents side-by-side and gives you a copy of the documents that merges the changes and shows you what they are.

Protect

The Protect group contains just one command: Protect Document. This rather ordinary little button is actually the entry point for Information Rights Management, which lets you control who can have this document and what they can do with it. See Chapter 6 for a much longer discussion on protecting documents and Information Rights Management.

The View Tab

The View Tab gives you the controls to handle how Word is going to display your document. (See Figure 2.37.) There are a number of useful commands here, so let's dig in.

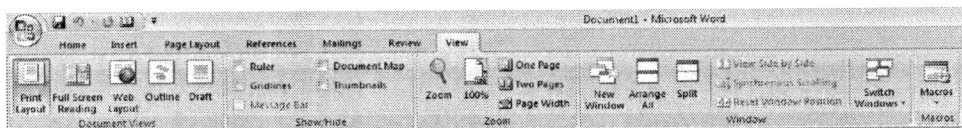

FIGURE 2.37

Document Views

The Document Views group lets you switch between the five basic views that Word offers.

- Print Layout—This is the default view that most people use, most of the time. It lays out the document on the page more or less how it's going to look if you print it. It's a familiar, comfortable, and capable view and that's why most people use it. Note . . . which printer you currently have selected under Office Button | Print | Print may affect how pages display and paginate in Print Layout view. If you're going to use this view, and I'll bet you are, try to have the printer you're actually going to print on already selected in the print settings in order to reduce the chances of a nasty surprise later.

- Full Screen Reading—This is a new view and one that users tend to either love or hate. When you open a Word document from an e-mail message, for example, Word 2007 defaults to showing it to you in Full Screen Reading view. This is a read-only view, no editing allowed by default (see sidebar), so you probably won't choose to use it that often. If you don't like it for viewing received documents, by the way, I'll show you how to turn it off in Chapter 9.

  > If you'd like to enable editing in the Full Screen Reading view, click the View Options at the top-right corner of the view and choose "Allow Typing."

- Web Layout—this view shows how your document will look as a web page. Very few lawyers will use this view; there aren't any page margins and the pagination and layout are going to be different from how the document will look when you print or send it.

- Outline—Outline view is a view optimized for outlining. It's occasionally useful for highly structured documents (or if you just like to use Word to create outlines), but you should be sure to switch back to Print Layout view to finalize your document formatting and layout.

- Draft—The draft view is a clean look at your document without all the bells and whistles that some find distracting. It can be somewhat faster than Print Layout view because it doesn't do foreground repagination—which is a fancy way of saying that it won't stall you while it tries to do administrative stuff with your long document. Do note, however, if you have images, charts or clipart pasted into your document they won't show up in Draft view. You'll need to switch to one of the other views (Print Layout most likely) to see them.

Show/Hide

The next group is the Show/Hide group, which is just a small collection of checkboxes that turn on/off some common features of Word.

- Ruler—Turning off the ruler saves you a tiny bit of space at the top of the document but does give you a slightly cleaner look. I actually do like to turn it off personally; especially since it's so easy to turn it back on for those rare instances when I want or need it. You can also turn the ruler on or off with the very discreet button at the top of the vertical scroll bar on the right edge of the window.
- Gridlines—if you need to do some really precise alignment of elements of your documents, or if you just have an odd fetish for typing on graph paper, you can turn on the gridlines. Primarily, this is used when you're doing some more advanced graphic design, such as laying out a graphically complex newsletter. I can honestly say that in 20 years of working with lawyers and technology I've never seen an lawyer who intentionally turned the gridlines on.
- Document Map and Thumbnails—I'm grouping these two together because they only *look* like checkboxes. In effect they're actually radio buttons—in other words they're mutually exclusive. These control what is going to show in the navigation pane on the left side (see Figure 2.38). The document map is a text-based outline

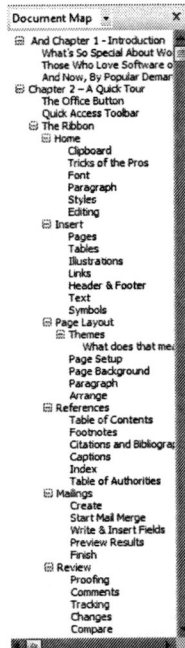

FIGURE 2.38

that shows you your document based upon the headings and helps you to navigate readily up and down in a long document. I use it quite often, especially when writing a document like this book.

Thumbnails gives you a graphical look at your pages. If your pages, like mine, are mostly text then it's really not that useful a view. If you're creating a more complex document with a lot of graphics and other distinctive formatting, then I suppose the thumbnails view might be more useful. In most cases, I don't think lawyers will find the Thumbnails view useful.

■ Message Bar—This option is going to be grayed out if there aren't any message bar items to display at the time. What are message bar items? Security alerts, policy messages, workflow tasks . . . that sort of thing. The message bar is displayed by default when one of those items exists on a document, you use this checkbox to turn the message bar off (and later back on) in those instances.

Zoom

The Zoom group gives you some quick controls that help you display your document in the most productive way for you. Important to note that *all* of these buttons and settings are basically just presets of various zoom levels. Clicking "Two Pages" for example sets the zoom level to a percentage that will show two pages on the screen, side by side, at the same time.

Clicking the Zoom button will open the Zoom dialog box you see in Figure 2.39. From there, you can more precisely control how your document is zoomed, including some of the pre-created zoom options like "Text Width" or "Page Width." What's the difference? Text width excludes

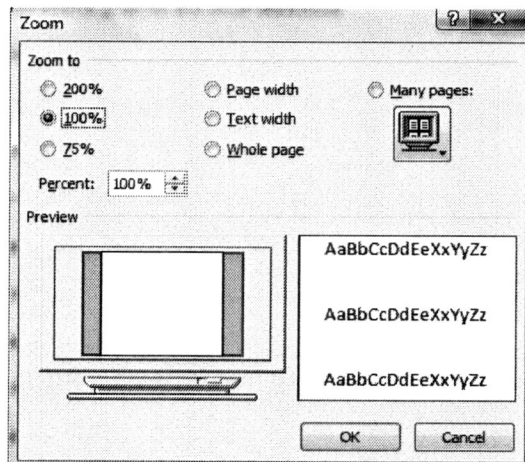

FIGURE 2.39

the right and left margins; page width doesn't. Whole Page is going to zoom the document so that you see the entire page, top to bottom, and left to right on the screen at once.

The other buttons in the Zoom group give you quick access to popular zoom options. 100% takes you quickly to the 100% zoom level; One Page and Two Pages set the zoom to display either one or two pages.

Window

Word has always allowed you to work with multiple documents at once in multiple windows. With Word 2007, the tools are just right out on the Ribbon instead of hidden under a Window menu.

If you already have a document open, clicking "New Window" might surprise you just slightly . . . rather than opening a new, blank, Word window it actually opens a second copy of your open document in the new window. That can be really handy if you're copying/pasting text from one part of your document to another, or if you're using cut/paste to move text from one part to the other and you want to be able to see both bits of the document at the same time.

Once you have opened one or more "New Windows," you can use the "Arrange All" command to lay those windows out side by side (actually one on top of the other, stacked vertically) on the screen. This will arrange *all* Word 2007 windows for you, by the way, not just windows you open using the New Window command. Most of the time, if you have multiple instances of Word 2007 running, it's because you opened documents from your document management system, from Windows Explorer or by just starting another instance of Word from the operating system—as opposed to using the "New Window" command. If you'd like to quickly arrange those multiple windows on the screen, the Arrange All command is your answer.

Another tool that lets you see multiple parts of your document at the same time is the Split Window tool. When you click it, you'll get a horizontal line you can place anywhere on the screen. When you place it, Word will split the screen at that point. You'll get two sections of the window, each with the same document as you can see in Figure 2.40.

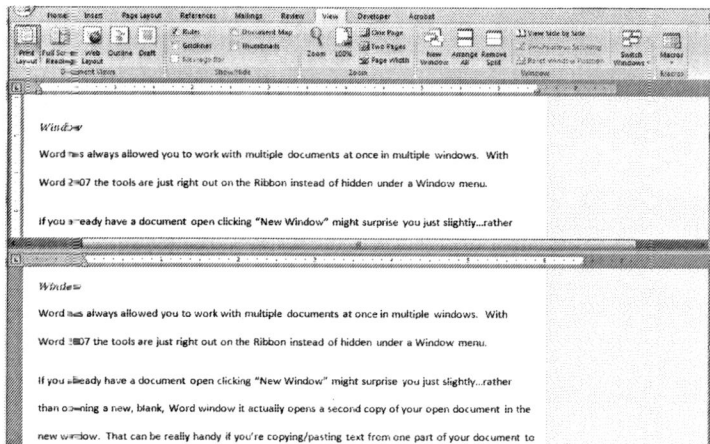

FIGURE 2.40

You can scroll up or down in either window to compare, copy, or paste text. When you're done with the split, just click "Remove Split" to turn it off.

Word 2007 provides you with a lot of tools to compare documents and one of them is the "View Side by Side" option. In this regard, they really heard the feedback from the users because this feature has been asked for a lot. And they even gave it a couple of nice bells and whistles.

> **Tricky bit**
>
> If you have the document map turned on, you can't Split the windows and Remove Split will be greyed out. If you have Thumbnails turned on, you still can't turn on Split . . . but Remove Split will be active and will turn the Thumbnails off. Go figure.

Clicking the Synchronous Scrolling command (which only works if you have View Side by Side enabled) sets the two Word windows to scroll in lock-step. So if you scroll up or down in one, the other will follow. This is a great feature when you're trying to compare two documents as it makes it easy to make sure you're always in sync.

If you happen to move or resize your documents when they're in Side by Side mode, so that one document is larger or off to another place on the screen and want to restore them to be equally sized and side-by-side, you can click the "Reset Window Position" button and it'll put your Word windows back the way they were when you first viewed side by side.

The Switch Windows command is reasonably self-explanatory—clicking that will let you choose among all of the Word 2007 windows you have open. You can do the same thing on the Windows task bar and I invariably do.

Macros

The final group on the View tab is the Macros group and it contains just one command. Clicking the Macros button will give you the options to record or manage Word macros. I suspect they put this command here because . . . well . . . they didn't really know where else to put it. (See next section.) We're going to talk more about Macros in Chapter 8.

The Developer Tab

I know what you're thinking . . . "Developer tab? WHAT Developer tab?" Well . . . the Developer tab is sort of an odd hybrid tab. There are some tabs that are standard: Home, Insert, Page Layout, etc. There are some tabs that are contextual: the Table or Drawing Tools tabs only appear when you have a table or when you have a drawing selected. There are tabs that will appear only if you have certain software installed—for instance Adobe Acrobat adds a tab if you have Acrobat installed. But the Developer tab is a slightly different animal—it's a tab that you can turn on and off in the Word Options (see Figure 2.41 below). By default it's turned off—so if you're one of the few folks who want it on, you'll have to hit the Office Button, then click Word Options, and on the Popular options you'll see it listed as the third one down.

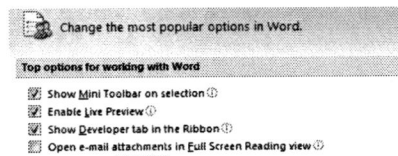

FIGURE 2.41

Once you've turned it on (see Figure 2.42), however, you get a number of features that are interesting to people who want to extend Word 2007 with some custom code. We'll touch on this a bit in Chapter 8, but since most lawyers don't have a lot of interest in programming Word, we're not going to spend a lot of time on it. If Visual Basic for Applications fascinates you and you really want to develop your own elaborate Word extensions, there are a number of books and resources out there for you and I'll list a few of those in Chapter 8. For now, let's just take a cursory run around the tab so you know what's on it and why.

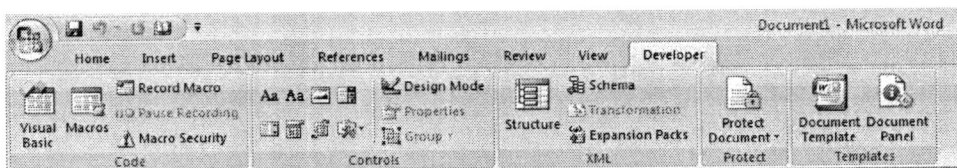

FIGURE 2.42

Code

The Code group contains the starting points for developing custom Word solutions. The Visual Basic button is going to launch the Microsoft Visual Basic editor, which you can see in Figure 2.43 below. From here, a talented programmer can make all sorts of magic happen. And even a total amateur can probably stumble around and at least create a program that inserts "Hello World" into a document over and over again with just a little time and effort.

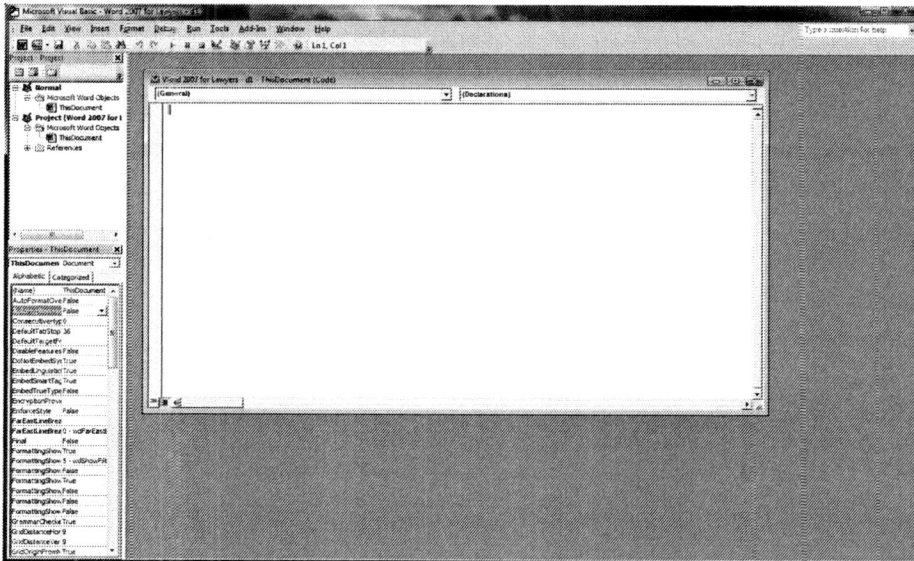

FIGURE 2.43

The Macros button launches the Macros dialog box you see in Figure 2.44. From here, you can also launch the aforementioned Visual Basic Editor to create or edit macro code or you can manage (read: Delete) your macros.

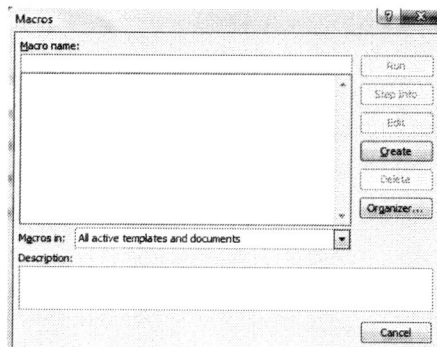

FIGURE 2.44

For most of you, the more useful option here is actually going to be the "Record Macro" command that lets you create a custom macro simply by starting the recording, performing a set of tasks, then stopping the recording, and saving that result as a macro. Anytime you want to do that set of tasks again, simply "play" the macro. Cool, huh? If that concept has your juices flowing then I suggest you hurry up and get to Chapter 8 because we'll go over it in more detail there. If that idea doesn't interest you at all, then maybe you'll skip straight to Chapter 9.

The final option of the Code group actually doesn't have a lot to do with creating code and has a lot more to do with securing Word against other people's code. Clicking the Macro Security command will open the Trust Center dialog of Word Options and let you control how Word handles a document it encounters that has macros in it. The default setting is to "Disable with Notification," which I recommend you leave as is. That will *not* allow macros in a document you receive to run, but will tell you there are macros in the document, just in case you didn't know, and give you the option to enable them. Continue with Chapter 9 if you want to learn more about these settings.

Controls

The controls group gives you a tribe of little controls you can use to insert things like date pickers, drop down lists, and such into your document. Mostly these are used when creating custom document templates that include some level of automation in them. Chapter 8 will mention these further and give a little demonstration on their use.

XML

If you're an XML guru and really want to get in and wrap your hands around the new Open XML Document structure, then this group is your playground. (See Figure 2.45.) Here you can play with the schema, view, or

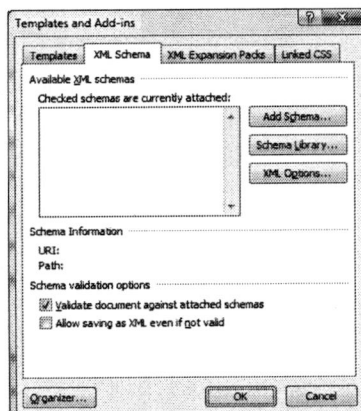

FIGURE 2.45

add XML Expansion Packs and even work with linked CSS style sheets. Sound like something you'd love to do? I didn't think so. Which is why I'm not going to waste much time talking about it in this book.

▼

A "schema" in this context is a structure that describes an XML document. The XML schema defines the data elements (like City, State, and ZIP) that can be tagged and identified in a document.

Protect

The Protect group may look familiar—that's because it's identical to the one you found on the Review tab. Same button, same purpose, same function. I guess anything worth doing is worth doing in two places.

Templates

The templates group rounds out our tour of the Ribbon and does so in style. It's one of those groups that is actually pretty useful if you're doing Word development (and if you're not, why are you on the Developer tab?). From here, you can manage your templates and document information panels.

We'll talk more about templates throughout the book—most notably in Chapters 5, 8, 11, and 13. But keep your eyes open, you never know where the little fellas might turn up.

Document Information Panels are a little different animal, however. They give you access to some of the basic metadata about the document in a handy panel.

From this panel, you can see and edit information, such as the document's title, keywords, author, and even add comments about the document. You can manually display the panel by clicking the Office Button and going to Prepare and then Properties. And you can see a sample panel in Figure 2.46 below.

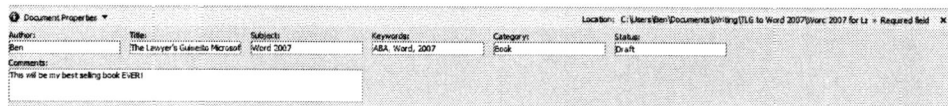

FIGURE 2.46

Clicking the Document Panel button in the Templates group, however, will present you with the Document Information Panel Options dialog box that you see in Figure 2.47.

Here you can specify a custom Document Information Panel if you want to, or simply select different settings to have displayed by default. Most significantly, though, you can choose to have the panel automatically displayed when a document is opened or saved for the first time. This is a great way to remind you what the document is about and to

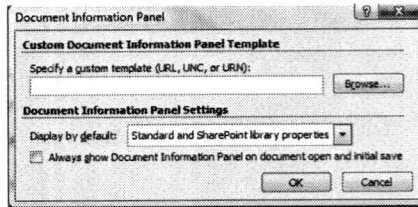

FIGURE 2.47

prompt you to add information (like the aforementioned Comments, Title, Subject, Keywords, etc.) to a document when you save it.

Those of you who are using document management systems, like DocsOpen or iManage, which prompt you for a document profile are familiar with the concept already.

The Customize Status Bar

At the bottom of the Word window is the new and improved Customize Status Bar. (See Figure 2.48.) This is one of the underappreciated features of Word and it's an area that lawyers can really get a lot of value from. From left to right across the status bar, you'll (usually) find the page count ("Page 9 of 30"), which tells you which page you're on and how many total pages you've got. The tricky thing about this display is that it's also a button—if you click it, you'll get the Find and Replace dialog box we discussed above that lets you go immediately to any page, lets you search for text (and replace it if you want to), and even lets you jump straight to bookmarks.

FIGURE 2.48

The reason I said "usually" above is that this status bar is very configurable. Right-click the bar and you can choose a number of things to add to the status bar. Among the choices you'll have:

- Formatted Page Number: This shows you the page number you're currently on. I usually don't bother with this one because I like the "Page Number" option below, better, and I find them redundant.
- Section: If you're using section breaks, this will tell you which section you're currently in. In my experience, most firms don't do much with sections so it will probably always read "1" for you.
- Page Number: This is on by default and it tells you which page you're on and how many total pages you have. "Page 53 of 125" for example.
- Line Number: Many documents prepared for courts have very specific line number requirements—so it can be handy to know which line number you're on.
- The Column field is a little deceptive. When you first see it you might think, as I did, that it refers to columns like newspaper columns. Legal documents frequently have multiple "columns" especially in the headers. So, you might expect that "Column" was going to tell you if you were in column 1, 2, or 3. But that's not what it is at all. In fact, "Column" in this context refers to the horizontal cursor position. In other words when your cursor is all the way on the left end of the line that will read "1." As you move across the line from left to right, that number will increment. Usually it's not that handy, but sometimes if you need to vertically align two words or characters, it can be useful to know that both of them are at "Column 17" or wherever.
- Word count: Right next to the page number you'll find Word Count—which tells you how many total words you have in the document at the moment. And yes, it updates live. Oooh, there's 18,043 for me. 18,046. 18,047.
- Track Changes: A *very* handy tool that I recommend *all* lawyers turn on—this will tell you at a glance if Track Changes is currently on or off for this document.
- Overtype: This item tells you if you're in "Insert" mode or "Overtype" mode.

Insert mode lets you place your cursor somewhere on the screen, between two characters for example, and whatever you type will be inserted, moving any content to the right of your insertion point.

Overtype mode will replace the content to the right of your insertion point with whatever you happen to type. If you typed "Farrah Majors" and want to add "Fawcett," you'd make sure you were in Insert mode, click in front of "Majors," and type "Fawcett" to get "Farrah Fawcett Majors." If you typed "John Cougar" and you want to change it to "John Mellencamp" (without having to release another album), you'd place your insertion point to the left of the "C" in Cougar, make sure you were in Overtype mode, and type "Mellencamp" to replace "Cougar."

Typically changing modes involves simply pressing the "Insert" key on your keyboard—it's a toggle that swiches back and forth. In Word 2007, you can also just left-click on the "Insert" (or "Overtype") on the status bar to switch back and forth between them. There are no features in Word 2007 that let you disable obscure 80s Pop Culture references, however.

Just to the right of the status bar you'll find some controls that affect how Word displays your documents.

First up are buttons that let you select one of the five document views that we discussed above.

- Print Layout
- Full Screen Reading
- Web Layout
- Outline
- Draft

Next up is the zoom level indicator previously discussed. To the right of that is a zoom slider that lets you zoom in and out on your document. Great if you're like me and your eyes aren't quite what they used to be, or if you have an especially large monitor and want to pull back to see more of the page at once.

All of the settings on the status bar, even the zoom settings on the right end, can be turned on or off quite quickly and easily in the Customize Status Bar dialog we talked about previously.

The Mini Toolbar

Word 2007 has another little time-saver in store for you. When you select some text in Word, a small floating Toolbar will appear that contains some

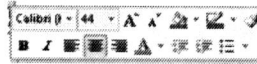

FIGURE 2.49

of the most common functions that people do with selected text. For instance: Bold, font size, font color, or even Format Painter. If you want to use one of these functions, just click the button on the Floating Toolbar and you're done. This saves you from having to mouse all the way to the top of the screen and possibly have to change to a different tab on the Ribbon to find the command you want. (See Figure 2.49.)

> The Mini Toolbar, like many Office functions, has gone thru several names internally at Microsoft. At one point, it was called the "Minibar." At another point, it was called the "Floatie." Mercifully they ultimately settled on "Mini Toolbar."

The Mini Toolbar will appear automatically any time you use the mouse to select some text in Word 2007, and it will go away automatically if you ignore it—it only persists if you actually move the mouse to it and use it. It can take a little practice to get good at the Mini Toolbar; it appears and fades away like a mischievous puppy hiding behind the couch. Once you've mastered the art of mousing with the Mini Toolbar, however, I think you'll find it quite handy. If not, you can easily turn it off; just click the Office Button, go to Word Options and the very first option on the very first tab is to turn on or off the display of the Mini Toolbar.

Summary

Word 2007 is perhaps the most dramatic update to the Microsoft Word program since Word for Windows debuted. The Fluent interface provides a bit of a learning curve as you try to re-learn where your favorite commands are located and discover new product features and existing features that are new to you. The Ribbon is the most distinctive change and brings every feature of the product out in front where you can find them. Other features of the new interface include the more sophisticated, useful and configurable status bar and the handy little Mini Toolbar that appears when needed to save you time in performing common formatting tasks.

Creating a Basic Document

3

At some level creating a basic document is just that: basic. If you know how to navigate the program, it becomes a matter of using the basic tools. In this chapter I'll try to familiarize you with those tools and give you some tips for using them more effectively.

Start from Scratch

We'll talk about using templates in Chapter 4 but for now let's look at how you can use Word to start from a totally blank sheet of paper. To get a clean sheet of "paper," click the Office Button and then click New.

The "New Document" window will appear (see Figure 3.1) and "Blank Document" should be selected by default. Click it and you'll get a new blank sheet of paper in Word that's ready to type in.

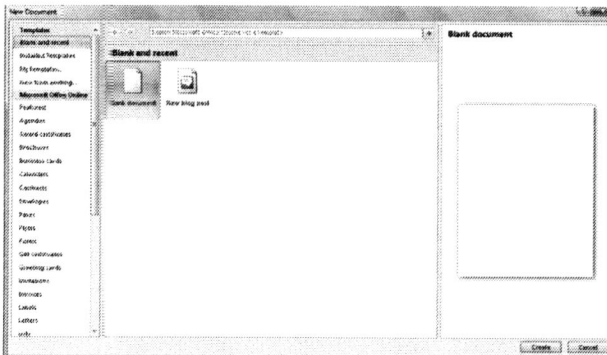

FIGURE 3.1

Another option for creating a new document is to right-click in the folder you want to locate the new document in and choose New | Microsoft Office Word Document. This will create a blank document in the folder that you can then double-click to open it in Word. Take note that when you first create the document this way Windows will have the name highlighted so you can change it. Presuming you don't really want to call it "New Microsoft Office Word Document.docx" you should change it. But don't change the .docx extension or Windows won't know what to do with it anymore.

Adding and Editing Text

Adding text in Word is quite easy—just point and click the mouse to place the insertion point where you want to put the text and start typing. The ability to click anywhere on the page and just start typing was actually introduced in Word 2003—it eliminates the need to insert a lot of carriage returns (enters) and tabs to get your cursor to a particular place on the page.

Find and Replace

Have you ever typed an entire document, then discovered that you repeatedly misspelled the defendant's name? Or, maybe you're reusing a document from a previous client and only making relevant changes. Well, if you've ever had to search a long document for every instance of a word or phrase with the intention of changing or correcting that word or phrase, then Find and Replace (see Figure 3.2) is a feature you're going to adore. It does more or less exactly what the name suggests: you tell it

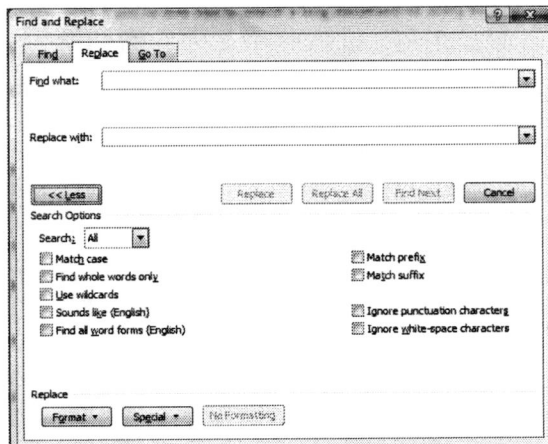

FIGURE 3.2

what to find and it will replace that text, either with or without prompting you at each instance, with a different string of text that you specify. Want to change every instance of "Smith" to "Brown?" Simple go to the Editing group on the Home tab of the Ribbon, click "Replace," then type "Smith" into the Find What field, and "Brown" into the Replace With field. Click "Replace" if you want Word to prompt you on

Be careful with "Replace All." There is a famous story of a newspaper that let their computers correct some of the text in one of their news stories and the next day their readers were surprised to discover that the "budget for the State of Massachusetts was back in the Afro-American." It's often worth letting a human approve the changes; or at least proofread the results.

each instance, or Replace All if you're confident that you need to change it everywhere. This is also handy if you need to change every instance of "Smith" to "Smyth."

If you look closely at the advanced options on the Find and Replace dialog (click "More" if you don't see them), you'll notice that you can match case so that only exact matches, case-sensitive, will be affected. That's helpful when John Matter sues Case Tractor Corp and and you want to replace the names but not the words.

There are three other useful options on this tool I want to point out:

- Use Wildcards—This option lets you use wildcards in your search terms to search for a broader set of matches. A "?" replaces a single character. "The?" will find "Them" and "They" but not "Their" or "Thessaly." An "*" replaces a string of characters. "Tw*" will find "Two" and "Twain" and "Twitter." An "*" by itself will find every word in the document, handy if you're just messing around I guess and want to see what a document consisting of 53,213 instances of "Gumbo" looks like.
- Sounds like—This should be an amazing feature but as it stands it's only pretty good. You can type a term and have Word find (and replace if you like) words that sound like the word you specify. That can be a fantastic way to find not only your specified terms but also perhaps misspellings of the word. It's also handy if you're not entirely sure how to spell the word. The downside to it is that it's not that accurate. It often finds words that are similar to your word but really don't sound that much like it. Still . . . a really good effort at this feature and sometimes handy.
- Find all word forms—this is a great tool because it will find variations on the word. For example, searching for "run" will also find "running" and "ran." But not "jog."

But Find and Replace has a lot of other nifty uses as well. At the bottom of the Find and Replace dialog are two more buttons of interest.

The Format Option

The format option lets you search for (and replace if you want) different formatting options. In fact, nearly every formatting option in Word can be accessed through this option. Need to change all of your Bold formatted text to Small Caps? Find and Replace can do it. You can remove all highlighting throughout your document. Now before you look at this as the best tool for controlling text formatting in Word you really should read Chapter 4 where we talk about Styles. But if you need to do something about direct formatting (we'll get to that in Chapter 4), this can be a good tool.

The Special Button

The Special button in Find and Replace lets you find (and replace) special characters. Click the Special button and you'll get a list of the characters you can work with like the one you see in Figure 3.3. One character that lawyers are likely to want to find is the Section Character (§).

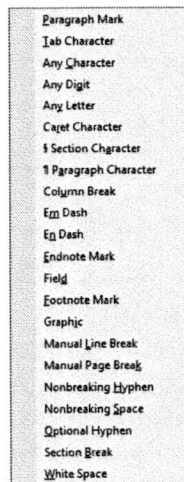

```
Paragraph Mark
Tab Character
Any Character
Any Digit
Any Letter
Caret Character
§ Section Character
¶ Paragraph Character
Column Break
Em Dash
En Dash
Endnote Mark
Field
Footnote Mark
Graphic
Manual Line Break
Manual Page Break
Nonbreaking Hyphen
Nonbreaking Space
Optional Hyphen
Section Break
White Space
```

FIGURE 3.3

Spell Check

Microsoft Word 2007 includes a powerful spell checker that is designed to help you with your document creation. I have to confess that I make considerable use of it myself. The nice thing about it is that you don't have to do anything to invoke it; it's running all the time by default. If Word thinks you've misspelled a word, it will underline that word with a red squiggly line that indicates Word has identified a possible problem. Right-click the word and Microsoft Word will offer you some suggested corrections.

If you're confident you have the word spelled correctly but Microsoft Word thinks otherwise (as it often will for proper names for example), you can add it to Word's dictionary when you right-click the word. Then Word will know what it is when it sees it again in the future.

AutoCorrect

AutoCorrect is one of those features of Word that enables you to type quickly and fixes little mistakes for you as you go. Among the things it will do for you is auto-capitalize the first word in a sentence, just in case you forget or just don't want to be bothered with it, and fix common spelling mistakes such as when you type "teh" but mean "the."

▼

If you really want to type "teh" one time, just click Undo or press CTRL + Z after it changes it to "the" and it will change back. You may have to click Undo twice.

The AutoCorrect options can be set under the Office button if you click "Word Options," then go to the Proofing group and click the AutoCorrect Options button to get the AutoCorrect options dialog box you see in Figure 3.4.

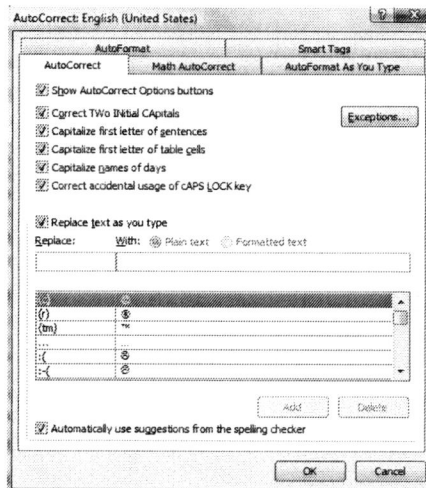

FIGURE 3.4

Grammar Check

A feature that was added to Microsoft Word a few versions back and has slowly improved is the grammar checker. This works in conjunction with the spell checker and will underline any perceived errors of grammar with green squiggly lines. To be honest, I find it mostly useless myself—it generally points out sentences it thinks are fragments and not a lot else. As you may have noticed, I have a sort of specific writing style and some of what I write is probably not grammatically impeccable . . . but I probably wrote it that way for a reason. It's very rare that Word suggests a grammatical correction that I accept so I usually turn the grammar checker off . . . just to save that tiny bit of performance. Besides, if my grammar were perfect how would my editor earn his keep?

Saving

If you're creating documents you care about, and presumably you are, you will at some point want to save them. Saving a document in Word is pretty simple, you can click the "Save" icon, which is one of the few default icons on the Quick Access Toolbar or you can click the Office Button | Save. The mouse-averse among you can press CTRL+S to save. If it's the first time you've saved the document, Word will prompt you to give the document a name and choose a location (if you want to save it somewhere other than the default location). If you've saved the document before, Word will just quickly and quietly save the document, overwriting the previous version of the document.

Your other basic saving option is to click the Office Button and Save As. What that does is prompt you for a new filename and/or location to save the file. This is great if you want to leave the original file as is and save this as a new file. (See the sidebar. I know, read it again.) The other reason you might want to use Save As is if you want to save this file in a different format—like Office 97-2003, Rich Text Format or maybe it was an older file format to begin with and you want to save it as an Office 2007 OpenXML file. You can also get to this option by pressing F12, by the way.

Caution!

One of the biggest mistakes lawyers make with Word (see Chapter 11 where I will beat you over the head with this one again) is reusing an existing document from another client or matter, making changes and then accidentally saving the new edits over the old version. Be careful!

New File Format

Either way that you choose to save your documents, Word 2007 gives you a brand new file format to save them in by default. Office Open XML is our new format and you can readily identify documents saved in that format by their file extension. .DOCX is the new default Word extension (replacing .DOC) and the "X" tells you it's an XML document. .DOTX is the new default extension for Word 2007 templates. You might occasionally see .DOCM or .DOTM—those are macro-enabled documents and templates respectively. They don't necessarily contain macros, but they can (and in practical usage usually do).

The Office Open XML documents have a few notable advantages. First and foremost they are quite a bit smaller than the old .DOC files. .DOCX files are actually ZIP files—compressed—containing several discreet files. A .docx file can actually be as much as 50% smaller than the same document in .doc format. That can really pay off if you have a large document library in terms of significantly reduced storage space requirements, significantly faster backups and faster transfer speeds when e-mailing documents or working with them remotely.

Another advantage of the new file format is interoperability. XML is a popular and open file format and is much easier for other vendors to work with than the old, proprietary, binary, .DOC files were. Exchanging documents with other applications or working with .DOCX files in other applications (like document management or indexing tools) is much easier in the new format.

.DOCX files are both more resilient and more recoverable than the old format documents were. They're less likely to corrupt or fail and if they DO corrupt you're a lot more likely to be able to get your data back. That's because rather than being one big file the .DOCX is actually, as I mentioned above, a compressed file that contains a number of smaller files. Your text is actually stored separately, within the .DOCX file, from the formatting for example. If a bit of your formatting gets corrupted, Word can probably still recover your text by simply deleting the file containing the formatting. You might have to go back through your document and reapply your formatting but that's a lot better than losing all of your text too. And, frankly, it's pretty unusual that you'd even have to do that with the new formats.

Naming Files

Folks who've used computers for a long time are familiar with the "8 point 3" naming convention. Back in the old days, before flash drives and Wikipedia, we used to have to name our documents things like "jonesbrf.doc" because of the limitations of the File Allocation Table (FAT) file system. But since FAT gave way to FAT32 (the 32-bit version of FAT) and NTFS (NT File System; the preferred file system of Windows XP and Vista), long filenames became possible and preferable. That means you can use up to 255 characters in a filename, including some symbols. You can now name your documents things like "Jones v Smith Memo.docx" or "Letter to Judge Steffey regarding jury selection in Brown matter.docx."

Especially if you're not using a document management system like DocsOpen or Worldox you should implement a sensible naming system for your documents in order to facilitate finding them later. What system you use is up to you, but don't neglect it.

By the way, don't get crazy with the filenames. Just because you CAN use up to 255 characters doesn't mean you should. If you start naming documents "Letter to Amstutz, Huddleston and Malcom requesting electronic production of all documents including but not limited to those documents relating to sales of Widgets in the Northeastern and surrounding sales territories during fiscal 2006.docx," then . . . well . . . just don't. It's excessive, annoying, and ultimately not useful.

If there are others in your firm, you should discuss your naming system with them so that you're all on the same page. Don't restrict the discussion just to partners or lawyers; encourage paralegals and legal secretaries to participate too. An experienced legal secretary can have some very valuable input to help you come up with the best solution. Plus, if you get them involved from the beginning, you'll make it that much easier to implement whatever policy you come up with.

Folders

If you're going to use the basic Windows file system to organize your files, then I would encourage you to adopt a system of folders. Don't just throw everything into one folder and then hope you can find it. The system you use is up to you but I would recommend something along the lines of:

- Clients
  - Client A
    - Matter 1
    - Matter 2
  - Client B
  - Client C
    - Matter 1
    - Matter 2
- Administrative
  - Accounts Payable
  - Advertising

And so forth. With an intelligent hierarchy of folders, it's easier to find what you need. In this example, Client B only has one matter (and isn't expected to have a second) so there really isn't a need to create any subfolders for them. Some lawyers I've seen will create subfolders of the Matter subfolders for different kinds of documents, but generally, I think that just adds a needless layer of complexity. Use the long file names to specify what kind of document it is and keep all of those documents in the single "Matter x" subfolder. Unless there are hundreds of documents, there really isn't a need to further subdivide the subfolder. In Chapter 12, I'll mention full text search—that's another tool you can use to help find files you've stored in subfolders.

Tags

When you save your document, Word will give you the option to apply a tag to the document (see Figure 3.5). Tags can be useful for categorizing your documents and making them easier to find later. You might tag items with the client/matter number of the case, or perhaps with a tag that explains what kind of document it is (Memo, brief, etc.). It's tempting to use the Tags feature to include keywords about the document, but you usually shouldn't bother using keywords that actually appear in the document because Instant Search will find those documents already. To add a tag, just click the Tags field and type in whatever you'd like to add. Separate multiple tags with a comma.

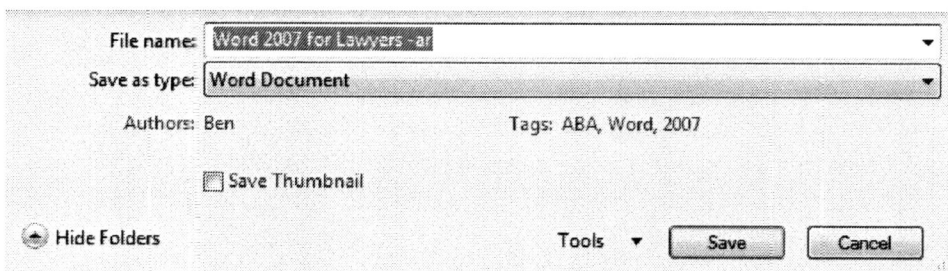

File name:	Word 2007 for Lawyers -ar		▼
Save as type:	Word Document		▼
Authors:	Ben	Tags: ABA, Word, 2007	
	☐ Save Thumbnail		
⊕ Hide Folders		Tools ▼	Save	Cancel

FIGURE 3.5

Printing

Before we go too far, it only seems appropriate to tell you how to Quick Print and, oddly enough, the quickest way to print may not be to use the Quick Print tool. Let me explain; on the Office Button, under the Print option you'll find a Quick Print option. You click that and Word just starts spooling your print job to the printer. No dialog box; no options to change. That's pretty quick. But it requires you to take your hand off the keyboard, grab the mouse, click once, highlight print, and click Quick Print. The faster way? Press CTRL+P to get the print dialog box and just press

Enter. Two keystrokes, no mouse, same result.

In the normal course, most users print Word documents just by clicking the Office Button and then Print, but Word 2007 has a lot of powerful printing tools that can be extremely useful.

Click Office Button | Print or press CTRL+ P to launch the Print dialog box. (See Figure 3.6.)

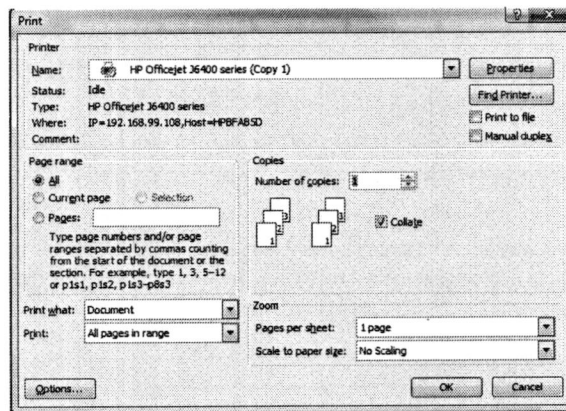

FIGURE 3.6

The settings at the top let you choose which printer you want to print to. If you have multiple printers in your firm, you can pick the one you want to print to here. Keep in mind that different printers have different features and so which printer you choose will slightly affect the options you have—in fact pretty much everything within the "Print" box is affected by which printer you have selected. Printing to a color printer will give you color printing options while printing to a network attached copier may give you options for duplexing and stapling for example. One option that is fairly universal is a "Print to File" checkbox, which sends the print job to a file on disk instead of to the printer. When you check that box and click OK, it will prompt you for a file name and location (such as your Documents folder or a flash drive). Next, when you save it, Word will create a .PRN file that contains all of the printer instructions like fonts, colors, and such that would be needed to print the file later. Typically, you would use that option if you were creating a document, such as a flyer or brochure, that you were going to send to a commercial printing company. You'd get it just the way you want it, print it to a file, and send that file to the commercial printer so they could print your brochures or whatnot.

Clicking the Properties button in the Printer box will give you access to that printer's properties (just like accessing it through the Control Panel | Printers tool) so you can make changes for this print job to low-level printer settings. This tool can be completely different from printer to printer so I won't even attempt to explain it here. Your printer documentation will probably cover that fairly adequately.

Page Range

You might not always want to print the full document and the Print Range section is there to help you with that. Here you can print just the current page, or you can print a range of pages. That's pretty helpful when you just need to reprint pages 11-14 of a contract because somebody, and I'm not saying who, Kim, accidentally spilled coffee on them.

The other option you have here is to print just the selected text. If you'd like to just print one specific paragraph, or some specific bit of a document but not an entire page or not a range of pages, you can just select the text you'd like to print, then press CTRL+P (or click Office Button | Print) and choose "Selection" under the Print Range group.

Zoom

Another section I find helpful when I go to print is the Zoom section. If I'm printing a long document and it's just for internal use, for example so I can proofread a draft on paper, I'll often choose to save paper by having Word print 2 or 4 pages on a page. The end result comes out looking something like Figure 3.7. The text is small, but still readable and, especially if I also use duplexing, I can save an awful lot of paper this way.

Tricks of the Pros

If you have a document with any kind of involved formatting or pagination try the Print Preview before you send it to the printer. You can confirm on-screen that the print job will look the way you expect it to look, rather than having to find out when you've wasted a lot of paper, toner, and time. Office Button | Print | Print Preview (or CTRL+F2) to take a peek. Also handy for troubleshooting weird printing issues.

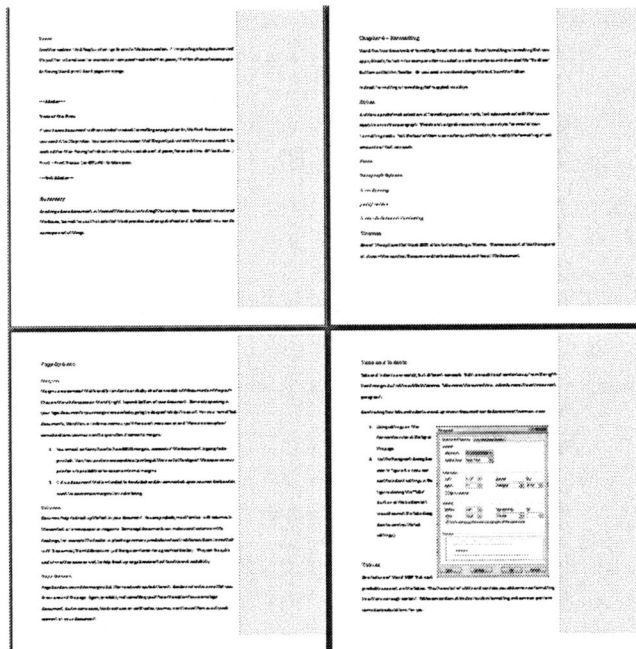

FIGURE 3.7

Another good use for the Zoom section is if you need to resize a document's printing. Let's say you have a document that was initially created for 11″ x 17″ paper and you decide to print it on 8.5″ x 11″. Just changing the paper type in Word isn't going to solve the problem by itself—you need to also go into Zoom and under Scale to Paper Size be sure to select the proper sized paper ("Letter" in this example).

Summary

Creating a basic document in Microsoft Word is a fairly straightforward process. Once you've mastered the basics, learned to use the tools that Word provides, such as spell check and AutoCorrect, and gotten a handle on the many print options available, you can do some powerful things.

Formatting 4

Word has two basic kinds of formatting: Direct and Indirect. Direct formatting is formatting that you apply directly to text—for example, when you select a word or sentence and then click the "Boldface" button on the Mini Toolbar. Or, you select a word and change the font from the Ribbon.

Indirect formatting is formatting that is applied via a Style. Many of the formatting problems you'll encounter with Word come about because of a conflict between an underlying style and some direct formatting applied on top of that style.

Styles

A style is a predefined collection of formatting properties; fonts, text colors, and so forth that you can apply to a word or paragraph. There are a lot of good reasons to rely upon styles for most of your formatting needs. Not the least of them is consistency and the ability to modify the formatting of vast amounts of text very easily. You can set a style to have 11 point text, for example, and apply it broadly across your document. If you later decide you want to change it to 12 point text, you need only adjust the style and just like magic all of the text assigned that style will be updated.

Word 2007 gives you quick and easy access to some commonly used styles right on the Styles Quick Gallery on the Home tab of the Ribbon. (See Figure 4.1.)

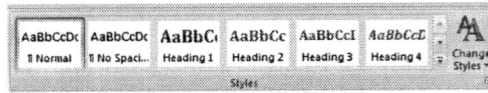

FIGURE 4.1

Fonts

A font is the combination of the typeface and other elements like size, pitch, and spacing that determines the shape of the letters in your document. You can take a basic typeface like Times New Roman and apply other characteristics to it like Boldface, 13 point, and underlined. One thing that can be a little confusing in Microsoft Word is that the font is sometimes used to refer only to the typeface (like "Courier" or "Times New Roman") and sometimes used to refer to the typeface AND the various characteristics applied to it (like "Calibri 12 points Italic"). I wish I had an easy answer for you on that one, you'll just have to try and understand from the context what is being meant. For the purposes of this book, I'll try to use "Typeface" when I mean just the typeface ("Courier," "Arial," etc.) and "Font" when I mean the whole thing.

Paragraph Options

In Word, the Paragraph is an important concept. Most of the styles you'll use will be paragraph styles and most of the formatting applied will be applied on a paragraph level. There are a number of options that apply to a paragraph in Microsoft Word.

Line Spacing

Line spacing refers to the amount of space between lines of text. Single, Double, etc. You can control your line spacing on a paragraph by paragraph basis using direct formatting with the Line Spacing button on the Ribbon (see Figure 4.2) or (better still) you can modify the line spacing for the style that your text is based on so that the line spacing is consistent across all of your paragraphs assigned to that style. Generally speaking in legal documents, your line spacing is going to be specified by the court anyhow so you probably won't have a lot of discretion in what it should be. But for correspondence, marketing materials, and other personal documents you can probably make your line spacing whatever you'd like it to be.

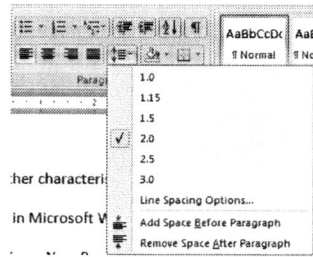

FIGURE 4.2

Justification

Justification relates to how the text aligns on the page horizontally, or from left to right. Typically our text is left justified, which means that it aligns to the left side of the page. As you type, your text moves across the page from left to right but it's always in a straight line down the left side of the page. The right end of the line can be somewhat ragged, as mine is here, depending upon the words in the line and how long it actually is.

Right justification aligns the text to the right side of the page. For illustration, I'm right-justifying this paragraph and you can see that my text lines up perfectly along the right side . . . but now the left side is a bit ragged depending upon the length of the line.

The next option is center justified, like this paragraph is. Now the lines won't necessarily line up on *either* side but they'll all be perfectly balanced along the horizontal center point of the page.

Finally, you have full justification. A line that is full justified will line up both left *and* right, but Word will play around with the word spacing in the line in order to make the line fit fully across the page.

Themes

One of the new options that Word 2007 offers for formatting is Themes. Themes are sort of like the superset of styles—they control the colors and fonts and basic look and feel of the document. I don't think most lawyers are going to take any notice of Themes so, other than observing that they exist in Word 2007 and giving you the heads up about what they do (Control the color and font scheme), I'm not going to spend too much time talking about Themes. The vast majority of what lawyers and law firms do in formatting can be addressed with direct and indirect formatting; and especially styles in the default theme. I seriously doubt many of you will ever care to change the Theme.

Page Options

Just as you have options that apply on a paragraph by paragraph basis there are also options that are relevant on the page level.

Margins

Margins are a concept that's pretty familiar to anybody who has worked with documents in the past—they are the white space on the left, right, top, and bottom of your document. Generally speaking, in your legal documents your margins are probably going to be specified by the court. For your non-official documents, like letters or internal memos, you'll have a lot more leeway and there are a couple of considerations you may want to give when it comes to margins:

1. You almost certainly have to have *some* margins, especially if the document is going to be printed. Very few printers are capable of printing all the way to the edge of the paper so your printer will probably enforce some minimal margins.
2. If it's a document that is intended to be studied and/or commented upon, you may deliberately want to leave ample margins for note-taking.

Columns

Columns help to break up the text in your document. You are probably most familiar with columns in the context of a newspaper or magazine. Some legal documents can make use of columns in the headings; for example, the header in pleadings in many jurisdictions have traditionally been formatted with three columns (the middle column just being a container for a graphical border). They can be quite useful in other cases as well to help break up large blocks of text for style and readability.

To set up columns in your document, go to the Page Layout tab of the Ribbon and click the Columns button to get what you see in Figure 4.3.

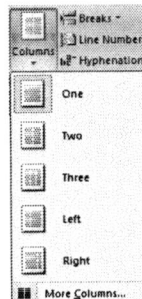

FIGURE 4.3

Here you can choose from the gallery to have one, two, three, or more columns. You can also do some unbalanced columns like left or right—which are excellent for setting up letterhead by the way.

▼ ▼ ▼ ▼ ▼

Tricks of the Pros

Preprinted letterhead is just so 1997. These days all the cool kids are printing their letterhead on demand as part of their documents. Just create a template with the margins you want, put your firm header at the top, create a column on the left (or right) to list your addresses, partners, associates . . . all the stuff you've got on your preprinted letterhead now. A good graphic designer or Microsoft Word expert (heck, even a savvy legal assistant!) can set up a Word Template for you that looks almost identical to your preprinted letterhead. Now that you've got that template, create all of your letters and such using that template and just print on plain blank paper (or bond if you like). It'll look like you printed on pre-printed letterhead but it'll save you a lot of costs both up front and in the future. Tell the truth . . . how many boxes of letterhead do you have in a closet preprinted with the names of lawyers who are no longer with your firm; or featuring the address of your old office? If you're printing your letterhead on demand, from a template, you make a simple change to the template when somebody joins or leaves the firm or when an address or phone number changes and voila . . . your new letterhead is ready. And, with Word 2007's new file formats, you can even retroactively change the template applied to previously created documents—so if you ever reprint those documents in the future they can be printed with the current letterhead template; instead of the template that was in use months or years back when the document was originally created.

Most of the time lawyers are happy with one of those default column choices presented in the gallery. For the rare instance when you need custom columns other than what you see there, just click the More Columns command at the bottom of the gallery to get the Columns dialog box you see in Figure 4.4. Here you can set up some extremely specific columns with custom spacing and everything.

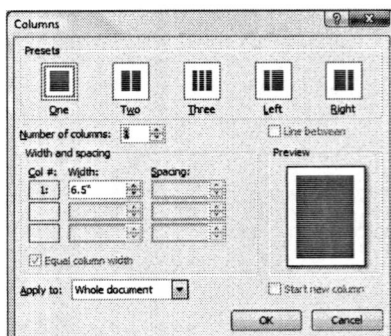

FIGURE 4.4

There are two really useful settings in this dialog box that I sometimes use even when I've only created a basic two-column page, for example:

■ Line Between: This will create a nice vertical line between your columns. Handy in pleading headers and other places where you want a vertical line to separate your columns. No need to create a bogus center column just for a graphical divider in your headings anymore.

■ Apply to: The default is "whole document" but the other option in that box is "This point forward." I'll use that to turn off columns, by setting the colums to "One," if I only want to have two columns for part of a page or if I want subsequent pages to have a different column layout.

Page Borders

Page borders sound like margins but they're actually quite different. Borders refer to a line that you draw around the page. Again, probably not something you'll have the option to use on a legal document, but in some cases, like brochures or certificates, you may want to use them as a stylized element of your document. Click the Page Borders control on the Ribbon to get the Borders and Shading dialog box you see in Figure 4.5. This dialog box is actually somewhat more powerful than simple page borders, though we'll start there. Here you can set a border around the page, or even have the entire page shaded. The border can be a solid line or a broken line or a dashed line or a . . . you get the idea. And, of course, you can specify the thickness of the line. You can have the border apply to the entire document or just to certain sections of it.

If you click the Borders tab of the Borders and Shading dialog box, you can create paragraph borders. For lawyers these are actually some-

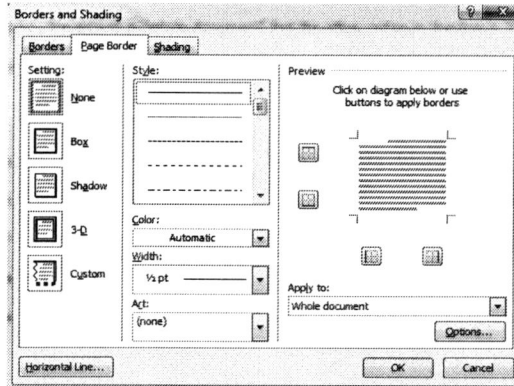

FIGURE 4.5

what *more* useful, though not something you'd use in a pleading most likely. They let you enclose a particular paragraph (or more) within a border, setting them off graphically for emphasis.

The other useful tool that's here is one that you might have used before and that you've spent a *lot* of time looking for and that's Horizontal Line. When I create training or instructional materials, I sometimes like to divide sections of the page or document with a horizontal line. When I first started using Word 2007, I probably wasted far more time than I needed to trying to find out where this command had gone and it took me two or three uses before I remembered that it was now semi-hidden under the Page Layout | Page Borders command. (I kept looking for it under Insert | Shapes.)

Tricks of the Pros

If you like to insert horizontal lines, you may want to just add this command to the Quick Access Toolbar (QAT). To do that, right-click the QAT and choose "Customize Quick Access Toolbar . . ." Change "Popular Commands" to "All Commands" and scroll down until you find "Horizontal Line" to add it.

Tabs and Indents

Tabs and Indents are related, but different, concepts. Both are used to align content horizontally on the page but with a subtle difference. Tabs set anchor points for you to align text on the current line. Indents move the entire current line or paragraph. You can have multiple tabs across the line, but a given paragraph will have just a single indent setting (well, one on the left and one on the right if you like).

Controlling how tabs and indents are set up in your document can be done one of two main ways:

1. Using settings on the horizontal ruler at the top of the page.
2. Via the Paragraph dialog box seen in Figure 4.6. (You can see the Indent settings in the figure; clicking the "Tabs" button at the bottom left would launch the Tabs dialog box to control the tab settings.)

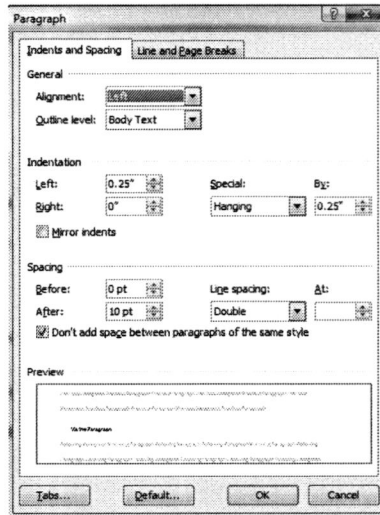

FIGURE 4.6

Personally, I prefer the Paragraph dialog box. I know the ruler is always there and I've seen people work their magic with a mouse and a few deft strokes, but to be honest, I never quite seem to get the results I want from setting tabs on the ruler and after a few minutes of trying I usually give up and fall back to the tried and true, well-understood, paragraph dialog box. If you really want to use the ruler to set your tabs and indents though, let's take a moment to look at how you do that . . .

Using the Ruler to Set Tabs and Indents

First of all, when you first look at the Word ruler, you won't see any defined tab stops, but you know (or you will after you finish reading this sentence) that the Normal template in Word includes default tab stops every .5 inches. And you can see that in action if you start at the beginning of a blank line and start pressing the TAB key . . . the cursor will advance to the right half an inch every time you press the button.

The first step in setting your tabs up is to place your insertion point in the paragraph that you want these tabs to apply to. For simplicity, we'll assume you're just going to set some tabs up to use in the current and future paragraphs.

The next step in setting up your tabs is to click the tab selector at the left end of the ruler as you can see in Figure 4.7. By default it looks sort of like a capital "L."

▼

There's a reason that tabs and indents are on the paragraph tab of the Page Layout group—they are assigned to paragraphs by default. If you set tabs on a paragraph, then continue typing the next paragraph the tab settings will follow. If you select an existing paragraph in the middle of a bunch of paragraphs, your new tab settings will only apply to the selected paragraph. Want to apply the tabs to multiple paragraphs? Select them, then set the tab settings. Want to apply it to the entire document? CTRL+A to select all, then set your tab settings.

FIGURE 4.7

Each time you click it you'll get a different cryptic little symbol. The first three to be addressed are fairly standard types of tabs:

- Left tab: looks like an L, sensibly enough. If you set a Left tab, then text that starts at that tab stop will continue, as you type, to the right. This is the sort of tab you're most commonly used to. You can see one above in Figure 4.7
- Center Tab: Looks like an upside-down T. Set a center tab and text you type will center off that point—in other words it will adjust left and right from that spot.
- Right Tab: Looks like a backwards L. Set this tab and text will proceed from that point to the left as you type.

The next two tabs are a little different:

- Decimal Tab: The decimal tab character looks like the Center Tab character (the upside-down T) but with a decimal point to the right side of it. When you set a decimal tab, the text (which is presumably numbers) will align along the decimal point. This is the way you can align a column of numbers with decimal places so that they align on the decimal just like what you see in Figure 4.8.

4.56
14.72
123.456
5.74
5.3
9.123
6.32

FIGURE 4.8

- Bar Tab: [Pause for laughter] This is a type of tab that is different from the rest in that it's not designed to align text. It creates a vertical line on the page—the sort of thing you might use to create the vertical line in a pleading heading. When you click the tab selector until it looks like a vertical line, that's the bar tab. If your waitress starts to look like a vertical line, it's probably a good time to ask for your bar tab . . . and call a cab.

> **Tip**
> If you're not sure which kind of tab you're looking at in the Tab Selector, just hover your mouse over the top of it and you'll get a tool tip that tells you.

After you've clicked through the five kinds of tabs, the Tab Selector button will, curiously, offer you two types of Indent you can set up:

- First Line Indent: The first line indent does pretty much what you think it does—indents the first line of the paragraph the specified distance. The icon for this one looks like a downward pointing triangle.
- Hanging Indent: The hanging indent moves the entire paragraph over the specified amount. This icon looks like a small box.

> **Tricks of the Pros**
> Want to quickly remove a tab you set manually? Just drag the tab indicator off the ruler using your mouse.

Once you've selected the type of tab or indent that you want to create, click on the ruler where you'd like to place the tabs or indents. You can place as many tabs as you like (within reason), but only one indent per paragraph.

Using the Tabs Dialog to Set Tabs

To get into the Tabs dialog press ALT+O, T and you'll get the dialog box you see in Figure 4.9. Here you can type in the placement of the tab stops you want and you can select what type of tab alignment you want.

The other setting you can select here that's interesting is the Leader setting. By default there's none, but if you want the tab to be prefaced by dots, a dashed line, or an underline you can select that here.

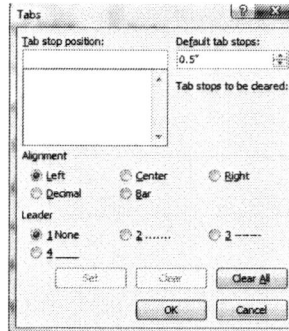

FIGURE 4.9

Tables

One feature of Word 2007 that you'll probably use a lot are the Tables. They have a lot of utility and can help you add some nice formatting to otherwise rough content. Tables can contain all kinds of custom formatting and can even perform some basic calculations for you.

Creating a Table

Creating a table is a pretty simple matter. Go to the Insert tab and find the Tables gallery (see Figure 4.10). The quick way is to just start at the top left corner with your mouse and drag down and over until you have the number of columns (up and down) and rows (left to right) you need. You can make a table of up to 10 columns and up to 8 rows that way. If you need something else, or you just can't get the hang of using the mouse for this task, you can click the Insert Table command to get the Insert Table dialog box you see in Figure 4.11. Then you can specify however many columns or rows that you need. If you guess wrong . . . don't worry about it. It's not that hard to insert additional rows and/or columns later if you subsequently discover that you forgot one.

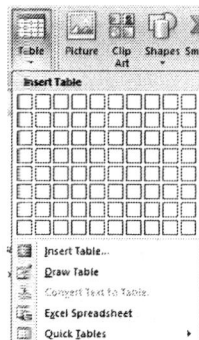

FIGURE 4.10

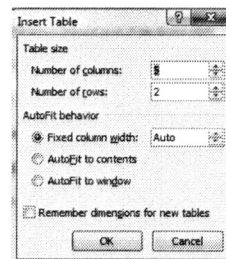

FIGURE 4.11

There are two other useful features you'll find in the Insert Table window. The first is a way to control how AutoFit is going to work in this table. That means whether or not Word will automatically adjust the width of the column to fit the content. By default, Word 2007 will try to make some intelligent guesses about how the table should be laid out and will auto-size the columns accordingly. Those intelligent guesses will be based solely on the number of columns and the width of available space though—they won't have anything to do with the contents of the columns. If you'd like the columns to resize based upon the content of the column, here's your chance; just click the radio button next to "Auto-Fit to contents." The columns will automatically size to accommodate the widest bit of content in the column. Naturally there are limits; you can't have five columns that are each three inches wide on a letter-sized sheet of paper for instance.

Quick Tables

Word 2007 provides you with some tools to help you create some tables that are a little more than basic. When you go to the Insert tab on the Ribbon and click the drop-arrow on the Table button, you'll see "Quick Tables" listed at the bottom of the menu. Highlight it and the Quick Tables gallery, like in Figure 4.12, will appear. These are predefined tables you can insert—calendars, matrices, lists, and so forth. The colors schemes may vary a bit because they depend upon which Theme you have assigned to your document but the basic content will always be there. If you want to create a fancy table, check here first and see if there is a predefined Quick Table for that. If so, you'll save yourself a lot of time trying to reinvent one.

The Table Tools Tabs on the Ribbon

What's this? New tabs? Yes, one thing Word 2007 does to try and keep the Ribbon a manageable size is that it does have the ability to do contextual tabs. There are a lot of tools for working with tables in Microsoft Word, but you don't really need those tools if you don't actually have any tables in your document. So, Word conveniently stashes them away by hiding those tabs from you until you actually insert a table into your document. Create a table and place your cursor anywhere within it and you'll magically be presented with two new tabs on the Ribbon under the heading "Table Tools."

> **❝**
>
> Any sufficiently advanced technology is indistinguishable from magic.
> —*Arthur C. Clarke*
>
> **❞**

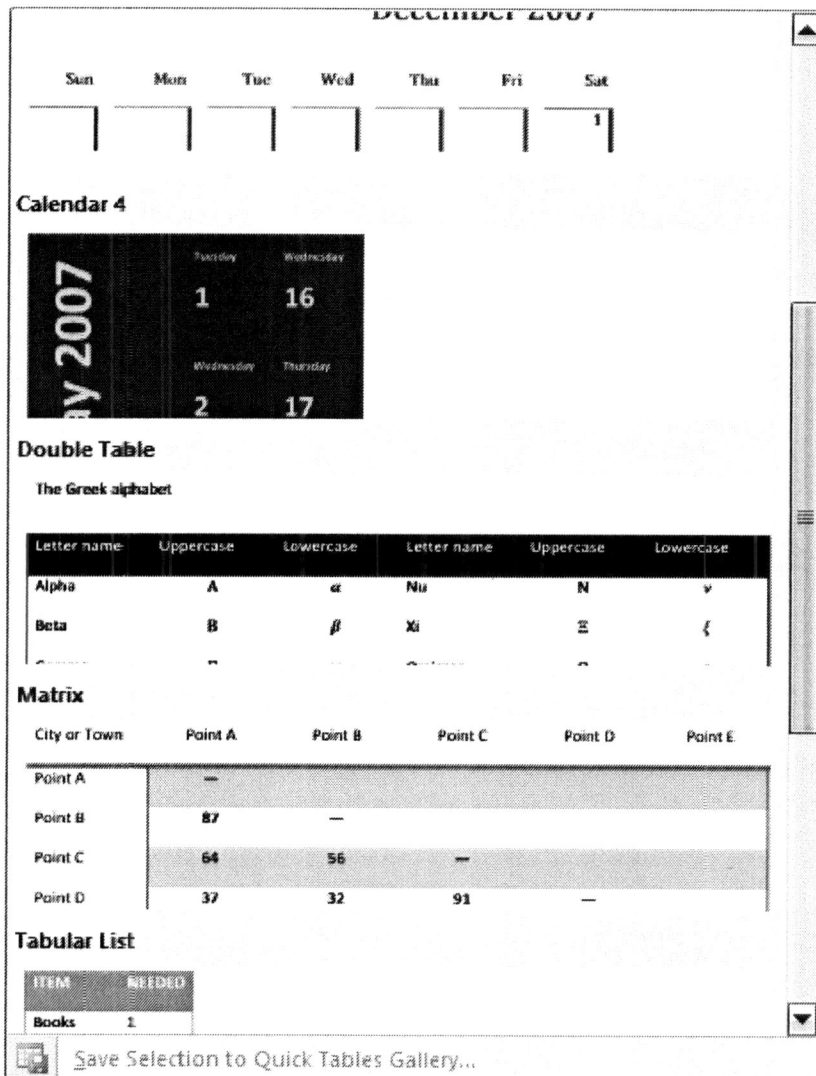

FIGURE 4.12

The Design Tab

The design tab gives you tools to control the basic look and feel of your table. Colors, lines, shadings, and so forth.

The first group of commands in the Design tab (see Figure 4.13) includes some checkboxes that let you specify if your table has special rows or columns in it. If you have a header row or first column that contains data labels, check the appropriate boxes. If you have a total row or a last

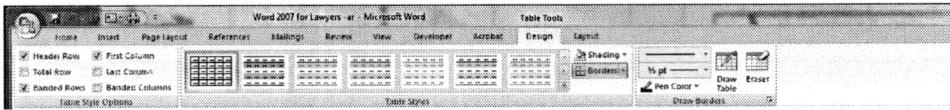

FIGURE 4.13

column that contains sums or summary data, check those boxes. Those will apply a bit of special formatting to set off those rows or columns a bit to make it clear that they're headings or summaries.

The checkboxes for banding just specify if you want the alternate rows to be shaded for easier reading.

The next group on this tab gives you a gallery of quick table styles (see Figure 4.14). By default, you've got a plain table (If you created your table with the Insert | Table tool), but you can pick from dozens of other choices in various styles, accents and even colors just by selecting it from the Gallery.

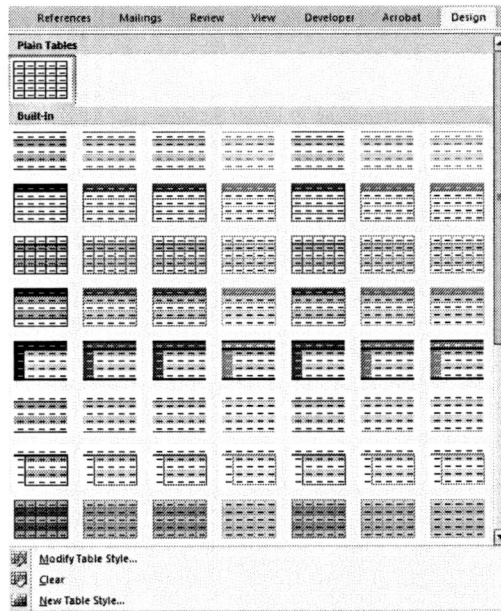

FIGURE 4.14

You also have the ability to customize the shading and/or borders of your table from the Design tab. Clicking the drop arrow next to Borders and you'll see Figure 4.15. Here you can do all sorts of tricky things with custom borders like adjust the thickness of the lines or have borders only along the sides or top/bottom of the cell.

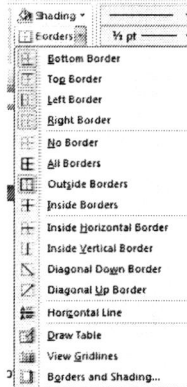

This is another example of Word 2007's live preview feature. Just by hovering your mouse over the sample tables in the gallery, Word will change your table to show you what it will look like *if* you select that option. No need to trial and error it, just move deliberately through the gallery until you find the look you like, then click on it.

FIGURE 4.15

The Layout Tab

The Layout tab is all about configuring the actual functionality of your table. Adding rows and columns, splitting cells, sorting or even inserting basic formulas. Let's take a moment to look at the most important features of the Layout tab. (See Figure 4.16.)

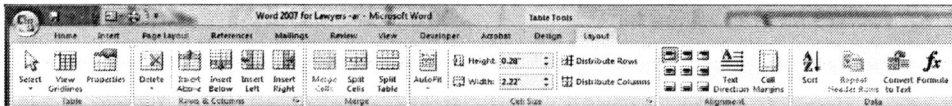

FIGURE 4.16

Properties

The table properties dialog box seen in Figure 4.17 lets you set various settings about the table, as well as the individual rows, columns, and

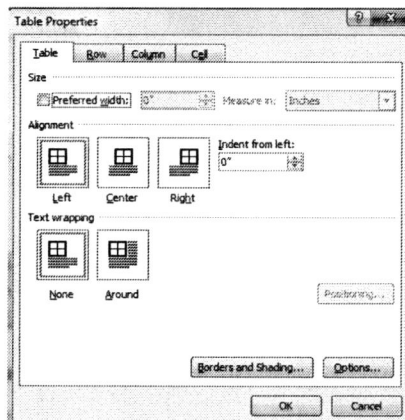

FIGURE 4.17

cells. You can specify the width, alignment, and how you'd like the text to wrap around it. If text wrapping is set to None (which it is by default), then the table will stand alone and no text will appear alongside it.

Rows and Columns

The Rows and Columns group contains commands for easily adding rows or columns to an existing table. If you underestimated how many you'd need, this is your solution. (You can also right-click your table and choose "Insert" to get at those commands.)

Data

The Data group (see Figure 4.18) contains some of the most interesting table features that Word has. First off, the "Sort" tool lets you sort any column based upon the data. Sort alphabetically, numerically, or by date depending upon the kind of data in the column. This is a great way to reorder data that you quickly input without having to worry about inputting it in a particular order to begin with.

FIGURE 4.18

▼ ▼ ▼ ▼ ▼

Tricks of the Pros

Lots of folks don't realize that you can actually sort lists of text that aren't in Tables in Word. Just select your list of terms and click "Sort" on the Home tab of the Ribbon. You'll get the Sort Text dialog box you see in Figure 4.19. You can do a three level sort if your data is that complex, but most of the time, you'll probably just do a simple ascending or descending (A–Z or Z–A) sort.

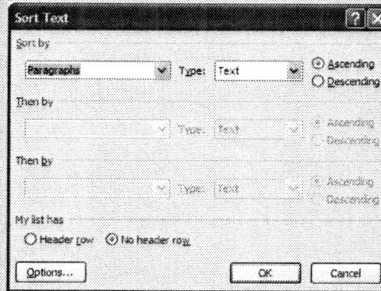

FIGURE 4.19

Notice the Header row options toward the bottom? That lets you tell Word if your list has a header row at the top that you don't want sorted into the text.

Convert to Text lets you break down your table without deleting the data within it. Essentially, this command will take a table and convert it directly to text.

The formula command gives Word limited, very limited, calculation capabilities. You can create formulas to do a lot of things, but don't get too carried away. Creating and maintaining more than a few simple formulas is a chore in Word.

▼ ▼ ▼ ▼ ▼

Tricks of the Pros

Most Microsoft Office pros wouldn't spend a lot of time creating a complex table, especially with a lot of formulas, in Microsoft Word. The tables feature just isn't that robust. Instead, we would create the table in Excel and just embed it into Word in the appropriate place. In Chapter 7, we'll dig into how to do that. Trust me, you'll like it.

Deleting a Table

Deleting a table is not quite as easy as you might think, but that's probably a good thing. If you took the time to create the table, you probably really wanted it and you wouldn't want to just blow it away casually. The best way to delete the table is to click somewhere in the table, then go to the Table Tools—Layout tab of the Ribbon (which only appears if you actually have a Table in your document and you are working with it), click the "Delete" button, and select "Delete Table" as you can see in Figure 4.20.

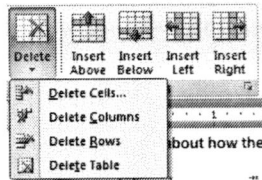

FIGURE 4.20

Reveal Codes

OK, I bamboozled you. This isn't really reveal codes but WordPerfect users are constantly looking for that feature and this is Word's best analogue: Reveal Formatting. (See Figure 4.21.) Word doesn't really have

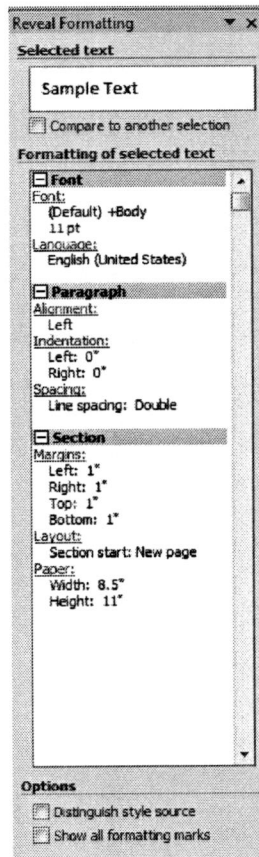

FIGURE 4.21

codes, as we discussed earlier, so the best it can do is show you what formatting has been applied to the current paragraph section or selected text. The Reveal Formatting task pane can be launched by pressing SHIFT+F1 and it will show you everything you need to know about the formatting applied to the selected text, current paragraph or current section.

If you want to make a change to one of the formatting elements, just click the hyperlinked title of the element and the appropriate dialog box will be opened that lets you make the changes you want. Take some time to learn to use this tool—it's worth it.

Introduction to Templates

A template is a starting point for a document. It generally includes formatting, layout (like margins and paper type), and even often contains boilerplate text to get your document started. One simple example might be if you print on a sheet of custom mailing labels frequently and you want to set up your page layout (margins, borders, etc.) to fit those labels, then save that as a template for later reuse. Or, a more advanced example might be if you have a standard retention letter that you send to clients to acknowledge the lawyer-client relationship, you could create the standard letter, minus the specifics like names, dates, addresses, and save that as a template. Then in the future when you want to send that letter you just start from the template, fill in the variables for that particular client, and you're ready to go.

Word has been based upon templates for years and there are two kinds of templates that you should be familiar with in Word:

- Global—Global templates are always open, regardless of what kind of template you based the document on. Normal.dotm, the default template in Word, is an example of a Global template.
- Document—A document template is the template that you base an individual document on. There are a couple of dozen of them that come with Word (Faxes, memos, letters, etc.) and hundreds more available (generally for free) from Microsoft Office Online. Or, you can build your own as we'll talk about in Chapter 8. Document templates are probably what you're thinking of when you think about templates.

Headers and Footers

Headers and footers are text elements that appear at the top and bottom of each page. In some cases, these may be empty or blank—simply margins. In other cases, they can contain highly formatted or dynamic data, such as a letterhead masthead at the top, page numbering, and document titles in the footer and so forth.

To create a header just go to the Insert tab of the Ribbon, click the Header command on the Header and Footer group and you'll get the gallery you see in Figure 4.22 with a number of standard headers you can add. You can use one of those; start with one and then modify it; or even start with a blank header and create your own content.

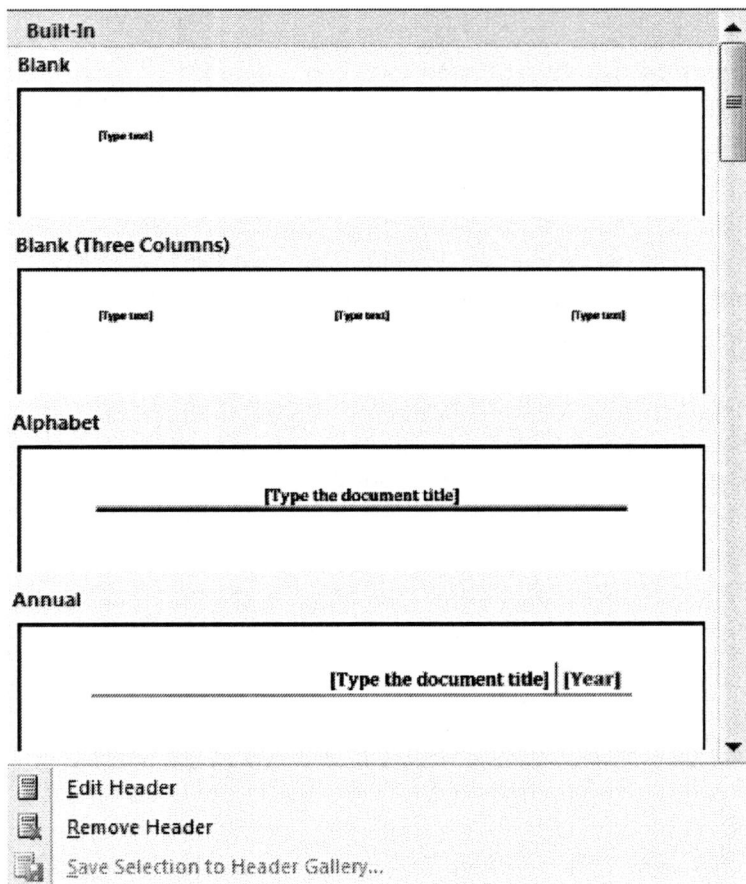

FIGURE 4.22

To delete a header, just click the "Remove Header" option.

Creating a footer is essentially the same process but with a slightly different gallery. (See Figure 4.23.)

In either case, if you build a custom header or footer and think you'll want to use it again in the future, you can simply select your custom

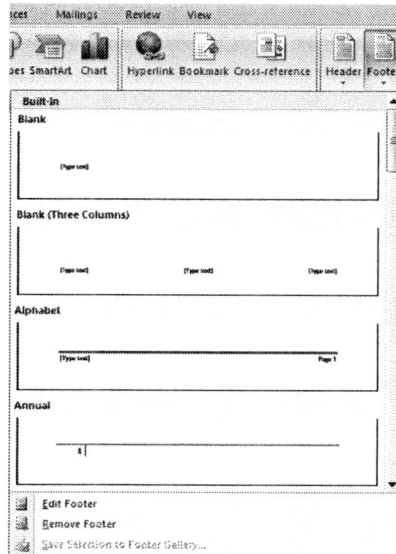

FIGURE 4.23

header or footer, then pop the appropriate gallery (header or footer) as described previously and then click the "Save Selection to [Header/Footer] Gallery . . ." button. The gallery is stored with the template so any future documents you create with the same template (Normal.dotm, usually) will have your custom header or footer in the gallery for your easy access.

When you have a header or footer in your document and you double-click the header or footer area to edit it, another contextual tab is added to the Ribbon and that's the "Header & Footer Tools: Design" tab as you see in Figure 4.24.

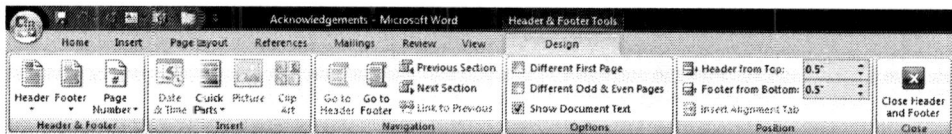

FIGURE 4.24

The Header and Footer group contains the same tools that the Header and Footer group on the Insert menu does and those tools, naturally, work the same way here. The Insert group contains four commands that you'll also find on the Insert tab of the Ribbon—these are things you might commonly insert into a header or footer. Honestly, I doubt that many lawyers will be inserting too many pictures or bits of clip art into a header or footer (though you could use that to insert a firm logo I suppose), but Date and Time would be a pretty common thing to insert and the Quick Parts include document properties like Author and fields like the document's path, which is quite popular with lawyers. You can also create and save custom quick parts like boilerplate text (a disclaimer perhaps?) that you want to reuse again and again.

The Navigation group has tools that make it a little easier for you to move around between headers and footers, though I rarely see these commands used by lawyers in practice.

The Options group, however, has some *very* useful commands in it; in particular "Different First Page" and "Different Odd & Even Pages," which lets you create documents that don't need the same header and/or footer on every page. That's especially handy if you're creating a document with a cover page (which you might not want the same header/footer on) or if you're creating a book-style document where the even/odd pages will face each other and you want to put unique information on those facing pages. We get a *lot* of requests for how to omit the footer from a first page of a document and "Different First Page" is the answer.

The Position group includes two very useful but confusingly named commands: Header From Top and Footer From Bottom. These commands actually let you specify the height of the header and footer respectively. If you have a lot of information you want to fit into your header or footer, you can make it larger, or if you want an especially svelte header or footer, you can make it smaller. Also handy if you're trying to match up the header or footer to a preprinted form or piece of letterhead. The third command in the position group lets you create an alignment tab in the header or footer. Alignment tabs are a new feature in Word 2007, and unlike other tabs that have an absolute position on the page ("at 2.5 inches" for example), alignment tabs are relative to the margins of your page. So, if you create an alignment tab that is 2.5 inches from the left margin and you later change the margins, then the alignment tab will move as well. In theory, it's a handy way to align text within your header or footer without having to worry about realigning it if you later change your page margins. In reality, legal documents have fairly well-defined and inflexible margin settings anyhow, so the chances you'd be changing the margins in a way that affects your header or footer text are pretty slim.

Finally, the Close Header and Footer button gets you out of the header and footer and back to editing your page. You can accomplish the same thing by merely double-clicking anywhere on your page (other than in the header or footer). If you want to get back into the header or footer . . . just double click it.

Summary

It's not just what you say, it's how you say it. Your content is critical, of course, but we all know that legal documents have very precise formatting requirements and you have to make sure you have complete control of how that content is laid out. It does you no good to make a brilliant legal argument if the court rejects it because it's improperly formatted.

Word provides you with some great tools to control formatting—styles, tabs, tables, columns, and more. Mastering those tools will give you mastery over how your work is presented. If you only have time to master *one* of these concepts though . . . spend that time on Styles.

Stuff Lawyers Use 5

Recognizing that I have no way of knowing what jurisdiction you're in (or even what country!), I can't get overly specific in this chapter. Each of you may have different requirements for documents in your specific jurisdiction. What I will try to do is show some of the features that tend to appear in legal-specific documents and hopefully you'll be able to evaluate these tips in the context of your own court rules and make any adjustments you need to make.

Pleadings

Word has, for quite some time actually, had a template for pleadings. Unfortunately, they don't make it terribly easy to find, but once you have it, you can use it all you like. Your best bet for finding it is to go to Office Button | New and at the very top of the New Document window is a search box for searching the Microsoft Online site for a particular kind of document. Type in "Pleading" and press enter as I have in Figure 5.1 on the next page. What you'll get is a list of templates that match that keyword—as you can see in this figure, I've gotten four hits that are types of pleadings and a form that says it's a petition for di-

> **Note**
>
> You'll need to do this, at least the first time, from a computer that is connected to the Internet. If you're on an airplane or otherwise disconnected at the time, you'll have to wait. Once you've downloaded the template the first time, you can save it to your local hard drive and you'll always have it.

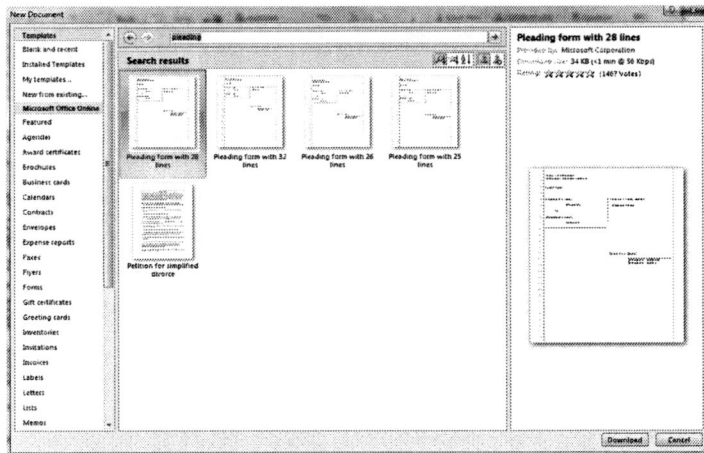

FIGURE 5.1

vorce. Select the pleading template you want, I picked the one with 28 lines for my test but you can select whatever fits your jurisdiction best.

These templates are provided free of charge, but it *will* check your Microsoft Office first using the "Microsoft Genuine Advantage" tool to verify that you have a legal and properly licensed copy of Microsoft Word 2007 in use. Assuming you do, the download should take mere seconds and you'll be ready to roll with your new pleading template.

Table of Authorities

Lawyers love to create tables of authorities. A table of authorities is a list of references in the document, along with the page number indicating where the reference can be found. Creating a table of authorities is pretty easy actually. You simply insert your citation into the document where you want it, then highlight it, go to the References tab on the Ribbon and click "Mark Citation" under the table of authorities group. Doing so will launch the dialog box you see in Figure 5.2. Here you can edit the short citation and change the category if you like.

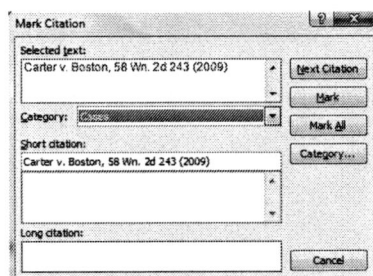

FIGURE 5.2

If none of the categories built into Word suit you, you can edit the list of categories by clicking the "Category" button on the right side of the dialog box. Add or change the categories to whatever you like.

Once you've got the category and short citation the way you want them, click "Mark."

To insert your Table of Authorities into the document, just go to where you want it and click "Insert Table of Authorities" from the like-named group on the References tab of the Ribbon. (See Figure 5.3.) If you subsequently add authorities that you want included in the table, just go back to the References tab and click the "Update Table" button in the Table of Authorities group.

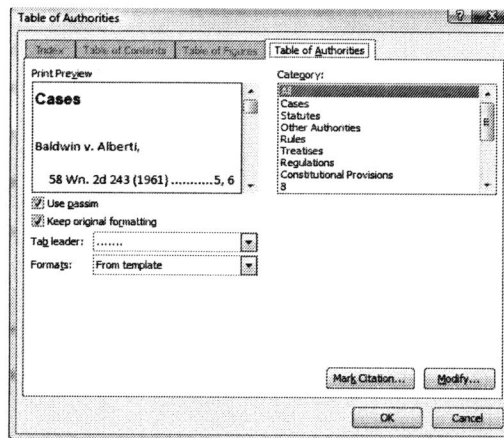

FIGURE 5.3

Numbered and Bulleted Lists

One feature that lawyers use quite often are lists—both numbered and bulleted. The difference is fairly straightforward—a bulleted list is used when the order of the items isn't as important. A numbered list is a way to create a list when you want to specify an order of events (like a set of step-by-step instructions) or when you want to create a list of items that are set off with unique identifiers so they can be more readily referred to later. Numbered lists are more common, for this last reason, in legal documents.

Word is pretty intelligent about recognizing when you want to create a bulleted or numbered list. If you just start a new paragraph with a "1." Word will assume that you intend to create a numbered list and will apply the default style for that. This is also true if you start an outline with the classic Roman numerals ("I." etc.) or an alpha list with "A."

If you want to start a bulleted list instead, you can just preface your line with an asterisk like this "*" followed by a space and Word will convert that automatically to the default bullet.

You can change the numbering format just by clicking the drop-arrow to the right of the numbering button on the Ribbon like in Figure 5.4. Here you can select an alternate format for your numbered list or define a new number format.

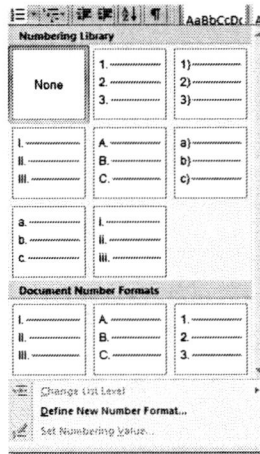

FIGURE 5.4

If you'd like to turn off Word 2007's proclivity to initiate numbered lists when you start a line with "1." or whatnot, you can do so by clicking the Office Button, going to Word options | Proofing | AutoCorrect Options | AutoFormat as you Type tab, as you see in Figure 5.5. Uncheck the box under "Apply as you type" for "Automatic numbered lists" and your worries are gone. Well, if your worries consist only of Word automatically creating numbered lists anyhow.

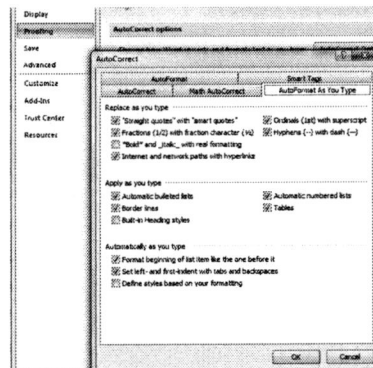

FIGURE 5.5

Understanding Numbering in Word

It's probably a good idea for me to give you a rudimentary understanding of how numbering works in Microsoft Word. We could do an extensive study of the subject, but if you're an lawyer, you've already had a lot of years of school and you probably don't want to spend two more just trying to figure out Word's little complexities in the area of numbered lists. So, let's try for the short-course version.

There are two basic kinds of lists in Word: Simple Lists and Multilevel lists (yes, I'm oversimplifying a bit but just come with me on this). The defining characteristic of a Simple List is that it has only one level, such as 1., 2., 3., 4 . . etc. or A., B., C. or even bullets. Whatever the delineating character, the point is there's just the one level of list. Multilevel lists are outlines and similar lists that contain multiple levels with different symbols or numbers (typically) to delineate the levels. Like this:

    I. This is the first level.
      a. This is a second level.
      b. This is another second level item.
        i. You can have a third level.
        ii. Or more levels, but you get the idea . . .
    II. And another first level item to finish my example.

All of these lists are really a series of paragraphs (each line is a new paragraph), which have been formatted as list paragraphs. Where you can sometimes run into problems with lists is that if you use the List Galleries to apply your list formatting.

There isn't any real difference between a bulleted and a numbered list as far as Word is concerned. The only difference between them is the kind of character prefacing each paragraph.

You can create a numbered list from scratch, or you can convert existing text to a numbered list.

To create a new list, click the Numbering (or Bullets or Multilevel list, depending upon which you want) button on the Home tab of the Ribbon to get the gallery of choices, as you see in Figure 5.6. Select the format you want and then just start typing your list. At the end of each item, press enter to get the next number.

> **Tip**
>
> If you want extra space after an item or if you want to type another paragraph within your list without preceding that paragraph with a number, press SHIFT+ENTER instead of ENTER. When you press ENTER again, Word will resume your list.

If you want to convert an existing set of text to a list, just select that text first and use the Numbering or Bullets gallery to apply your list format. Each paragraph in your selected text will be formatted as a separate list item. Note . . . you may have to clean it up a bit by separating or recombining items, depending upon how diligent you were in using paragraphs to create the text to begin with. If you want to separate something

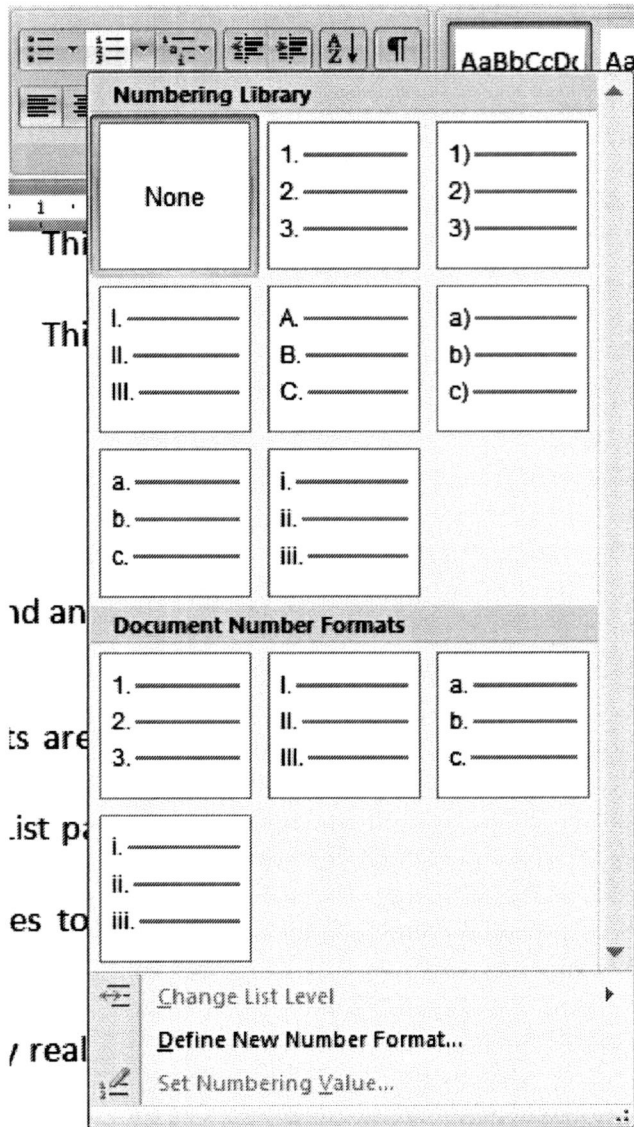

FIGURE 5.6

as a new list item, just move your cursor to the beginning of that word or phrase and press ENTER to make it a new paragraph (and thus a new list item). If Word has made two list items (1 & 2 perhaps) out of something that should be a single list item, just go to the beginning of the second item and hit backspace to delete the paragraph definition and move it up onto the previous line.

Automatic Lists

Word will often create lists for you automatically, sometimes whether you want it to or not, if you just start typing one. To start a numbered list automatically, just start a paragraph by typing "1." and pressing the space bar. Word will start a numbered list. "A." or "a." or "I." will have the same effect with different numbered list formats. To start a bulleted list, type an asterisk ("*") then press the space bar.

If that behavior annoys you and you would like to have more control over your lists (and non-lists), you can turn it off. Like a lot of the things Word automatically provides that capability by AutoCorrect. To turn it off, just click the Office Button, go to Word Options | Proofing and click the "AutoCorrect Options" button. Then go to the "AutoFormat As You Type" tab and under the "Apply as you type" group you'll find entries for "Automatic bulleted lists" and "Automatic numbered lists." (See Figure 5.7.) Clear one, or both, of the checkboxes as you desire and Word will stop making automatic lists for you.

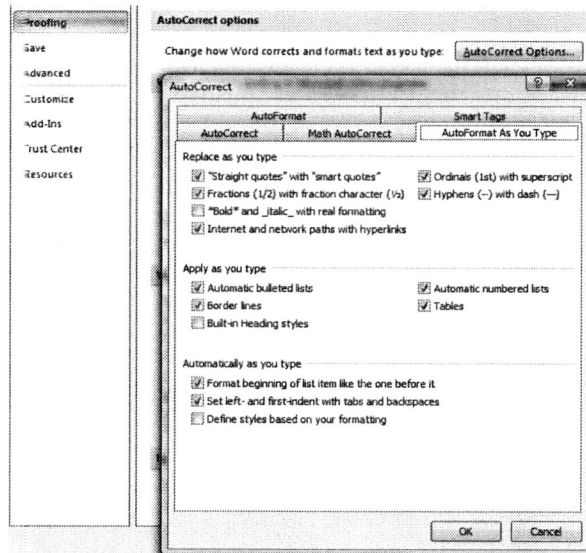

FIGURE 5.7

Continuing a List

Maybe you've ended a numbered list and somewhere later in the document you want to resume that list, or maybe you got tired of pressing SHIFT+ENTER to insert un-numbered paragraphs and decided it would be easier to just end the list, type your additional paragraphs, and resume the list later. Either way, there is a fairly simple way to continue a previous list. Just start a new list, either automatically as above or by clicking the numbering button from the Ribbon. Then right-click your first new item and select "Continue Numbering" from the context menu (see Figure 5.8). Word will pick up your list from where it left off . . . usually. The exceptions? If your new list uses a different number format than the previous one did or if you've been messing around with the list indents.

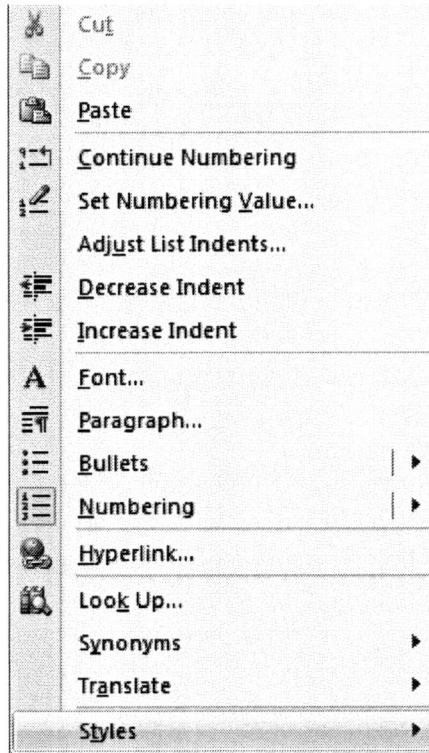

FIGURE 5.8

If that happens to you and you can't seem to match up the number formats, don't throw in the towel. Turn on the display of paragraph marks (CTRL+SHIFT+8), select the last correctly numbered list item, and be sure to include the paragraph mark (that's what contains the number formatting). Then use the format painter to "paint" that format onto your resumed list.

If none of that works don't give up hope, the "Set Numbering Value" dialog box will come to your rescue. Start your new list items and click the drop-arrow next to the Numbering button to get the Numbering Gallery. Select "Set Numbering Value" to get the Set Numbering Value dialog box you see in Figure 5.9. From here, you can try "Continue from previous list" but that would be the triumph of hope over experience because if Continue Numbering didn't work . . . Con-

One gotcha with this solution . . . a nice feature of Word's numbered lists is that if you decided to insert an item in the list, all of the other numbers below that will update to reflect the new addition. But it won't work if you have used the "Set value to" trick to fix a list, that's actually a *separate* list. So if you add a new #4 to your first list, you may now have two "#7s" as your previous #6 became #7 and your manually continued list knew nothing about it. Just keep an eye on that if you resort to using "Set value to" to continue a previous list.

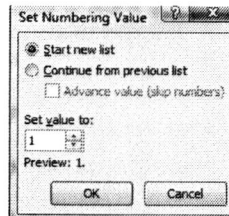

FIGURE 5.9

tinue from previous list won't either. But what you *can* do is change the "Set value to" setting to whatever your next number is supposed to be and let Word just continue from there as if this was a new list that just happens to start at 7 or 12 or whatever. Ideal? No. But if all else fails, this will help you get your work done.

Restarting Numbering

The "Set value to" option I mentioned just above has another good use . . . starting your numbering over again. Sometimes Word will want to continue a previous list even when you don't want it to. If you want to manually reset the numbering to "1." (or some other value), you can use "Set value to" to manually set the numbers back to "1." (or whatever) and then continue your list from there.

When you're ready to end your list, you can click the Bullets (or Numbering) button again to turn the style off, or just press ENTER twice.

Table of Contents

Building a table of contents is somewhat like creating a Table of Authorities. You mark text and then insert the Table of Contents and Word will build the table for you and update it whenever you ask. Marking the text is actually a little more automatic with the Table of Contents than it is with the Table of Authorities because the Table of Contents builds with the pre-defined "Heading" styles in Word that you're probably already using.

Whenever I create a long document, I use the Heading 1, Heading 2, Heading 3, etc. styles to format section and sub-section headings. If I want to add a Table of Contents, it's thus quite easy to do; just go to where I want the Table of Contents, switch to the References tab and click the "Table of Contents" button to display the Table of Contents gallery of pre-defined styles. I can also create my own if I don't like any of the built in tables. When you select a Table of Contents from the gallery, it will be inserted in the document at the current insertion point.

Electronic Filing

Electronic filing is rapidly becoming the rule rather than the exception and Word 2007 is even more compatible than any version before with those e-filing rules. Though the specific requirements will vary slightly from jurisdiction to jurisdiction, virtually all of them will accept your e-filing in PDF format, which means that Word 2007's (almost) native PDF capability gets you to where you need to go in order to file electronically. If you're in a jurisdiction that accepts Word documents, it probably still requires the .DOC (Word 97-2003) format files, which you can also easily produce with Word 2007 by simply doing a Save As and changing the Save As Type to "Word 97-2003 Document." (See Figure 5.10.)

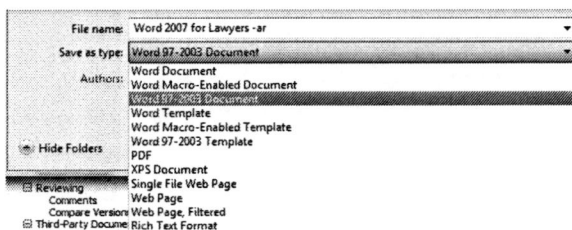

FIGURE 5.10

Using Bibliography

Word 2007's Bibliography function is surprisingly capable. When you type some text that you would like to include a citation for simply click where you'd like the citation included, then go to the References tab of the Ribbon. Make sure that the Style is appropriate for your document (APA is the default and what I generally use) then click "Insert Citation."

If the citation is one you've used before, in this document, it will appear on the drop list. Select it and the citation will be inserted at your cursor. If not you can click "Add Source." Adding the source will let you specify author, title, publisher and other information you need for the Bibliography.

▼ ▼ ▼ ▼ ▼

Tricks of the Pros

The drop list of citations will initially only include cites that you've used in this document. If you'd like to add citations you've used in previous documents go to the References tab, and click Manage Sources. You'll see the Master List on the left which includes all of the sources you've added in previous documents. Select the ones you want to use in this document and click the "Copy" button to move them to the list for the current document.

You can also use the Manage Sources tool to delete or edit previously used sources, or add a new one.

If you want to insert a citation but you don't have that citation on your list yet and you're not ready to enter that information, then click "Add New Placeholder" instead of "Add New Source." Word will let you name and create a placeholder and later you can go back and update those placeholders with the cite information so that they can be replaced with the actual content. When you're ready to fix those placeholders just go to the References Tab and click Manage Sources. You can select your placeholder and Edit it to replace it with the actual citation info.

When you're ready to create the bibliography just go to the place in the document (near the end, generally) where you want it, go to the References tab of the Ribbon and click Bibliography to drop the gallery. On the gallery select a Bibliography style you like, and it will be created for you with all of your sources.

Later if you add new cites and you want to update your Bibliography just click on the Bibliography and a "Update Citations and Bibliography" button will appear.

Summary

Lawyers make heavy use of a number of pretty specific features of Microsoft Word in the creation of the documents we use in our practices. Among those features, the Table of Authorities, Electronic Filing, and list formats have improved dramatically in Word 2007. Master those capabilities and you'll be more effective than ever before.

Collaboration 6

Microsoft approached Office 2007 with a very heavy emphasis on collaboration and this plays nicely into how lawyers tend to use their tools. Partners, Associates, Co-Counsel, Clients, Witnesses, Paralegals . . . on any given document there may be anywhere from one to many authors and editors. Effectively working together to produce a professional finished document is key to running a great law practice.

> 66
> I've always believed in writing without a collaborator, because where two people are writing the same book, each believes he gets all the worries and only half the royalties.
> —*Agatha Christie*
> 99

SharePoint

SharePoint is Microsoft's browser-based collaboration portal. If you have Windows Server 2003, then you already have a license for Windows SharePoint Services 3.0, which is all you need to create shared document libraries and a fair set of other collaboration tools. Creating and configuring SharePoint sites is a little beyond the scope of this

▼
Want to know more about how to collaborate to produce documents in your practice? Visit the ABA Web store and pick up a copy of Dennis Kennedy and Tom Mighell's excellent book, *The Lawyer's Guide to Collaboration Tools and Technologies* (ABA, 2008).

book, but I'll try to offer you a few tips for working with SharePoint from a user's standpoint.

Windows SharePoint Services 3.0 (WSS)

Windows SharePoint Services (WSS) is the basic set of services that provide collaboration and a web-based interface. Microsoft Office SharePoint Server (we'll talk about that next) is built on top of WSS. However, WSS is all you need for most collaboration. WSS installs right on top of any Windows 2003 or Windows 2008 server and runs there as a service. Check with your IT consultant or systems administrator—you may discover that you already have WSS installed and running in your firm. Did I mention that if you have a Windows 2003 (or 2008) server then you already own the WSS license? Effectively, it's free.

Microsoft Office SharePoint Server 2007 (MOSS)

Microsoft Office SharePoint Server (MOSS) adds a lot of bells and whistles on top of WSS. Most of those bells and whistles involve search and personalized portals. For most firms, especially small firms, MOSS is overkill—especially because MOSS is not even remotely free. You'll have to buy it separately to install on your servers.

Using SharePoint

OK, so you've got SharePoint installed on your server. Now what? Before you start saving to your SharePoint site you should add it to your Network Places—that'll make it easier to save there. To do that, click the Office Button and Save As. Toward the bottom of the Save As dialog box, click the "Tools" button to get the drop-list you see in Figure 6.1.

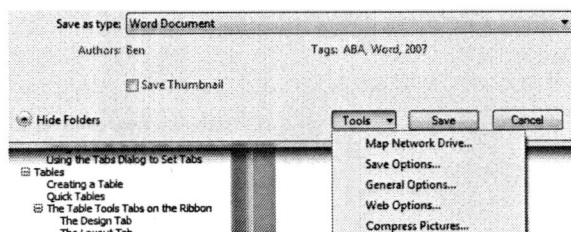

FIGURE 6.1

Select "Map Network Drive" to get the dialog box you see in Figure 6.2 below. (Note—this was done in Vista, your dialog box will look a little different if you're using Windows XP but the process is basically the same.) Once you get there, click the link that says "Connect to a Web site that you can use to store your documents and pictures." That will start the "Add Network Location Wizard," which walks you through the process. Make sure to select "Choose a Custom Network Location" instead of "MSN Communities" when you get to that step. When you get to the screen that asks for the location, type (or copy and paste from your browser) the address of your document library in SharePoint. If you're not sure what it is, ask your network administrator, he or she should be able to tell you. After you specify the location, you'll be asked to give it a name; just pick a friendly name that makes sense to you. "Our SharePoint Server" or something like that is fine. When you're finished, Word will add the location to your folders list so it will be able to save documents in the future without going through the mapping steps each time.

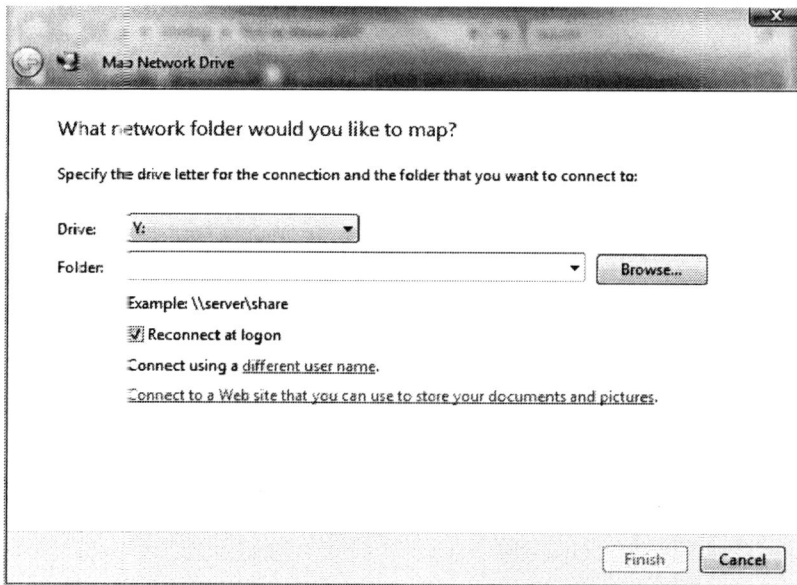

FIGURE 6.2

Uploading Existing Documents to SharePoint

If you want to upload documents you've already created, just go to your SharePoint site in your web browser and click the Upload button on the document library's toolbar (as you can see in Figure 6.3).

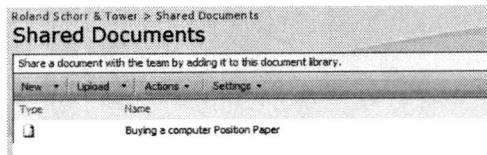

FIGURE 6.3

It will ask you where the document is and walk you through the up-load. Easy enough for one document. If you want to copy a *bunch* of documents, however, you may want to use a slightly different technique. On the right-side of the SharePoint view, you'll find a view setting that looks like Figure 6.4.

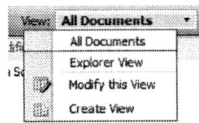

FIGURE 6.4

Click the "All Documents" and drop-down list appears as shown in the figure and select Explorer View. That will open your document library in a view that looks just like Windows Explorer. Now open the real Windows Explorer (Windows Key + E will do it) alongside and navigate to the folder that contains the documents you want to upload. Select those documents and just drag and drop them to your SharePoint Explorer view.

Groove

The question I get all the time is "What is Groove?" And my answer is usually "Well . . . umm . . . Groove is sort of hard to explain." Groove is one of those really cool products that Microsoft bought and is now developing to improve and to integrate into the rest of their product line.

Groove is a utility that each of the folks who are going to participate on the team will install on their workstations. You create a Groove workspace for your case or project, and within that workspace, you can have document libraries, calendars, contact lists, and all sorts of other project-related content. (See Figure 6.5.)

Adding files to a Groove document library is much like adding them to SharePoint. Open the Groove workspace, navigate to the files library where you want the document(s) to reside, then drag and drop files from

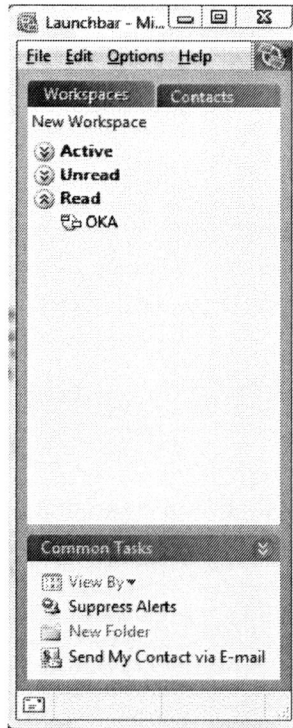

FIGURE 6.5

Windows Explorer to the Groove workspace. (See Figure 6.6 below.) Once you've placed the documents in Groove, your collaborators who subscribe to the same workspace (you can invite them from the "Workspace

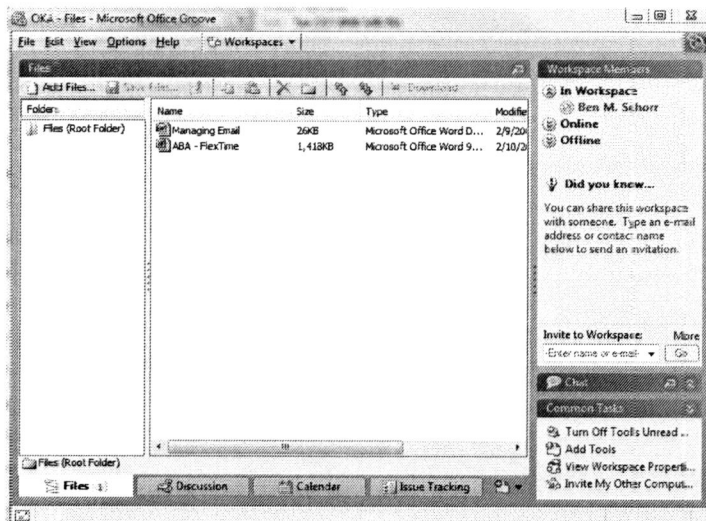

FIGURE 6.6

Members" tab on the right side of the workspace) will automatically receive those documents on their own stations. Groove synchronizes the document library of the workspace transparently in the background among all of the connected members of the workspace. Go offline and the library goes with you—it will automatically update, including uploading any changes you made while offline, the next time you connect.

Generally speaking, Groove is best for small teams—between two and 20 members or so—as larger teams can tend to generate too much synchronization traffic and lead to inefficiencies.

For more information about Microsoft Groove, you might want to check out these sites:

- http://office.microsoft.com/en-us/groove/default.aspx—The Official Microsoft Groove home page.
- http://technet.microsoft.com/en-us/magazine/2006.10.intothe groove.aspx—A little more technical introduction to Groove from TechNet Magazine.
- http://grv.microsoft.com/help/—A bunch of helpful documentation and resources for getting started with Groove, including a tutorial and deployment guide.

Groove is not free.

Collaboration via E-mail

Over the last decade or so lawyers have gotten very comfortable collaborating via e-mail; by sending documents back and forth. This method is tried but not really true . . . and that's because this method tends to generate an unwieldy number of document versions, and especially, if you're working with more than one other party, it can become a nightmare of tracked changes and trying to merge different versions of the content into a single master document.

Tracking Changes

One of Word's most controversial features—if a word processor can be said to have "controversial features"—has got to be tracked changes. The reason is that if you're not careful, you can inadvertently transmit those tracked changes to other, potentially adverse, parties in your case. And that can be bad. Really, really bad. See Chapter 11's section on metadata for more on that. But here we're going to focus on using Tracked Changes' power for good and not evil.

Track Changes features can be found on the Review tab of the Ribbon (see Figure 6.7).

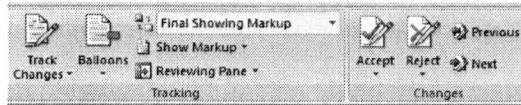

FIGURE 6.7

If you're going to use it, then the first thing you'll need to do is turn Track Changes on. Just click the Track Changes button to do that. On the status bar (see Figure 6.8), it should change from "Track Changes: Off" to "Track Changes: On."

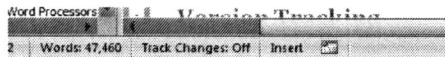

FIGURE 6.8

If you don't see the "Track Changes" status on your status bar at the bottom of Word, then you really *do* want to turn that option on. Right-click the status bar and click where it says "Track Changes" to turn that on and add it to the status bar. Believe me . . . if Track Changes is on, you *want* to know it.

There are also a number of options you can set/change for Track Changes. To get to those, click where it says "Track Changes" on the Ribbon to drop down the menu, and select "Change Tracking Options." (See Figure 6.9.) That will display the "Track Changes Options" dialog box that you see in Figure 6.10 below.

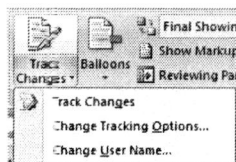

FIGURE 6.9

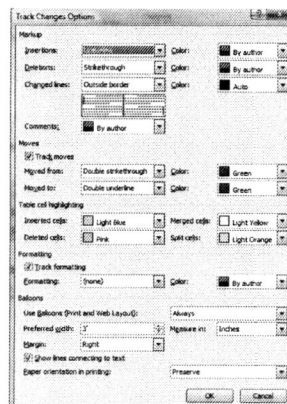

FIGURE 6.10

Most of these options just have to do with how the changes will be displayed—which colors or font effects you want to apply—but a couple of them are especially useful. For instance, I find it hard to read a document that has *too* many highlighted changes and I want any substantive changes that get made to really stand out. So, I tend to turn off the ability to track formatting changes. Not many formatting changes are going to get made to a legal document anyhow (since the formats are fairly proscribed), and for the stuff that I write, I don't care much about the formatting. To turn tracking of formatting changes off, just uncheck the box next to "Track formatting."

The other interesting settings here allow you to customize how the balloons (those are the pop-out colored text boxes that explain or display the change) are formatted. You can set little things like how wide they should be, and which margin you want them in. These are all personal preference settings and I tend to leave them alone since the defaults are fine with me; but if you'd rather have the balloons in the left margin instead of the right or 2" wide instead of 3," then you can make those changes here.

One other configuration change I'll encourage you to make is to how the balloons work. If you click the drop arrow on the balloons button of the Ribbon, you'll get a menu that controls how the balloons are going to function. The default is to show all Revisions in Balloons, and if you like to work that way that's fine, but I think most lawyers are actually more comfortable with revisions being displayed inline—which means the affected text is struck out and the replacement text, in a different color, inserted in its place. This has the "redline" effect that most lawyers are familiar with. I do like to see comments and formatting in balloons, as those can be easily set off to the side. But for actual text revisions, I like to see them inline, where the editor wanted them to go. So, my setting would look like Figure 6.11.

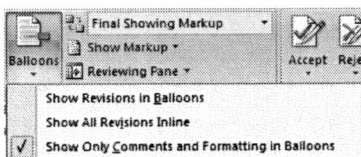

FIGURE 6.11

The next field I want to point out in Track Changes is the Display for Review field and it really is important. You want to make sure that if Track Changes is on that you either have one of the ". . . Showing Markup" options selected *or* that you are *very* aware of the fact that you

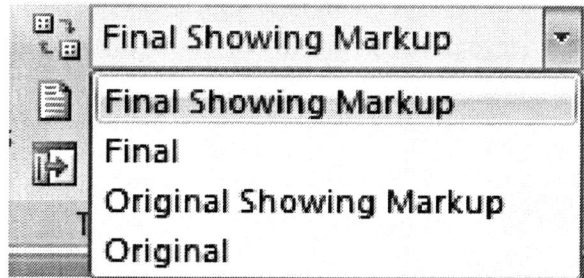

FIGURE 6.12

don't. (See Figure 6.12.) Again, Track Changes can be great but it can also be seriously bad if you accidentally allow a document with tracked changes into the hands of another party who shouldn't see those changes. If you change your "Display for Review" to "Final" or "Original," Word will hide the tracked changes from you, even though they will still be embedded within your document. If you find editing a document with the markup displayed to be too distracting, it's ok to turn the markup display off . . . but be darned sure you turn it back on and give the document a look-over; plus run it thru a metadata checker, before you send it along to anybody who isn't collaborating on its creation. That may include the client or court, as well as adverse parties.

Under the Show Markup button (see Figure 6.13) you can control which markup is going to display. Again, with the possible exception of formatting, I think that you really should have *all* of it showing.

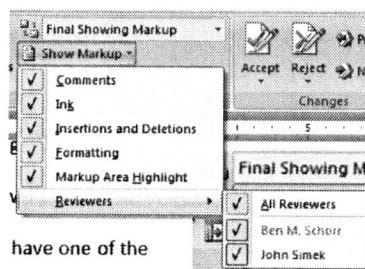

FIGURE 6.13

The Reviewers list lets you control which reviewers you want to display markup from and, cleverly, shows which color their particular edits will appear in. In my document, John Simek's comments are going to appear in purple; while mine will appear in red. If you want to hide markup from a particular reviewer, you can turn them off (or back on) here. Usually you should leave this alone though so you can see all markup from all reviewers.

The other tool you're going to find handy, I predict, is the Reviewing Pane. When the Reviewing Pane is turned on, it shows a summary (either vertically along the left side of the document or horizontally at the bottom) of changes and lets you quickly navigate them. I use this tool all the time when I'm dealing with the many comments and edits my editors come back with. When you have 71 edits in a 200 page document, it can be nice to have that tool there to help you quickly address them.

Once you have changes in your document and you want to start merging (or rejecting) those changes, the next Ribbon group, appropriately titled "Changes," provides just the tools you need. (See Figure 6.14.)

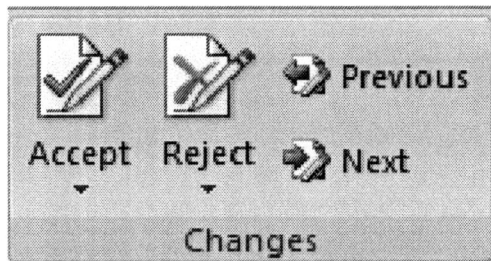

FIGURE 6.14

When you select a particular change in your document, you can click "Accept" to make that change part of the final document or "Reject" to delete that change and leave the document as it was before the change was made.

Clicking the drop arrow on "Accept" (or "Reject") will give you a couple of tools that may speed up the process somewhat. Most notably the ability to Accept (or Reject) ALL changes in the document in a single stroke (well . . . a couple of clicks anyhow). (See Figure 6.15.) If you have supreme confidence in your editor, or if you've already reviewed and agree with (or hate) all of the edits they've suggested, you can accept (or reject) them all at once. A huge time saver!

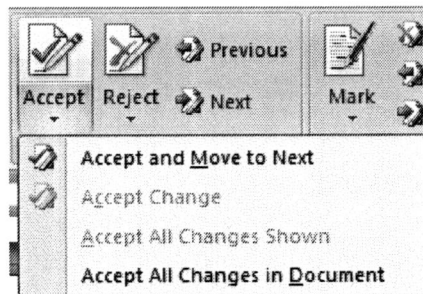

FIGURE 6.15

▼ ▼ ▼ ▼ ▼

Tricks of the Pros

If you want to accept or reject all changes made by one particular reviewer, there *is* a way to do that in Word 2007. On the Review pane of
the Ribbon, click "Show Markup," highlight "Reviewers" and uncheck
"All Reviewers," which is the default. Annoyingly, Word will now
make you again click "Show Markup" and highlight Reviewers. Now
you want to select only the reviewer (or reviewers) whose changes
you want to work with. With that done, you can go back to the Accept button, hit the drop arrow (as we did above) and select "Accept
all changes shown" and only the changes from that reviewer will be
accepted en masse. Yes, you can also use this trick to reject all
changes from that reviewer.

The Previous and Next buttons in the Changes group just take you to
the Previous (or Next) change in the document without doing anything to
the current change. Handy if you're just reviewing changes without wanting to take any action on them. As a
general rule, however, I recommend
acting upon the changes while you're
there—it's poor time management to
touch the same change twice if you
don't have to.

Carpe See-um

Do it while you're looking at it!
(Yes, I just made that up.)

Version Tracking

When you're creating and/or collaborating on documents, it is often
handy to have some way to track what version you're currently working
with. Word provides a rudimentary way to do that automatically, in the
advanced properties. Click the Office Button, then Prepare, and then
"Properties" to display the properties bar at the top of your document. At
the left side of that, click the Property Views and Options button similar
to what you see in Figure 6.16 and select Advanced Properties. What
you'll get is a dialog box similar to Figure 6.17 and on the Statistics tab
you'll find the "Revision Number." All that really is, unfortunately, is a
count of how many times the document has been modified and saved. If
you press CTRL+S after every word, you'll increment the Revision Number
awfully quickly.

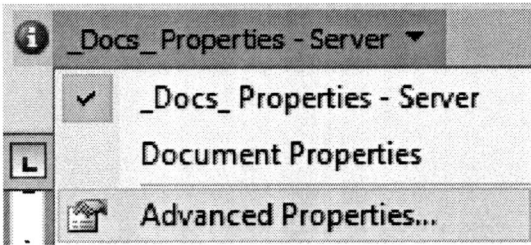

FIGURE 6.16

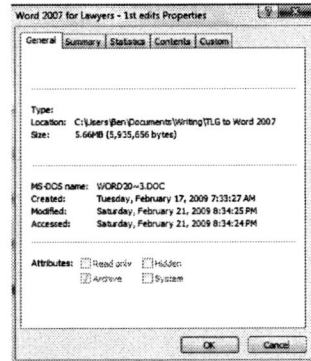

FIGURE 6.17

If you're using a fancy third-party document management system, it will handle the version tracking for you.

There is also a simple, manual, way to track versions and also keep old versions around and that's to simply always use "Save As" on your document and save it with a name that includes a version number. Like "Smith Memo v1," "Smith Memo v2," etc. The new version won't overwrite the old version, and if you're faithful to this system, you'll always be able to easily tell which version you're on. The downside to this is that your folders may quickly fill up with a bunch of outdated versions of your documents and you may find yourself frequently needing to do some cleanup to get rid of them.

The key is to find a balance—using Save As for major revisions but a simple "Save" to reflect minor changes to the current version when you're going with updating the revision accordingly.

Reviewing

An important element to collaborating is reviewing the results of that collaboration. Microsoft Word 2007 provides you with some tools to use in reviewing those documents. The Review tab of the Ribbon (see Figure 6.18) provides quick access to those tools.

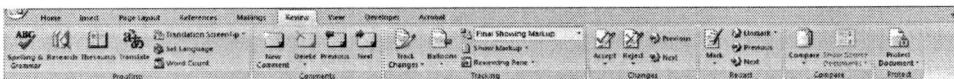

FIGURE 6.18

Comments

When you're reviewing a document, you can use Word's Comment feature to add your own comments to the document for review. Select the text you want to comment on and click "New Comment." Type your comment in the balloon that appears and it's just that easy. Your comments will appear in one color and comments by other reviewers will appear in different colors.

Tip

Comments can be one of the more dangerous bits of metadata in a document if you're not careful. There have been a number of instances where a document with inappropriate comments ended up in the hands of a client. Be circumspect about what you say and be sure to use a metadata checker to remove the comments (see Chapter 11) before you send it on to somebody who shouldn't read those comments.

You can quickly navigate to the next (or previous) comment in the document with the buttons on the Ribbon.

Compare Versions

One of the features that gets a good workout by law firms is the black lining feature (what we often call "red lining"), which is where you have the system compare two versions of a document and Word will highlight the changes for you.

To use it, click the Compare button on the Ribbon and select "Compare Two Versions of a Document." You'll get the Compare Documents dialog box (see Figure 6.19), which lets you specify the documents to com-

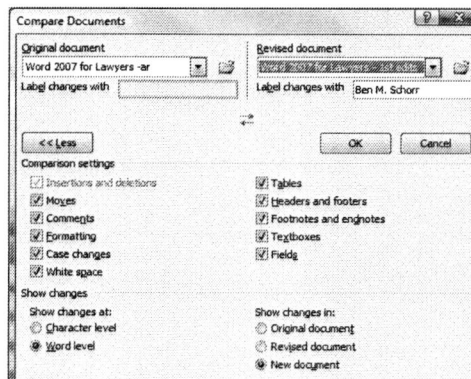

FIGURE 6.19

pare and set some of the options for the pending comparison. I usually just accept the defaults but there are one or two settings here I want to spend a moment on.

First of all, under Show Changes you should leave the "Show changes at" to "Word Level" instead of character level. Character level is ok, but tends to be rather distracting since most character changes that don't also change the word . . . aren't worth looking at. Any character change of significance also changes the word and would be flagged anyway.

The second setting you should be aware of is the "Show Changes In" setting. You can have the changes reflected in the Original or Revised documents, but I prefer to have a new document created showing the changes. The reason for that is that I like to leave the original documents unchanged, just in case I need to go back to one of them at some point.

Once you're satisfied with your options, click "OK" and you'll get something that looks like Figure 6.20. The original document is at the top on the right side, the revised document is on the bottom on the right side and the compared document (showing the changes) is right in the middle. On the left side of the screen, you'll see a list of the changes and you can quickly navigate to a change by clicking it on that list.

Tip

If you don't want to see the source documents, click the "Show Source Documents" button and you can hide one or both of them. Or, you can close any of the four default windows by clicking the "X" in the top right corner of that window.

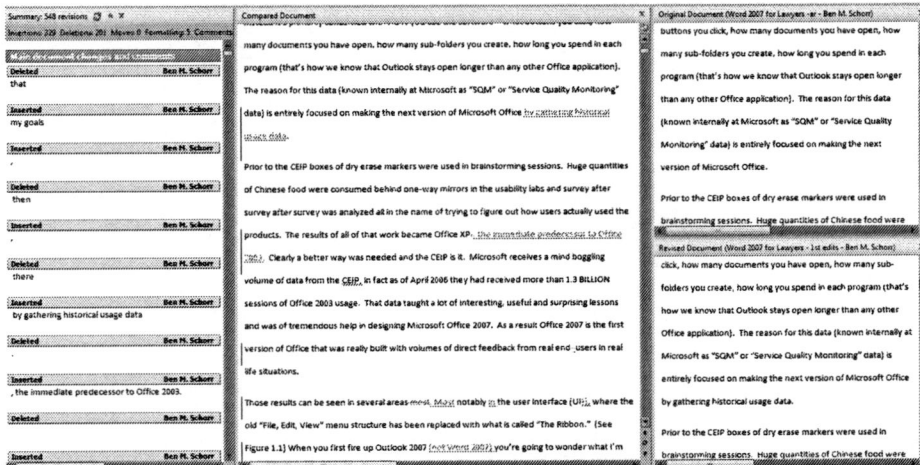

FIGURE 6.20

At the top of the revisions list you'll see a summary of the revisions in the compared documents. (See Figure 6.21.) Here you can see the total number of revisions along with a breakdown of how many insertions, how many deletions, how many comments, etc.

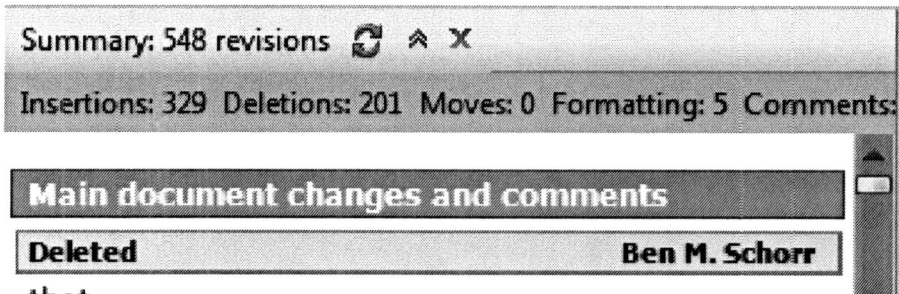

Summary: 548 revisions ⟳ ⌃ ✗

Insertions: 329 Deletions: 201 Moves: 0 Formatting: 5 Comments:

Main document changes and comments

Deleted   **Ben M. Schorr**

FIGURE 6.21

When you're satisfied with the combined document (and yes, you can edit the combined document right there in that window), just click Save (or press CTRL+S) and you'll be prompted to give the new document a new name and save it.

Third-Party Document Management Systems

I have to admit that I sort of resent third-party document management systems. They're an expensive crutch whose sole reason for existence is simple human weakness. With any modern computer if you use an intelligent file naming convention in a disciplined fashion and a good file searching system—Copernic Desktop and Windows Desktop Search (WDS) are just two such options that are also free—then you really wouldn't need a third-party document management system. Document management exists to help you and your colleagues intelligently save, store, and find documents. You can accomplish the same thing by setting up a policy that says "All memos will be saved to the client's folder, under the matter subfolder, with a file name in the format of "Memo to [X] regarding [Y]," and then adhering religiously to that policy. Everybody would be able to find a document they were looking for and the search tool (like WDS) would help cover those scenarios where simple good file names and directory structures didn't fit the bill.

Unfortunately, in the real world people get rushed and corners get cut. Pretty soon the root folder of the structure starts to fill up with files named "Memo1," "Memo2," "Jonesmemo," and so forth as people cut the handful of steps required to save the file properly and just save it as quickly as they can with whatever name they can bang in fast and move on. Soon you have the filing equivalent of kindergarten and nobody can remember which cubby they put their shoes in.

Document management systems solve this problem by automating some of the process (extracting keywords from the document itself; and inserting the author and editor IDs) and by forcing other parts of it—requiring the user to type in a client/matter number for example. They also generally include a search engine that can be used to search the document profiles as well as the document itself. In addition to the purpose-built document management tools, I'm going to mention momentarily many case management suites like ProLaw or Client Profiles have the capability to do some document management. If you already have a full-featured case management suite deployed, you might want to check and see if it can already suit your document management needs before you invest in a separate document management tool.

DocsOpen by Open Text (formerly "Hummingbird")

The venerable DocsOpen system is one that just about any lawyer who has been around a decade or two has probably run across in at least one firm. It was, for a time, the most popular system among the AmLaw 100 and if it has fallen from that perch it has only been due to cost, competition and perhaps some disillusionment among firms with the product— which, to be honest, is probably inevitable with a product as complicated and ubiquitous as a document management system is.

More information is available at: http://www.opentext.com/2/global/ sol-products/sol-pro-edocs-products2/pro-llecm-docsopen.htm. If the URL is any indication, you can already sense this is going to be complicated.

Interwoven WorkSite (formerly known as iManage)

Probably the other leading vendor in the AmLaw 100 for document and content management is Interwoven. Their WorkSite is extremely modular and can be customized for a particular firm.

More information is available at: http://www.interwoven.com.

Worldox

Worldox has been around since the late 1980s and is widely deployed in small- to mid-sized firms. Unlike its competitors, Worldox has always been Worldox and hasn't evolved through acquisition and change of ownership. It started out as a small, reasonably-priced, solution for smaller firms and has grown a bit from there. It's still pretty reasonably priced for what you get.

More information is available at: http://www.worldox.com.

Protecting Your Documents

Office 2007 extends the Information Rights Management (IRM) features that not that many people used in Office 2003. Basically, it's a powerful file-level technology that lets you control who can access documents and what they can do with them. It's not without its limitations, of course, and while you can prevent somebody from printing or forwarding your document, but you can't really prevent somebody from calling their friend over and showing them the document on the screen. You can prevent them from getting a screen capture of the document, but you can't prevent them from whipping out their camera phone and taking a photo of the screen. Basically, the old adage holds—try not to send sensitive documents to people you don't trust. But if you have to, then IRM can help make it a lot more difficult for your document to be misused or fall into the wrong hands.

▼
Don't see IRM? You might not have it. It's only included in the Office Ultimate, Professional Plus or Enterprise editions.

What IRM Can Do

- Prevent an authorized recipient from copying, changing, printing, forwarding, faxing, or copy/pasting the content. It also blocks the Print Screen function in Windows and the screen clipping feature in OneNote. (However, it doesn't necessarily block *all* third-party screen capture applications.)
- Lets you set an expiration date on a file so that the recipient can only access the document for a limited amount of time if you like. It's sort of the "Mission Impossible" feature—except without as much smoke.

▼
.XPS files are the "XML Paper Specification" format, which is sort of Microsoft's version of an Adobe .PDF file.

IRM in Office 2007 can protect a wide range of file types—not just .DOC and .DOCX files, but also templates (.DOT and .DOTX), macro-enabled documents and templates (.DOCM and

DOTM) as well as XPS files. As you might expect, IRM doesn't only apply to Word, but Excel, PowerPoint, and Outlook all respect IRM settings too.

In order to use IRM, you need the Windows Rights Management Services (RMS) Client with at least Service Pack 1 installed (as of this writing Service Pack 2 for RMS Client is available so you should get it if you don't already have it). If you're a Vista user, then you already have the RMS client—it's just that easy. If you're running Windows XP, then you'll have to download and install the RMS client. You can get it for free from Microsoft's web site.

> ▼
>
> Installing and configuring the RMS client isn't that difficult but you might be more comfortable having your systems administrator or consultant help you with it. If you're going to use RMS, you want to make sure it works properly.

Installing the Windows Rights Management Services (RMS) Client

Installing the client is pretty simple—the first time you try to use it you'll get led thru the process of installing it. By the way, that's true whether you're trying to protect a document or access a protected document.

The first time that you try to open a document that's protected with IRM the client software will try to connect to a licensing server to confirm your credentials and download what's called a "Use license." That use license will define what level of access you're going to have to the requested file. The level of access determines if you'll be able to open it, edit it, print it, or whatever . . . and for how long. The sender of the file not only gets to determine what actions you're allowed to perform, but he (or she) can expire those actions as of a certain date as well.

This process has to be repeated for every IRM-protected file you receive. The good news is that it only has to happen once per file—so once you've obtained that use license you don't have to download it again on that computer.

> ▼
>
> If you use multiple computers and attempt to access the same protected document from different computers, you'll have to install the Rights Management client on each of those computers and it will have to obtain the use license for you on each computer. There's no cost to you to do that—you just have to make sure that each computer has Internet access for this process.

Another permission you can control is whether to allow the recipients the ability to forward the document to a third party. If they try to, they'll get a dialog box that offers to contact the author for updated permissions. If you choose to, you can give somebody "Full Control" permissions, which allows them to do just about anything with the document including forwarding it to others and even assigning permissions to other people. Essentially, you give them the authority to specify what third parties can or can't do with it.

Rights management permissions are generally assigned on a per-user basis—you give Susan and Mike and Vivian permission to read but not edit, for example. But you can, in limited cases, give access on a Per Group basis. As an example, you may want to give the Immigration department permission to edit the document for the next five days. The tricky bit with assigning permissions on a per-group basis is that it's really only going to work for users and groups inside your firm. That's because IRM requires access to your Active Directory (that's your network's authentication directory) in order to confirm who is actually a member of the group. If you send the document to another firm, then you won't have access to their Active Directory to select their group and they won't have access to your Active Directory either. Lots of things in computing and permissions get trickier when you have to travel between firms—when the document leaves the friendly confines of your own network.

Document Retention

One of the hottest topics in Law Technology, as evidenced by the volume of books and articles about it and the fact that it's one of the hottest tracks at ABA TECHSHOW®, is eDiscovery. Now I may not be an expert on eDiscovery but I can tell you this . . . they can't discover what no longer exists. You may be required to keep certain documents for a certain length of time. Certainly, if you're in a field that has to operate under HIPAA, Sarbanes-Oxley, FCRA, or any of a number of other regulatory and compliance instruments, then you're going to be required to keep certain documents for a certain period of time. If you're an OB/GYN, you know you're keeping your patient records for at least 18 years for instance. But once you don't need to keep them anymore . . . don't keep them anymore. Rarely does anything good come from having outdated and expired documents in your files.

If for no other reason than efficient record-keeping and tidiness, establish a document retention policy that specifies how long you need to keep documents, how long you want to keep documents, and what you're going to do with those documents once those periods have expired. Will they be shredded? Returned to the client? Figure it out now, get the policy in place, document it carefully and start enforcing it immediately.

By the way, if you're not already familiar with the term, you should also get friendly with the term "Litigation Hold."

Electronic Media

Your document retention policy doesn't just extend to paper documents. It's not enough to toss that old client file in the fireplace and heat the lobby in the winter. If the documents were created on your computers, then there is a good chance that copies (yes, plural) of that document exist in your system. A few places you might want to grab a metaphorical flashlight and go looking:

- The Document Management system. Whatever you happen to have, whether it's Interwoven, WorldDox, some other commercial system, one you rolled yourself or even just a fancy hierarchical directory structure on a simple file system. The first, and most obvious, place to find the document is right there in the document management system. Archive it or delete it as appropriate when its time has come.
- Backups. It does you no good to shred the paper and delete the file from your document management system if that document is still sitting on a backup tape on the shelf above your server. Make sure you have a policy for how long to keep old backup tapes. Chances are that your document retention intervals will be measured in years anyhow, so any tapes that old aren't likely to be useful anymore—don't bother erasing them, in most cases you should just have those ancient tapes destroyed.
- E-mail. If the document went to the client, co-counsel, opposing counsel, or was collaborated on within the firm there is a good chance that one or more drafts of the document (which could be far more damaging than the finalized document by the way) may exist in your Sent Items folder or other e-mail folders. It's probably a good idea to clean those out; in fact you may not be required to keep e-mailed drafts of the documents for any specific period of time, especially if you *do* have a copy of the final document in your document management system. So, it may pay to be especially aggressive about cleaning out attached document drafts from your e-mail.
- Home computers. Lots of lawyers like to work from home these days and you may have a system set up that lets them do so. If so . . . might they have copies of documents they've worked on

stored on their local hard drives at home? What about that brief they slaved over all weekend and stored a copy of to their My Documents folder at home?

- Personal e-mail. Lawyer wants to work from home or while on vacation (defeats the purpose of "Vacation," no?), so they e-mail certain documents they're currently working on to their RoadRunner, Yahoo, Hotmail, Gmail, or other personal e-mail account. The case long over, they never think to delete the e-mail with the attached document(s) from their personal e-mail. No, they

Lawyer works at home occasionally on his trusty but aging desktop computer. He brings home files on a flash drive or maybe even e-mails them to his personal e-mail account so he can access them at home and saves them in his My Documents folder. Copies the finished product back to the USB flash drive to take back to the office on Monday to finalize, print, or send to the client. A couple of years go by and lawyer decides it's time for a new home computer. Good dad that he is, he donates his old trusty desktop to his kid's school. Not knowing any better he also just donated 2.5 years of client work product to his kid's school too. Uh-oh.

didn't delete it from the Outlook Express Inbox on their home computer either.

- Mobile devices. These days a lot of lawyers are carrying BlackBerries, iPhones, Treos, and other mobile devices on which they can get their e-mail. Any documents e-mailed to them are probably on their mobile devices too, as attachments, unless they have cleaned those messages out. Don't forget about USB flash drives, iPods, and other USB storage devices the lawyer might have used to transport documents to and fro.

Don't think your folks would ever e-mail documents to their home accounts or use their iPod to transport documents here and there? If you don't have some system in place to easily allow them to work on documents from home or on the road, then you can almost guarantee that even the most vaguely savvy among them has already improvised some system of their own. Google for "Free Document Sharing Service" and be prepared for more than 300,000 hits. Google and Microsoft are just two of the companies that as of this writing offer more than 1GB of free file sharing space to anybody who can fill out a short registration screen and click "OK." Don't be surprised if some of your people are using it. And that's not the sort of thing your firm wants to find out about when they are compelled to produce documents they thought were long-since expired.

Collaborating with Other Word Processors

As much as Microsoft would like to make it so, the reality is that not everybody is using Microsoft Word 2007. You may have to interoperate with people who are using older versions of Microsoft Word or even, Bill forgive me for saying so, products from other vendors like Corel's WordPerfect.

Older Versions of Word

Operating with older versions of Word is actually fairly easy. The Office 2007 OpenXML file formats are all new and the older versions of Word don't understand them natively. Microsoft has found a great way to accommodate users of the older versions, however. They've created "file converters" that you can install on older versions of Microsoft Office (Office 2000 or later), which enable those versions of Office to read *and* write the newer file formats natively! How cool is that?! Better still, these file converters are free. I won't try to post the cryptic URL for them here, just Google for "Office 2007 File Converters" and you will quickly find the site to obtain and download them, along with simple instructions. Most, but not quite all, of the document features will be available to them after they've installed the File Converters.

OK, you dragged it out of me. Examples of what might not be available to a Word 2003 user running the File Converters include things like equations created using the new Word equation editor. When the Word 2003 user opens a 2007 document with equations in it, they will be converted to images. The equations will be; not the Word 2003 user.

Even if you're *not* interacting with Office 2007 users, the file converters convey the benefits of the new file formats to the older software—such as the smaller file sizes.

If the other party isn't interested in installing the file converters, all is not lost. You can still click the Office Button, do a Save As and choose Office 97-2003 Document (see Figure 6.22) to save the document in the old binary, .DOC format. It shouldn't surprise you that if you do that you lose all of the benefits of saving in the new OpenXML formats. You've simply created a classic .DOC file that can be opened and edited by any application capable of working with those documents (such as Word 2002, AKA Word XP).

When you save a document in the older file formats, you're saving in what Word calls "Compatibility Mode." Word will caution you that certain elements of your document might not quite translate properly into Compatibility Mode. Luckily, most of those things are not elements

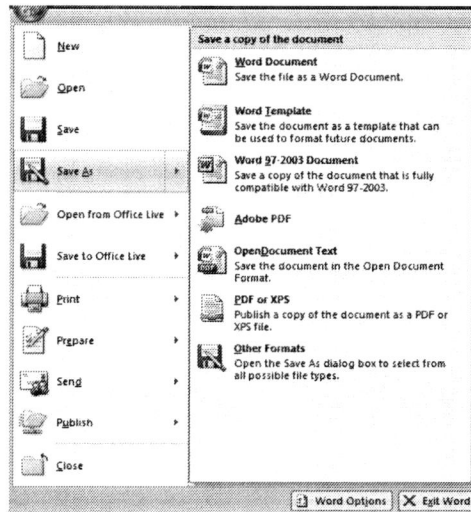

FIGURE 6.22

that most lawyers will care about. Mostly it's about themes and SmartArt, for example.

Microsoft Word for Mac

If you happen to be collaborating with one of that small, but vocal, contingent of users who believe that putting an "i" in front of anything and painting it white makes it cool then you're in luck—Microsoft Office 2008 for Mac supports the Office OpenXML format (.DOCX) natively. There are file converters for older versions of Office for Mac; just like the PC versions.

WordPerfect

Amazing how times change. When I first started in legal technology, about two decades ago, WordPerfect (for DOS back then) was easily the dominant word processor in law firms. Today, you still find it here and there, but for the most part, it's a distant second to Microsoft's Word. You obviously know what I mean, since you bought this book. Unless you're my mother and just bought a copy to give my Aunt Susan, I suppose.

That said, if your colleagues are using Corel WordPerfect Office X4, then Microsoft Office 2007 file formats are already supported, natively. No special hoops to jump through for you. For the Corel users, however, they should save their documents in Office OpenXML format (.DOCX) before they send to you so that you can read them.

Corel's WordPerfect X3 support for Office OpenXML is a little more uncertain. There are a number of vague statements inferring that X3 would support Office OpenXML, but X3 didn't support it when the product was new and there are a lot of documented instances where working between X3 and Office 2007 (and even older versions of Word for that matter) resulted in some fairly frustrating issues; particularly around the way fonts were translated between the two products. Your best bet, if you have to work between those two products, would be to use a format that is more common to both products. You could try saving the documents as Word 97-2003 format, but again, be prepared for possible formatting inconsistencies.

▼ ▼ ▼ ▼ ▼

In It for the Short Term

If you have to collaborate with somebody who has an obscure, or rather old, word processor and it's only going to be a short-term collaboration (a few weeks perhaps), then maybe you can persuade them to download and install the trial version of Microsoft Office 2007. It's fully functional and free, it just stops allowing you to edit documents after about 60 days. Great solution? No. But may be better than beating your head against the wall trying to share documents with somebody who uses StarOffice 5.2.

OpenOffice

OpenOffice is the open source productivity suite that is nominally authored by Sun Microsystems. At the time of this writing, it's at version 3.01 but like all things open source, that could change at any time. Working with OpenOffice users is relatively easy since OpenOffice supports OpenXML natively and Word 2007, with Service Pack 2, supports the OpenOffice formats natively too.

Working on the Road

We're an increasingly mobile bunch and the technology has evolved to the point where we don't have to be sitting at our desks in order to access and edit our documents. A number of technologies have emerged (and continue to emerge and impress) that allow you to work from anywhere at anytime.

Mobile Devices

Just about everybody is carrying a mobile device these days—many of you are carrying phones that function as personal information devices. Windows Mobile 6, for example, includes a version of what we used to call "Pocket Word" or "Word Mobile" (depends a bit upon which version you have). It's a mobile-enhanced version of Microsoft Word that you can use to read, edit, or even compose documents on . . . if you're really desperate. Let's be honest, working on a document of any size on a 2″ diagonal screen with a thumb keyboard is not exactly an optimal experience. You can create bulleted lists, use primitive fonts, add and edit text, and even send your completed document via e-mail when you're done (assuming your device is configured for e-mail).

To use Word Mobile, just transfer the document to your mobile device either via the USB Sync cable, Bluetooth, wireless, SD card, or whatever other file transfer mechanism may be available to you. Once it's on your device, just go to Start | Programs and look for either "Pocket Word" or "Office Mobile" | "Word Mobile" and when the program opens you'll be able to navigate to your document and open it.

I think I can safely say that this is not something you'll choose to do if you have other options, but it's nice to know that in a pinch, if you really have to review/edit a document while you're stuck in traffic somewhere and can't get access to a real computer to do it, this option can get the job done if you're patient enough.

That applies to DataViz's "Word to Go" too.

Telecommuting

One of the things technology is increasingly enabling is the ability to work from anywhere at any time. This can be a blessing and a curse. There are three main technologies for telecommuting—which you use is up to you and your IT department/consultant.

Remote Node

Remote node computing is the "VPN" or "Virtual Private Network" solution where you connect to your office via the Internet and establish a secure "tunnel" across the Internet that lets you join your local computer (home computer or laptop typically) to your office network. Then you work on your local computer just as if you were sitting in your office. You have access to all of the files and resources of the office network just as you do from your desk—albeit probably a little slower since you're limited to an Internet connection.

If you have Microsoft Word 2007 installed on your local computer, then you can use it just as you would Word 2007 on your desk at the office. Easy as that. All of the processing occurs on your local computer. One nice advantage of Remote Node is that it's not too hard to work offline (which means disconnected from the office) because your local computer is a stand-alone machine with Word 2007 installed. You can simply copy or check-out documents to your local hard drive, disconnect from the office, and work on those documents locally. Later when you connect back up, you just copy or check-in those documents back to the office.

This is pretty handy if you're taking a laptop on an airplane and want to work rather than watch the movie.

Remote Control

Remote Control is the old "pcAnywhere" or "GoToMyPC" solution. With this solution you connect to the office, again across the Internet typically, and with an application on your local computer you take control of a remote PC sitting idly at the office—usually your office computer. As the name sort of implies, you are remotely controlling your office computer and that means you quite literally have everything you have at the office. The office computer is transmitting to you images of the screen and you are transmitting to it keystrokes and mouse movements. All of the processing occurs on the office computer.

Remote control is fairly easy to set up but does have one big drawback . . . if you don't have an Internet connection, you're out of luck. You *have* to be able to connect to the office to use it; which means that you really can't do it from airplanes (at least not quite yet; aerial WiFi is almost upon us) or other disconnected areas. It also means you probably have to remember to leave the machine you're remotely controlling turned on when you leave the office, which may introduce other security issues. Also, if the office machine is shared with other users, it won't be accessible to you while another user is logged into it, either remotely or locally (sitting at the keyboard).

With Remote Control, you're literally using the same machine you use when you're sitting at the office so you are using the same copy of Microsoft Word 2007 (complete with any customization) that you are used to.

Remote Host

The third basic technology you'll find is Remote Host. This is the "Citrix" or "Terminal Server" solution where a server at your office hosts some number of simultaneous users who connect in remotely with virtual Windows desktops. The advantage to this is that you don't need to leave your office computer turned on—you're connecting to a server that is always on. Also, if you have a number of remote users, you don't need to provide office machines for each of them; they can remote into the Terminal Server from their home machines or laptops and work from there. It may be a little pricier to set up and configure than "GoToMyPC," but the results are a tad more professional, especially in an office where you may have a lot of simultaneous remote users.

With Remote Host, you can install and run Microsoft Word 2007 on the Terminal Server or Citrix Server and all of the functionality we've described in this book would still apply.

> **Note**
>
> If you have a Remote Host server and you want to install Word 2007 on it, you have to make sure you get the Volume License version of Word 2007. You can't install the Word 2007 that came with your PC (known as the "OEM" or "Original Equipment Manufacturer" version) or a retail version of Word that you bought at the computer store or from Amazon.com. Volume license versions are actually less expensive than the retail version, and contrary to popular belief, you don't have to have 50 machines to qualify. You need only buy five (or more) licenses to get volume licensing.

Summary

Collaborating and working remotely help to maximize your productivity and Microsoft Word 2007 has been designed with these benefits in mind. The new Office OpenXML format is the most open and portable format yet for Microsoft Office, and increasingly other word processing products, such as Corel's X4 and OpenOffice 3.01, will be able to comfortably support it natively. Additionally, with Service Pack 2 installed, Word 2007 now supports the OpenOffice formats natively.

Working with Data 7

One of the advantages of purchasing the Microsoft Office
Suite is that the applications in the suite tend to work well
together. Office 2007 takes this idea further than ever.

Outlook

Outlook is the application that is open the longest during the
day for most users of Microsoft Office and it's the place
where a lot of information that is useful to Word documents
(like names and addresses for instance) are stored. Naturally,
there is an interest in wanting to be able to use that information in Word as seamlessly as possible.

Mail Merge

Commonly, lawyers and firms keep a list of clients in Outlook
in the form of a Contacts folder. You can leverage that list of
information to create mailing labels or form letters in Word.
The way you do that is called a "mail merge" and basically
involves creating a document template with fields where
your variable data goes; things like "Name," "Address,"
"City," etc.

You can start your mail merge from either Word or Outlook, but I generally recommend you start from the Outlook
side because Outlook offers better filtering capabilities than
Word does.

1. To begin, you'll want to switch to your Contacts folder in Outlook and select the contact items you want to use for your merge. If there are only a handful of them, just hold down the CTRL key and click on each one to select them, or if they are contiguous hold down SHIFT and click the first and then last one in the group. If you want to select All of the contacts in the current view, then you can skip right to the next step.

▼ ▼ ▼ ▼ ▼

Tricks of the Pros

Mail merge is a great reason to use categories in your Contacts. Categorizing your contacts as "Clients" or "Holiday Card" or whatever and then filter your view either with the Search Contacts tool at the top right or by setting an actual Filter on the view with View | Current View | Customize Current View | Filter | More Choices. Once your Contacts folder is only displaying the contacts from the category you wish to merge from, then you can proceed with step 2 of the merge.

2. Click Tools | Mail Merge in Outlook. You'll get the "Mail Merge Contacts" dialog box like you see in Figure 7.1. If you're sending to ALL of the displayed contacts, then check the "All contacts in current view" radio button. If you've selected specific contacts and only want to merge those, then select the "Only selected contacts" radio button. Leave "Fields to merge" to "All contact fields."

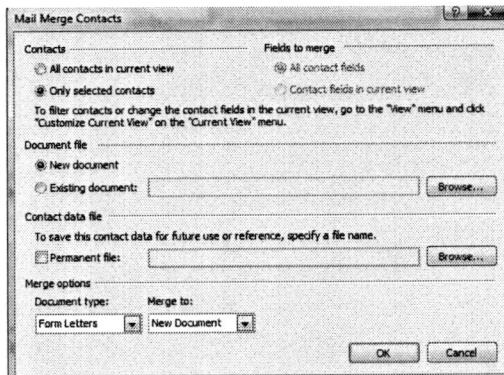

FIGURE 7.1

3. Select the Document you want to merge to. Usually it will be a new document, but there may be times when you have a preexisting main document (that's what Word calls the document that contains the text and information you're merging into) that you want to use.

4. If you plan to do this merge repeatedly with the same, unchanging group of contacts, you can save this contact data to a permenant file. I discourage this except in *one* scenario: you want to keep a snapshot of the merge data for reference—to show who you sent the newsletter to or what address you had on file for them at the time.

5. Under Merge options, select the Document Type. Normally it will be either Form Letters, Mailing Labels, or Envelopes. (See Figure 7.2.) A "Catalog" is essentially a directory. I've yet to find a practical use for that option in a law firm setting.

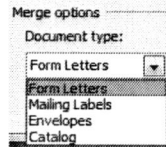

Merge options
Document type:

Form Letters
Form Letters
Mailing Labels
Envelopes
Catalog

FIGURE 7.2

6. Under Merge options, you can change the "Merge to" setting from New Document to either "Printer" or "E-mail." I discourage using "Printer" because that's going to perform your merge to the printer, and if something isn't right with the merge, the first indication you might have is blowing through 50 pages of paper before you realize it. I always merge to a New Document so I can preview my results *before* I send them to the printer or out via e-mail.

7. Click OK. Word will open with what looks like a blank document (assuming you chose "New Document" in step 3) but there is a key difference . . . the Ribbon will open to the Mailings tab and a number of the buttons will be active.

8. Create your document as you would like it to appear. In those places where you want to insert data from the merge (like Full Name or Mailing Address), click the "Insert Merge Field" button to get the gallery of possible fields from your data set to merge (see Figure 7.3). Select the field or fields you want to insert there.

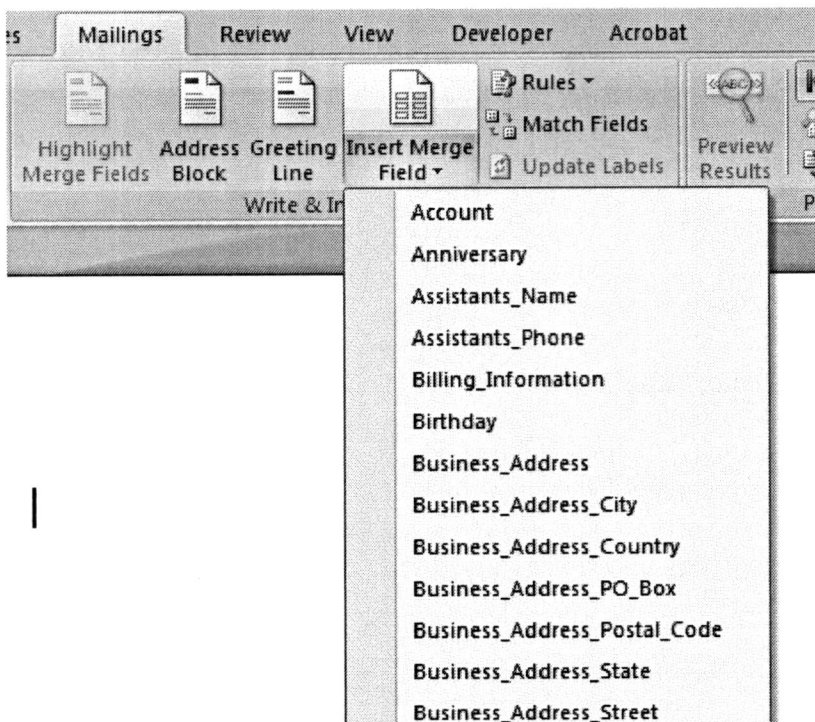

FIGURE 7.3

9. When you have the document completed, with fields in those places that will be replaced with Outlook contact data, you can preview your results by using the "Preview Results" button. Click that button and Word will perform the sample merge. (See Figure 7.4.)

10. Use the forward and back arrows on the Go To Record command to move forward and backwards through your previewed results and make sure everything looks the way it should.

FIGURE 7.4

▼ ▼ ▼ ▼ ▼

Tricks of the Pros

When merging Addresses from Outlook, rather than use the "Home Address" or "Business Address," use the "Mailing Address." That's because some of your contacts may want their mail sent to their home address and some to the business. It could be a nightmare figuring out which is which and doing two merges, so just use the "Mailing Address" option. Mailing Address is controlled by a checkbox in Outlook that lets you specify which, of multiple addresses, is the mailing address. (See Figure 7.5.)

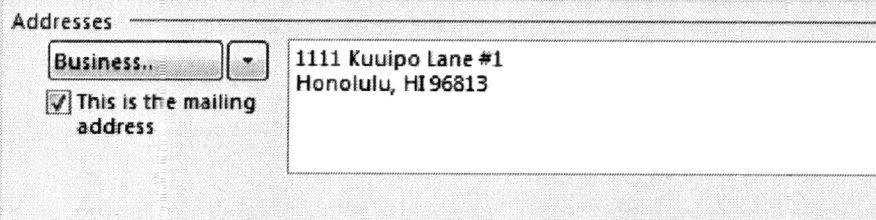

Addresses

| Business.. | ▾ | 1111 Kuuipo Lane #1 |
| ☑ This is the mailing address | | Honolulu, HI 96813 |

FIGURE 7.5

11. When you're happy with the results, click the "Finish & Merge" button and then you can print the results.

One-Off Envelopes

One of the features I've liked since the days of WordPerfect 5.1 for DOS (Remember that one?) is the ability to print envelopes. It just looks a lot more professional to have a printed envelope and it's a pain to have to load your envelope into a typewriter and type the address on. If you don't want to have to do a whole mail merge just to print a single envelope, then Word's Envelopes feature is for you.

To print an envelope with Word, just go to the Mailings tab and click the Envelopes button. That will give you the Envelopes and Labels dialog box you see in Figure 7.6. You can type your delivery (destination) address in the provided field or click the address book icon just above it to the right to access your Outlook address book and have Word pull the ad-

Word 2007 does take a step backward in one respect—I've always liked being able to print a barcode on the envelope for the destination address. Word 2007 does away with that feature. The reason it was pulled was that the POSTNET codes that the Barcode field in Word produced were no longer compliant with USPS regulations. It could be argued that Microsoft could have fixed the POSTNET codes, but to be honest, the US Postal Service is using high-speed scanners on all mail now and they are perfectly capable of reading a printed address on an envelope. So, there really isn't any advantage to printing the barcodes on the envelopes anymore.

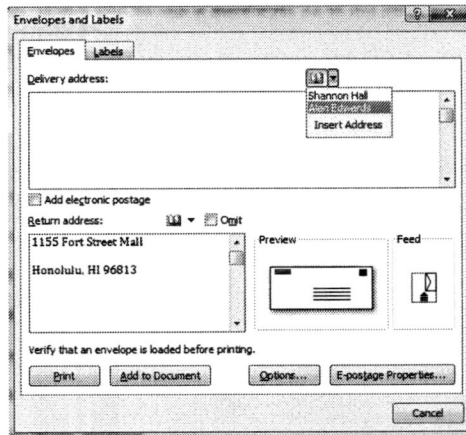

FIGURE 7.6

dress from there. If you click the down-arrow *next* to the address book (as I have in the figure), you'll see the last few addresses you've selected so you can reinsert a common address if you need to.

▼ ▼ ▼ ▼ ▼

Tricks of the Pros

If you have your destination address in the document, such as in an address block at the top of a letter, just select that address first, then click the Envelopes command in the Mailings tab. When the Envelopes and Labels dialog opens, that selected text will already appear in the Delivery Address field.

You can add your return address or check the "Omit" button if you have preprinted envelopes or if you're going to use a sticker for it. When you're ready to print the envelope, just load the envelope into your printer and click the Print button. Voila, a lovely envelope.

Excel

Word and Excel make it easy to embed Excel data into a Word document—either as a static table or even as a live link that updates as the data in Excel updates. There are a few different ways to do it, but let's start with the easiest way. Create your spreadsheet in Excel, select the cell/cells that you want to embed in your Word document, and click Copy. Switch to your Word document, place the insertion point where you want the data, and click Paste. There's your data (see Figure 7.7). Easy as that!

Important	Test	Data
1	2	3
4	5	6
7	8	9
12	15	18

FIGURE 7.7

Of course that's a static representation of the data. If it changes on the Excel spreadsheet it won't change in the Word document. If that's what you want, great. If, on the other hand, you were hoping for something more dynamic, then there is one more step you need to take. See the little clipboard at the bottom-right corner of Figure 7.7. That's a tool that gives you paste options and in this case it's pretty useful. If you click it, you'll get the options you find in Figure 7.8. The four basic options, at the top, relate to how the table of data will appear. Keeping source formatting means that any formats in Excel (including colors and lines) will come over. Match Destination Table Style will bring the data but replace those formats with a table style from your document.

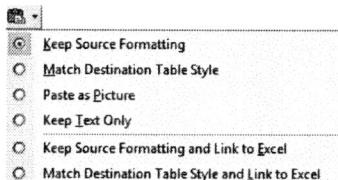

- Keep Source Formatting
- Match Destination Table Style
- Paste as Picture
- Keep Text Only
- Keep Source Formatting and Link to Excel
- Match Destination Table Style and Link to Excel

FIGURE 7.8

The default is to paste the data in as a table, but Paste as Picture won't paste it as a table at all, but rather as a static image. That's a good one to use if you want to maintain the source formatting and also make sure the data can't be easily edited.

Finally, Keep Text Only doesn't paste the data as a table but rather as plain text. This is good for simple content but not very good if you have a lot of data to paste.

All of those options differ in how the data is presented but they're the same in one very important way: They're all going to paste the data statically. In other words, the data is the data and that's it—there's no link back to the source Excel Workbook. If the data changes in the source workbook, it won't be updated in the Word document.

The last two options in Figure 7.8 address that shortcoming. Basically, you're just going to choose if you want to keep the Source Formatting (e.g., have the data look like it does in Excel) or if you're going to match the Destination Formatting (e.g., have the data look like a default Word table), but either way the data *will* be linked back to the Excel workbook. If the data in the workbook changes, then the data in the Word document will change as well.

The converse is not true, by the way. If you change the data in Word, it will *not* update the data in the Excel spreadsheet. In fact, the next time you make a change in Excel any changes you made to the Word version of the data will be lost—overwritten with the current version of the Excel data.

I guess I should point out that this only works as long as the Excel workbook is available. If you e-mail this Word document to a colleague at another firm, then the link will be broken since your colleague doesn't have the source workbook. They'll see the Excel data as of the last time you updated it, but any subsequent updates won't be reflected. If you move the Excel file to another location in your organization, Word will cleverly update the link to reflect the new location . . . so future changes will still be reflected, as long as you can still access the Excel file from that computer.

This is a pretty useful feature for documents that are a work in progress—for example, if you have a complicated purchase offer and you're still running all the "what-ifs" and scenarios in Excel. You can link the relevant Excel data to your Word document and Word will always reflect the latest numbers for you until you're ready to send or print. When you've got what you want, just print it or PDF it and send it off. When you PDF the document, you essentially affix the numbers as they are—they won't change in the PDF no matter what happens to the Excel workbook.

The other place this feature is really handy is in recurring reports. You can set up your report in the Word document and link in relevant data from Excel workbooks. For each period, your Word document will already have the relevant numbers from your Excel workbooks—making much shorter work of preparing the report.

If you'd like to break the link so that Word no longer automatically updates the data, just right-click the table in Word and choose Linked Worksheet Object and then Links, as I have in Figure 7.9.

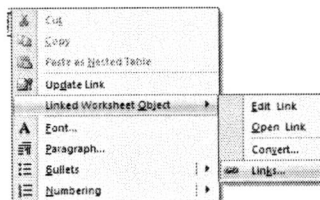

FIGURE 7.9

The Links dialog box (see Figure 7.10) includes a number of clever tools for working with the linked data, which includes a "Break Link" dialog that will effectively convert your linked table to a static table. If you only want to prevent the link from updating temporarily, click the "Locked" check box under Update Method on the Links dialog box instead of the "Break Link" button. Later, when you want to resume updating, just go back in and uncheck "Locked."

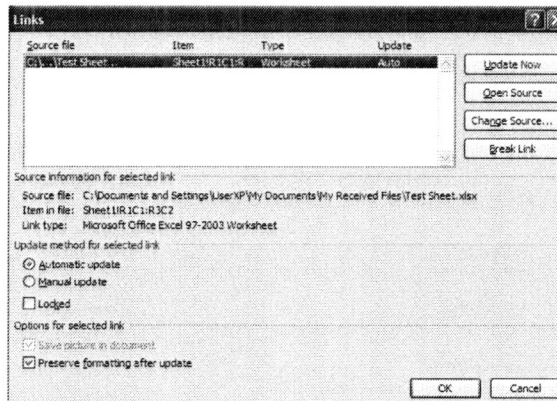

FIGURE 7.10

OneNote

OneNote is Microsoft's free-form note-taking software. It's an application that should be extremely popular with lawyers because it is essentially an electronic version of the yellow legal pad but with a *lot* more power. One of the things that OneNote is exceptionally good at is serving as a starting point for Word documents. When I start to write a long memo (or a book for that matter), I'll often start it as an outline in OneNote. I can do my Internet research, collaborate with colleagues, and reorganize things until I'm ready to write the actual detailed content. In OneNote (see Figure 7.11), you can create your outlines and other content, and when you're ready to send it over to Word for finishing and formatting, you just click File | Send to | Microsoft Office Word as you see in Figure 7.12. When you do that, you'll get a fresh new Word document with your outline ready for content.

You can also readily copy/paste content, images, diagrams, and other items from OneNote to Word.

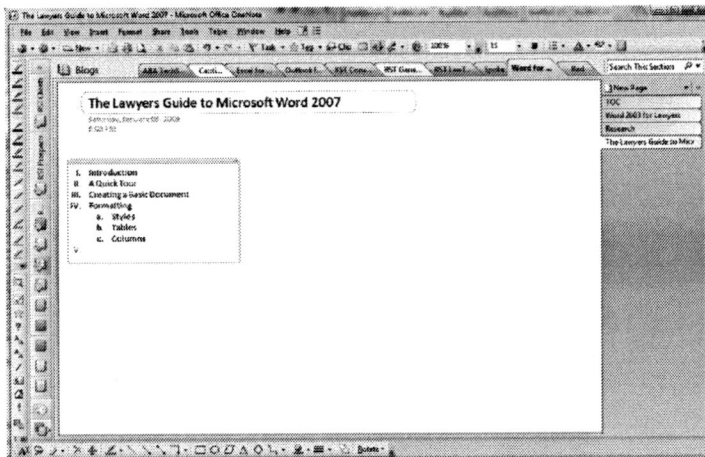

FIGURE 7.11

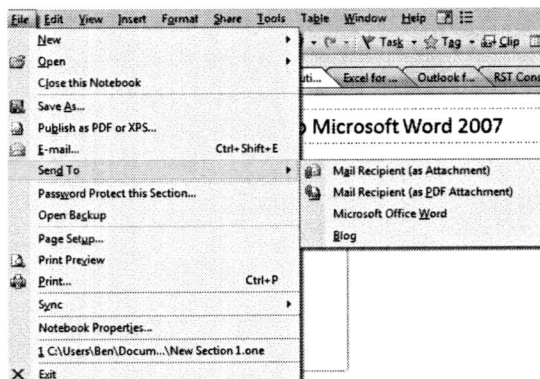

FIGURE 7.12

Pictures and Diagrams

They say a picture is worth a thousand words and there may well be times in your documents when you'll want to include a picture, diagram, or graphic. Word 2007 makes it pretty easy to do so. Go to the Insert tab, click Picture and use the Insert Picture dialog box to navigate to the picture you want to insert. When you've found it, click once to select it and then click insert.

Tricks of the Pros

If you're working with an image that you might change in the future, consider inserting the picture as a link to the file by clicking the drop-down arrow on the insert button. Later if you want to change or update the image, simply replace the image file on your hard drive with the new file using the same name.

Once you have the image inserted in your document, you can resize it by pointing at one of the tiny squares around the edge (called "handles") with your mouse cursor and drag the handle to resize it. If you need to be more precise in your image sizing, just right-click the image to get the context menu you see in Figure 7.13 and choose "Size . . ." In the size dialog box, you can not only specify the size of the image but you can also rotate the image or crop it.

As long as I'm on the subject . . . there are a couple of items on the context menu in Figure 7.13 that you should be interested in. The "Change Picture . . ." command lets you select a different image—handy if you realize that you inserted the picture of what was supposed to be a photo of a disputed property line, but is actually a shot of your family at the Grand Canyon.

✂	Cut
📋	Copy
📋	Paste
	Edit Picture
🖼	Change Picture...
	Bring to Front ▶
	Send to Back ▶
	Hyperlink...
	Insert Caption...
	Text Wrapping ▶
	Size...
	Format Picture...

FIGURE 7.13

Scanned Documents

Just like inserting pictures, there may be times when you'll want to insert a scanned document. There are two basic ways you might want to do that:

1. As an image. You want the other person to see and probably be able to read the document, but not edit it. Perhaps it's just an exhibit that you're including in your document.
2. As editable text. You've received the document in paper form and now you want to be able to edit the text like any other word document. To do that, you'll have to scan the document and run it through an OCR (Optical Character Recognition) program.

When you first scan in a file, or receive an image of a document via e-mail or other electronic transfer, the computer just sees a picture. It doesn't know a document from a building or an elephant, it's all just pixels to the computer. When you run the OCR program, it will look at the image and try to recognize the text so that it can be converted into As, Bs, Cs, and so forth. The results are saved as a document file that you can then edit.

The best OCR programs include spell checkers and some context-sensitive capabilities that make good guesses at what a word should be, but even so, they're not perfect. Even the very best tend to average only about 99% accuracy.

▼

When it come to Optical Character Recognition (OCR), the cleaner your original the better your results. If your original is clearly printed, in a nice clean font, black text on white paper, then you'll probably get very good results. If your original is a little wrinkled, colored text, highlighters, handwritten notes scrawled in the margins, and so forth, then your results may be somewhat unpredictable. Either way, be sure to carefully proofread the results before you trust them. Especially in legal documents, a single word or number that's wrong could have serious consequences.

Summary

Word is part of an suite of applications that are designed to work together. Over the years, that statement has garnered chuckles or snarls from users who have tried to make them work together without much success, but Word 2007 and the Office 2007 Suite go further than ever before to try and help the applications work together more smoothly. Whether you're doing mail merges from Outlook or embedding data from Excel, Microsoft Word 2007 can help you be more productive, more effective, and generally happier.

Automating Word

8

Microsoft Word 2007 offers some very powerful tools for automating your document creation and editing—reducing repetitive tasks and giving you better quality control while reducing errors.

▼

Power Corrupts. Absolute power is really kinda cool.

Document Assembly

Document assembly is the usage of tools like macros, scripts, or applications to automate the building of standardized documents. Mail merge is a form of document assembly too. There are a lot of third-party tools that can do it, as well as some tools built right into Word. The key to Document Assembly is to create a library of reusable parts (phrases, images, even entire pages of boilerplate text) so that you don't have to recreate them from scratch every time.

HotDocs (and others)

HotDocs (owned by LexisNexis) is an example of a third-party document assembly application. The premise is pretty straight-forward—you create a model document that is going to be the basis for all of the future documents of this type. In the document, you identify those bits that are going to vary from document to document—the client's name, dates, amounts, locations, and so forth. Once you have your model document completely built, you run the document assembly software and it performs an "interview" where it asks you for the variable information you previously specified for the document. The assembly software will take your answers, plug them into the places you specified in the model document, and the result is a fully built document!

Building Blocks

A popular feature among lawyers in previous versions of Word was the AutoText feature. Commonly, lawyers and staff would create custom Auto-Text entries with oft-used phrases or paragraphs and then use the Auto-Text to quickly and easily insert those bits where they needed them. In Word 2007, Building Blocks have replaced the AutoText feature making it simultaneously more powerful and more difficult to use. Building Blocks let you create and save snippets of a document that you expect to reuse often. One way Building Blocks improve on AutoText is that they're not just limited to text. You can make a Building Block out of just about any element of a document. For lawyers, that will still usually mean text but it could just as easily mean an image like a logo or scanned signature file.

To create a Building Block, you just select the element—highlight the text for example—you want to add to the Building Blocks gallery and then go to the Insert tab, Quick Parts, and Save Selection to Quick Parts Gallery. What you'll get is what you see in Figure 8.1.

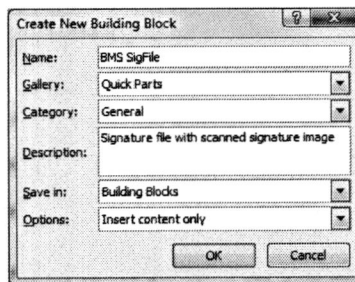

FIGURE 8.1

Give the building block a name. The name I have in this figure "BMS SigFile" is not ideal, actually, because the name you have needs to be descriptive, but should be fairly easy to quickly type. (I'll explain why in a moment.)

Pick a gallery to add your new part to—you'll see several of the known galleries like "Cover Pages" listed. Generally speaking, you'll want to choose either AutoText or "Quick Parts" if you're just adding text or maybe a scanned signature image as most lawyers will. Choosing "Quick Parts" has the added benefit that your new Block will appear on the Quick Parts gallery under the button on the Ribbon.

The next field is for Category and this one is purely up to you. You don't have to use Categories if you don't want to—put everything in General. But if you're going to use a lot of custom Blocks, you might want to organize them a bit by creating custom categories. Click the drop arrow for Category and you'll see that "Create new category" is a choice.

Give your new Block an optional description and then choose which template to save the Block in. For the most part, you'll want to just save in the Building Blocks template. The one exception I can think of that many of you might encounter would be if you were going to create a Building Block you want to share with others. In that case, you might create a custom template and save to that—then you can send that template to those you want to share with and they can open it.

To share Building Blocks with others, create a new template by saving a new document (create a Word document with a brief description of your intended Building Blocks, for example) as a template. Click the Office Button | Save As | Change the File Type to Template and give it a name. Save your Building Blocks to that template and send the template to the people you want to share with. They can save the template to Word's Startup folder (C:\Users*USER NAME*\AppData\Roaming\Microsoft\Word\STARTUP is the default in Vista) and the next time they start Word the custom Building Blocks will be available to them.

Finally, you have an Options field that lets you configure how your Block should be inserted into the document you're working on.

- Insert Content Only just inserts the contents of the Block at the current cursor point. This is what I usually use as most of my Building Blocks are just bits of boilerplate text that I save as Building Blocks to save myself the time of having to retype it or having to search it out and copy/paste it from another document.

- Insert Content in its own Paragraph sets off your Block as a paragraph of its own. Useful for signatures or if your Block is . . . well . . . a paragraph.

- Insert Content on its own Page creates page breaks before and after your Block. This is a nice option if you have an entire page of boilerplate that you want to be able to quickly add to your documents. For example, a biography page or one or more pages of standard contract language that you don't change often.

▼ ▼ ▼ ▼ ▼

Tricks of the Pros

If you have pages of text that change only a bit, create Building Blocks from them that are their own pages. Then when you need to build that document, insert the pages and then go back make the subtle changes to each of those pages. Building Blocks, once inserted, are edited as easily as any other bit of text. This way you can quickly build a several page document with the benefits of, but not the hazards of, document reuse.

With the old AutoText feature, you'd type the name of your AutoText entry and it would offer to replace your AutoText name with the actual text. With Building Blocks, you have to type the name of your Building Block (which is why we want it to be something easy to type) and then press "F3" to activate it (e.g., replace the name with the actual block).

To organize your Building Blocks, go to the Insert tab and click on the Quick Parts button. You'll find the "Building Blocks Organizer" pictured in Figure 8.2 below.

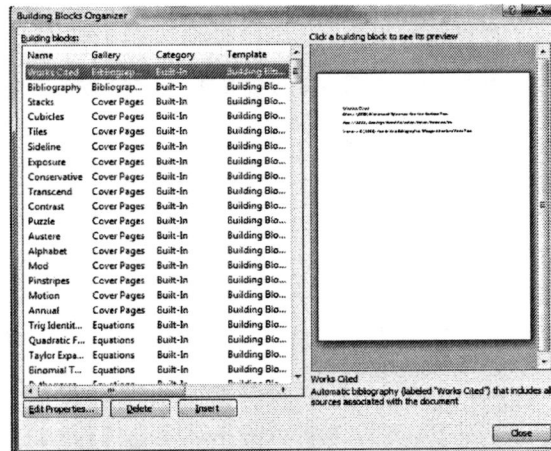

FIGURE 8.2

The Building Blocks Organizer is how you can edit the properties of a Building Block after the fact—for example, if you decide to change the category you assigned the Block to or what Gallery it appears in. You can also preview and insert your Building Blocks from the Organizer.

If you want to edit an existing Building Block, however, that's a bit of a different matter. There isn't any really easy way to do it—the best I can offer you is that you can insert the building block you want to edit into a blank document and make the changes you want. Then highlight and save the edited text as a new building block with the same name as the old one. Word will prompt you if you want to "redefine" the existing Building Block. Click "Yes" to replace the old one with the new version. If Word doesn't prompt you to redefine, then double-check to make sure you used the same name and saved the new version of the Building Block to the same gallery/template as the old one.

Macros

Word's macro language is amazingly powerful. So powerful, in fact, that it became the basis for a number of Word macro viruses a few years ago. The macro language that Word uses is Visual Basic for Applications (VBA). Entire books far thicker than this are devoted to the subject, so I won't attempt to cover it in detail here, besides the reality is that most of you will never do any VBA coding. What I'll do instead is show you how to use the Macro Recorder to create simple macros yourself and then later in this chapter give you a taste of what VBA is capable of, walk you through a couple of things that are especially useful for lawyers. and point you toward some resources if you want to know more.

Recording Macros

The easiest way to create a new macro is simply to record it and Word provides a capable facility to do just that. To access the Macro recorder, you can go to the View tab of the Ribbon, to the Macros group on the far right-end of the Ribbon, and click the drop-arrow on the button (see Figure 8.3) to find "Record Macro."

FIGURE 8.3

So, let's say for our example that you'd like to create a macro that prints the current page of your document only. All we need to do is start recording, name our Macro, then step thru the actions we want to record, then stop the recording and save it as a Macro. So let's give it a go . . .

1. Go to the View Tab, Macros, and Record Macro. The Record Macro dialog box (see Figure 8.4) will appear. Give your macro a name. I called mine "CurPrint" for "Current Page Print."

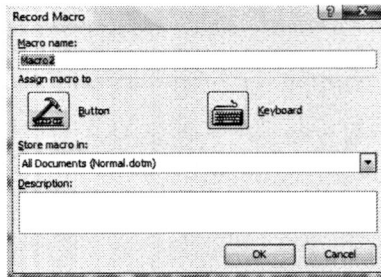

FIGURE 8.4

2. You can assign the macro to a button that you might put on the QAT (Quick Access Toolbar), which we covered in Chapter 2, or you can give it a keyboard shortcut. If it's not a macro you'll run often or if you want to invoke it using something like AutoHotKey, then you can do neither and just save it by name. I chose to assign it to CTRL+ALT+P, replacing "InsertPageField," which I rarely do.

3. If you only want this Macro to be part of a custom template, you can change the "Store In" field, but realistically you'll almost always leave that alone. If you're sophisticated enough to want finite control of which template the macro gets saved in, then you've probably skipped these simple step-by-step instructions anyhow.

4. You may want to give a description for what your macro does; especially if you have a lot of them and may not remember later or if you're going to share it with others users and want to make sure they know what it does.

5. Click OK and you'll be returned to your document and your mouse pointer will have a small "cassette tape" (remember those?) icon attached to it, which indicates that recording is currently on.

6. Perform the actions you wish to record. In our example, we're going to click the Office button, then highlight Print, and select Print. When the print dialog appears, check the radio button for "Current Page" and click "OK."

Your document should print and you should find yourself returned to the editing screen. Since clicking "OK" was the last step of your macro, you can go back to the View Tab | Macros button and click "Stop Recording." Recording will stop and your macro will be saved for future use. The next time you invoke that Macro—via View | Macros, or the button or keyboard shortcut you selected—the *exact* same set of steps will be repeated. Those steps can do anything in Word

▼

When recording Macro actions the speed with which you perform the tasks is irrelevant. The macro will be replayed much faster than it was recorded. But you don't want to record mistakes so I tend to move very deliberately when I'm recording. Plan ahead, click on things deliberately, pause to make sure you know what your next action is, then take that action. You'd rather not record mistakes or have to stop and start over.

that you can do—including type entire documents of text, perform a series of actions, order a pizza . . . well, ok, ordering pizza requires somewhat more advanced programming skills.

What Can VBA Do?

Just about anything you want it to do and even a few things you don't. You can manipulate data or files, automate repetitive tasks, or even roll your own more advanced application extension. In the previous section, we used the Macro Recorder to record a Macro, but what that really did was create some VBA code for us. We could have written that code manually, but in that example, we used the recorder to automate the process of creating the code.

Other Tools

VBA isn't the only way to do Macro and scripting in Microsoft Office. There are tools both built-in and from third parties that can help you with that as well.

AutoCorrect

Word's built-in AutoCorrect can be found under the Office Button | Word Options | Proofing | AutoCorrect Options, which launches the dialog box you see in Figure 8.5.

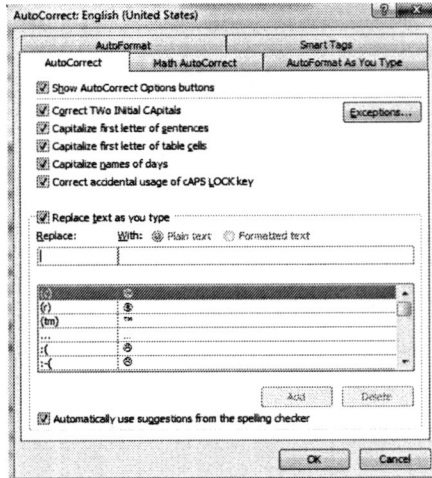

FIGURE 8.5

AutoCorrect is a handy tool to fix typos as you go. If you accidentally type "teh," Word's AutoCorrect will fix it to "the" on the fly. In fact, I had to undo an AutoCorrect in order to type that example! That's the typical usage of AutoCorrect, but it can also be customized to replace any text with any other text. Leaving aside the potential for clever practical jokes, this gives you a tool for replacing short strings of text with much longer ones. For instance, perhaps you work for "Jones, Smith, Jones, Smith, Jones, and Rumpelstiltskin." Naturally you don't want to have to type that out very often. It would be easy to add an AutoCorrect entry so that if you type "JSJSJR" (or even just "JSJ") Word would replace it with the full firm name (which I don't feel like re-typing here).

> If you're typing away and Word has autocorrected something for you that you didn't want it to auto-correct, you can press CTRL+Z to Undo that auto-correction and it will restore your originally typed text this time.

Hopefully you're seeing a lot of possibilities here. Have a client you work with a lot? You can put their name in and have it replace their initials with their full name. Use it for addresses, location names, court names, or other words and phrases you use a lot. It'll save you a lot of typing time *and* reduce the chances that you inadvertently send out a document in which you refer to your firm as "Jones, Smith, Jones, Smith, Jones, and Rumpledsuitman."

That's great for working in Word but what if you want those same replacements to work in other apps? Keep reading . . . our next tool gives you a universal AutoCorrect capability.

AutoHotKey

One of my all-time favorite free tools, AutoHotKey (http://www.autohotkey .com), is an all-around scripting language that, with a little bit of effort, you can use to automate tasks not only in Word but in the entire Office suite and, in fact, any application in Windows. You can launch programs with it, you can script installations in it, you can create blocks of text that will be inserted with a short string of characters, you can create mouse gestures, and you can do a lot of really cool things.

▼ ▼ ▼ ▼ ▼

What's a Mouse Gesture?

A mouse gesture is an action with the mouse that triggers an action. For example, if you hold down the right mouse button and move the mouse to the left you could have that action tell your web browser to go "Back." Or, hold down the right-mouse button and draw a clockwise circle to make your browser refresh. With a little effort, you can create just about any gesture you like and have AutoHotKey do whatever you'd like it to do in response.

For example . . . I have a little bit of script in AutoHotKey that whenever I type "bwa" and press the spacebar it will replace that with "Best wishes and aloha," which is my typical e-mail sign-off. Easy way to insert a signature block.

Coding something like that in AutoHotKey is quite easy. You just open the AutoHotKey script in any text editor (like Notepad) and add lines that say this:

::bwa::Best wishes and aloha,
return

The first bit defines what keystrokes you're going to type; "bwa" in my case. The second bit tells you what it's going to replace that with when you do so; "Best wishes and aloha," in my case. (In fact, I just used my bwa tool to put that in!) and the "Return" just tells AutoHotKey that you're done with what that action does.

While AutoHotKey is a good way to insert text quickly and consistently, it can also be used to automate any repetitive series of keystrokes or mouse clicks, and since it's not tied to any one application, scripts you create in AutoHotKey are available everywhere. I use it to launch applications too.

Did I mention it's free?

Customize Word's Hotkeys

One feature most people don't realize Word 2007 has is the ability to customize the hotkeys that Word uses. Don't want to use CTRL+B for boldface? You can change it. To get to the Customize Keyboard dialog box that you see in Figure 8.6, just go to the Office Button | Word Options | Customize and at the bottom left you'll find a button for "Customize Keyboard."

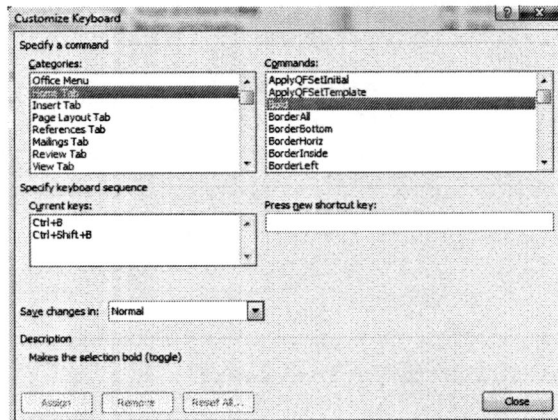

FIGURE 8.6

Let's try a useful exercise. One of the symbols that lawyers commonly use is the section symbol: §. So, let's assign it to a keyboard shortcut to make it easier to access. Go to the Customize Keyboard dialog box (instructions are still above if you need a refresher) and on the left side where it says "Categories" scroll all the way down to where it says "Common Symbols." It's the very last thing on that list. Then in the box on the right that now says "Common Symbols" scroll down until you find the Section Symbol. Select that one and you'll notice that under "Current Keys" the box is empty. There aren't any keys assigned to it yet. On the right where it says "Press new shortcut key," click there and press "ALT+S." You'll notice that when you enter that in the box you'll get a little message below the "Current Keys" box, which tells you what that hot key is currently assigned to (as far as Word knows). By default, it's available. Well, it's sort of available. By default ALT+S will open the references tab on the

Ribbon. But you can still get to the References tab by pressing and releasing ALT, then pressing S. So you can assign ALT+S to the section symbol and just use ALT, then S, to get to the References tab.

Word can only tell you about hot keys that it knows about. If some other program, like AutoHotKey, has ALT+S for something there's no way Word can know that and warn you about it. The other limitation here is that any hot key you set up in here is only going to work in Word.

To finish assigning ALT+S to your Section symbol, click the Assign button. Then you can exit back out to your Word document and give it a try. Sure enough, ALT+S should immediately put a § at your insertion point. Nice, eh?

The Roland Schorr 10-Most Method

If you're a fairly quick typist, I want to encourage you to use keyboard shortcuts and automation to make your Word experience substantially more efficient. Here's the way you do it . . .

1. Put some kind of notepad next to your keyboard. You can use an online thing like Vista's Notes sidebar gadget if you want to, but I really think it'll be easier to just have a piece of paper and a pencil.
2. Use Word in the course of your normal workday.
3. Each time you grab the mouse to click an icon or launch a command (like print, save, boldface, etc.) quickly note down what it was. The first time you do it make a note and each additional time you do the same thing you can just put a check mark next to the first one to indicate a repeat.
4. After you have enough of a sample size—perhaps a day or two—go back and try to figure out what the 10 most common tasks you used the mouse for were.
5. Learn, or create if necessary, the keyboard shortcuts for those tasks. If the shortcut takes more than two or three keystrokes to do it, then use AutoHotkey or Word's Macro Recorder to automate the task down to a single keystroke. It may be too much to try and master all 10 in a single day, so it's ok to break it down into chunks. Start with the most common tasks and learn two to three a day.

Tip This is also a great use of Building Blocks. If you can identify bits of text that you type often and can convert to Building Blocks, you can save time. Bonus . . . use AutoHotKey to insert a Building Block and then perform some common action upon it like applying a style.

If you can get to the point where your 5, 10 or 15 most common non-editing tasks (i.e., formatting, printing, launching applications, etc.) can be done with a just one or a few keystrokes or hotkey combinations, you can save yourself a lot of time in the course of your normal day.

Resources

Like all URLs ("Uniform Resource Locators" AKA web addresses) you see in print, these could change between the time that I type them here and you read them there. In those instances . . . Google is your friend.

- http://msdn.microsoft.com/en-us/isv/bb190538.aspx—This is Microsoft's MSDN site for Visual Basic for Applications. A lot of useful resources and tools here for people doing development with VBA.
- http://en.wikipedia.org/wiki/Visual_Basic_for_Applications— Wikipedia's article on Visual Basic for Applications. Nice starting point with some general background. Also includes a nice collection of references and links to more information.

Summary

Microsoft Word is an application that requires a high degree of user interaction—by that I mean that unlike some applications where you start a process and just let it run, Word is an application where virtually everything that happens occurs because the user pressed a button or clicked a mouse. A lot of those interactions the user has with Word are repetitive so there are a lot of efficiencies to be gained by learning to automate Word and make those interactions easier and faster. Lawyers and legal staff in particular tend to create a lot of repetitive documents—documents that don't vary greatly from one to the other. Using tools for document assembly and automation can help make the law office operate more effieciently and with fewer mistakes.

There are a number of tools available to help in that process.

Document assembly lets you automate the process of building standardized documents. By asking only for the variables (e.g., the stuff that changes; names, dates, places) and placing it in the document where you need it, document assembly software can significantly reduce the time it takes to build standard documents and ensure consistent quality and accurate content.

Visual Basic for Applications is a very powerful macro language. In fact, I daresay it's the most powerful Macro language ever implemented in an office productivity suite like Microsoft Office. It can manipulate data, run various functions of the application, and even interact with the operating system in powerful and potentially dangerous ways.

AutoHotkey is a free utility that can help you create powerful scripts that not only automate tasks in Word but in any other Windows application as well.

AutoCorrect and hotkeys are built-in Word tools that can be extended by the user to help automate tasks or simplify how things are initiated.

With just a bit of thought and practice, you can easily find a lot of new efficiencies! Especially as law firms and in-house legal departments move increasingly toward value-based billing, it's important to find new and powerful ways to streamline the process of practicing law and creating documents while improving accuracy and quality.

Managing and Maintaining Word 2007 **9**

In this chapter, we'll take a look at some of the configuration options of Microsoft Word. To get to these options, click the Office Button and toward the bottom of the menu you'll find a button labeled "Word Options."

Popular

The aptly-named Popular group (see Figure 9.1) contains a few of the most commonly used options in the program. If

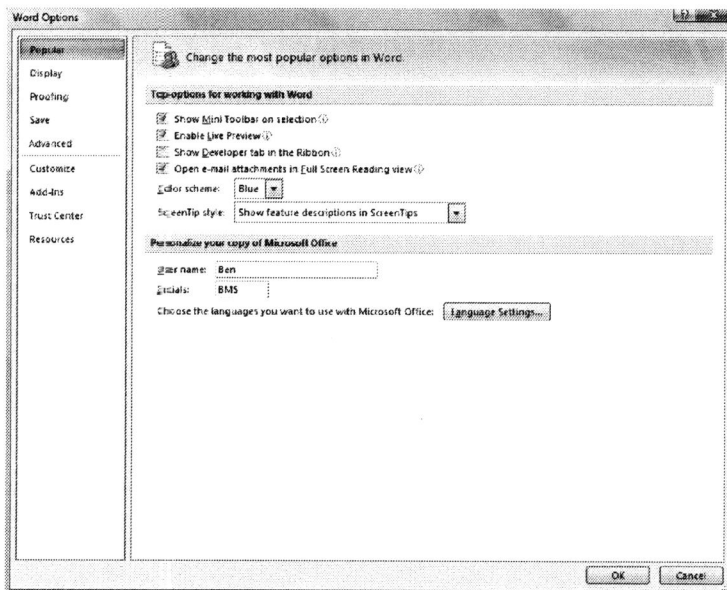

FIGURE 9.1

you find the Mini Toolbar more annoying than useful, you can turn it off right here. Likewise the Live Preview (Galleries) may be a burden to a slower system, though if they're not causing you problems I would leave them on. They'll save you more time than they could cost.

The other settings on this tab you should be concerned with are whether you want e-mail attachments to open in Full Screen Reading view. This is a feature I get a lot of questions on—lawyers receive e-mailed document attachments, and when they double-click to open them (after acknowledging all of the "Are you sure you want to open this?" prompts), they expect it to just open in Word the way they're used to seeing it. Instead, it opens in this curious "Reading View" that looks a bit odd and can be unsettling. That view *is* useful in many ways, but if you'd rather that Word just do what you expect it to, uncheck the "Open e-mail attachments in Full Screen Reading View" box and Word will just skip that screen and open normally for you.

> "Skin" is the term used to describe the color and layout of the interface in software. Some programs let you do a lot of creative things with the skin, others (like older versions of Office) gave you almost no control over it. With Office 2007, you can change the color scheme, but that's about it.

The next option we're interested in is new to Microsoft Office and that's the Color Scheme option. Here you can change the "skin" of Office to a different color scheme.

The three options are "Blue," "Silver," and "Black." Blue is the Office default and it's what most people use (in part because most people don't realize you can change it). Silver is a pleasant look and the one that I tend to use. Black is a dark skin which I have tried, but personally found to be just a little too dark for my taste. Whatever you choose is personal to your user profile and you can change it every few minutes if you want to—so feel free to play around and figure out which of the three schemes is the most pleasing to you.

The last settings on this page that interest us allow you to customize how Word identifies you. It lets you tell Word what your initials and full name are. These are used in instances like inserting comments, metadata about last editor and author, signature blocks, and such where this information can be automatically inserted for you. If you inherited this copy of Word and user profile from a previous user and their name/initials are still appearing in the product, this is one place you should go to change it.

Display

The Display group (see Figure 9.2) lets you control how Word will display applications.

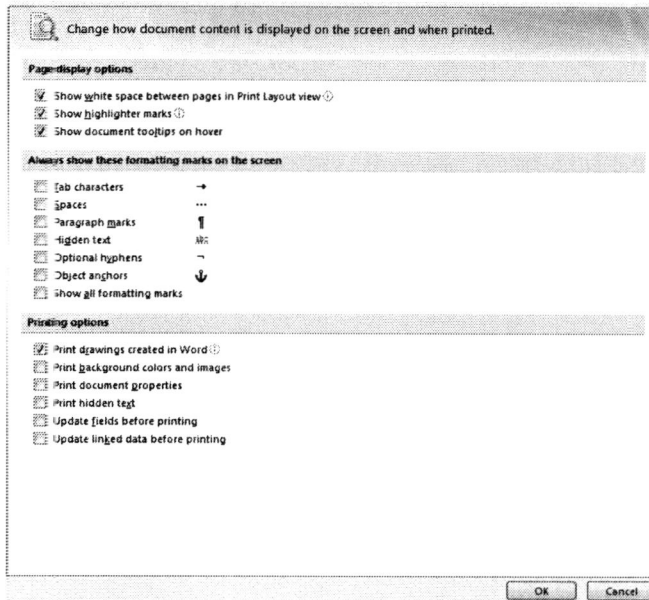

FIGURE 9.2

The first option is "Show white space between pages in Print Layout view." That option basically just shows the top and bottom margins, just like you'd see on the printed page. If you want to save a bit of screen real estate, you could turn that option off or just edit your documents in draft mode.

The problem with draft mode is that you lose a lot of the layout features, especially any embedded images. Most people work in Print Layout mode because that's the default. I work in it because as you may have noticed I have a lot of screen shots and figures in the book and the figures don't display in Draft mode.

This option will also show the headers and footers on a page. If you want to quickly turn it off (or back on), just point to the top or bottom edge of the page and double-click.

If you've used any highlighter marks in your document, which is a pretty common action when reviewing and collaborating on documents (you did read chapter 6, right?), you may want to turn off the display of highlighter marks. Worth noting that turning them off here not only suppresses the display of them on the screen but also keeps them from printing too.

"Show document tooltips on hover" turns off (or on) the display of balloons detailing the changes made to the text when Track Changes is turned on. Essentially, if you make a change to the text, then later hover over that text with your mouse and the change will be displayed in a tooltip that will "magically" appear above your cursor. If those balloons annoy you, here's where you turn them off.

The next section of the dialog box is where you control the display of formatting marks. I tend to leave all of these off myself. I may occasionally have it display paragraph marks because those can be significant in document formatting, but unless I'm troubleshooting document formatting issues (we'll talk about that in Chapter 10), I tend to just leave them all off. It's just a much cleaner look to the document.

If you want to turn all of the formatting marks on (or off) at once, you can just press CTRL+SHIFT+8 from within the document or click the button on the Home tab of the Ribbon, which looks like a Paragraph Mark (¶).

Proofing

The proofing section (see Figure 9.3) contains tools that are essential to your document assembly (see Chapter 8). It handles how Word will take care of spell checking, grammar checking, and autocorrect. A few of the default settings are worth noticing—for example, "Ignore words that are in UPPERCASE" or "Ignore words that contain numbers." In those cases, Word is going to assume that you're typing an acronym or a custom word/formula for which traditional spell-checking is likely to be of limited value. If you're in the habit of typing regular words in ALL UPPERCASE, then that's a habit I strongly suggest you break. Typing in ALL CAPS is really rather hard to read and looks like you're shouting. However, if you really insist upon shouting, then you might want to have Word not ignore those words and you can make that happen by unchecking the box here.

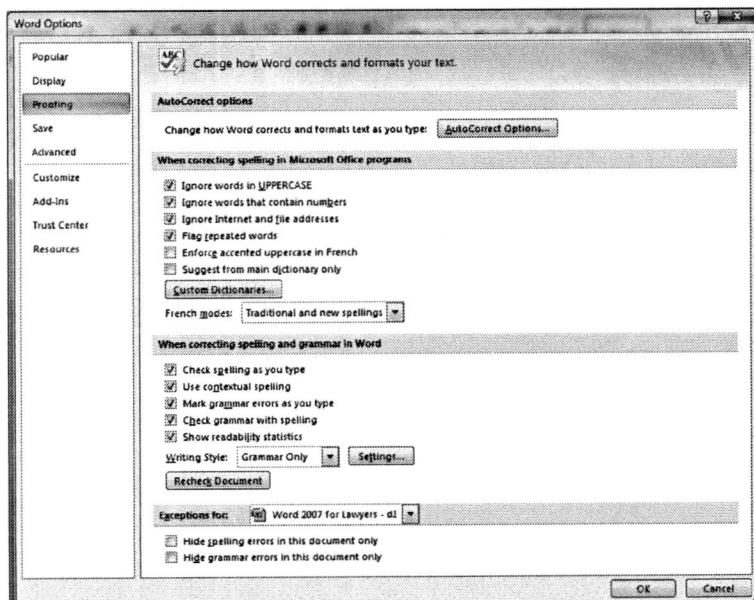

FIGURE 9.3

Another interesting option that appears on the main proofing page is the option to have custom dictionaries in Word. Click the Custom Dictionaries button to launch the dialog box you see in Figure 9.4. Here you can see the custom dictionaries that Word is going to use—the CUSTOM.DIC file is there by default and contains all of the words that you've added to the dictionary yourself—you can add new custom dictionaries, remove dictionaries, enable or disable them, edit the Word lists, and do all sorts of other tricky things.

You may be tempted to add or buy—or even create—a "legal" custom dictionary to Word, but in my experience, it's rarely needed. Most legal words ("abatement," "jurisprudence," even "venire") are already in the Word 2007 dictionary, and for the ones that remain ("voir dire" may trip your red squiggly lines), you can easily right-click the misrecognized word and select Add to Dictionary to just add it to your main dictionary.

Medical dictionaries are a little more useful as the words are somewhat more complex and esoteric.

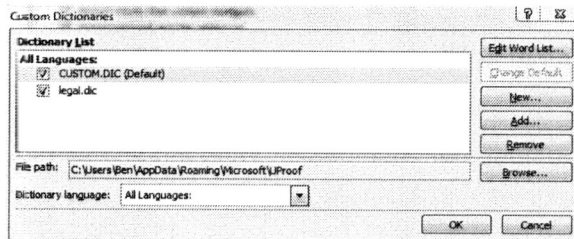

FIGURE 9.4

We already talked in Chapter 8 about configuring the AutoCorrect options so here we'll talk about some of the other settings on the Auto-Correct Options dialog box. To start with, let's look at "AutoFormat As You Type" (see Figure 9.5). These settings are, as you might have guessed,

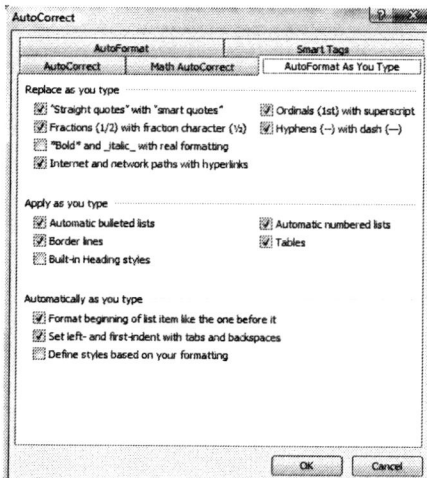

FIGURE 9.5

primarily concerned with automatically applying some stylish tweaks to your documents. For example—changing straight quotes to "smart quotes" which are the curly quotes and changing fractions to the fraction characters.

The next section on the Proofing tab offers a few useful choices.

- *Check spelling as you type* lets you turn off the live spell-checking. I recommend you leave this on, but if the red, squiggly lines distract you too much, you can turn it off.

- *Use contextual spelling* will make intelligent guesses about how words are supposed to be spelled based upon the context. This is a new feature in Word 2007—it's supposed to help you figure out when to use words like "than" versus "then" and so forth.

▼

The fractions character option is a lot more limited than it may seem. There are "hidden" ASCII characters for three of the common fractions: 1/4, 1/2, 3/4. If you type one of those three fractions, Word will automatically replace it with the ASCII character for that: _, _, _. (assuming you have the setting enabled in AutoFormat As You Type, which it is by default). Type any other fraction and you'll just get what you typed since Word has nothing to change it to.

Tip

There is also an occasionally handy button in this section. "Recheck Document" will run the spell check against your document, just as pressing F7 will, except "Recheck Document" will reset the "ignore" options you may have previously selected. You can use this if you suspect you may have "ignored" actual spelling errors and would like to reset those.

Save

The Save section of the Word Options helps you control options with how (and when) Word will save things.

First up, you can control the default document format. You'll probably want to leave that set to "Word Document (*.docx)," which lets you take advantage of the new document formats. But if you have to share a lot of documents with users of older versions of Word, who refuse to install the File Converters, you can change the default here. Even if you change the default to .DOC, you can still manually save a new document as a .DOCX file, you'll just have to manually set that each time you save. (See Figure 9.6.)

Some of you may remember the days when computers crashed fairly often (no Vista or Windows ME jokes, please!) and losing the document you'd been working on was a real possibility. A lot of old-timers (like me)

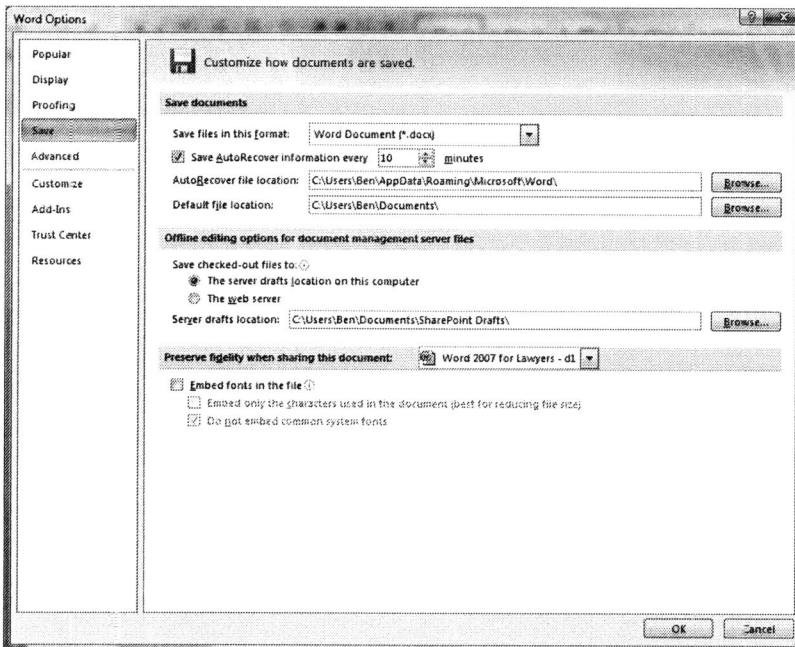

FIGURE 9.6

are in the habit of saving quite often, specifically so if the machine re-
boots suddenly you aren't going to lose your work. Word is, and has been
for quite some time, smarter than that however. It saves AutoRecover information on a regular schedule. What's AutoRecover information? It's
what enables Word to offer to recover your work for you when you restart
Word after a crash. By default Word will save this information, quietly in
the background, every 10 minutes. If you're paranoid or have a machine
that crashes a lot, you can set that to be a little more often—every five
minutes perhaps. If you're supremely confident, you can set it to a longer
interval, though really there isn't much reason to unless your machine is
so underpowered that saving AutoRecover information actually slows it
down or if you're really trying to milk every ounce of battery life out of
that laptop and want to reduce disk activity.

The Default File location is where Word is going to save documents
by default. Usually that's set to your own "My Documents" folder. You can
change it to be anything you like—including a server location if you have
one.

The only other setting in this section I want to point out is under the
"Preserve fidelity when sharing this document" section and it lets you
embed fonts in the file. Usually that's a waste of space, but it can be
handy if you're using a non-standard font in your document and you're
sharing the document with a user who doesn't have that font installed or
for whom the document just doesn't look quite right. Embedding the fonts

in the file does just that—saves a copy of the fonts you used within the document file so that when the other party opens the document they get the fonts too. The upside to this is that it helps the person you're sharing the document with see the document as you intended it. The downside is that it inflates your document size somewhat using more storage space. If you're e-mailing this file to your collaborator, the extra file size may also slow down (or even prevent) the transfer.

Advanced

The Advanced page has a lot of sections and options in it. We'll take it section by section, but I'm only going to spend time on those options that I think you're going to care about.

In the Editing options section you can control how Word 2007 is going to behave while you're editing. (See Figure 9.7.) The first option I'll explain, so you know what it does, but I don't recommend you change it. Basically if you select some text and then start typing, Word will delete the selection and replace it with whatever you type. That's the default behavior and what most people expect to happen. If you clear that checkbox, Word will instead *insert* what you're typing before the selected text. In which case, forgive me for suggesting it, there's no point in selecting the text to begin with. Just place your insertion point where you want to insert the text and type away.

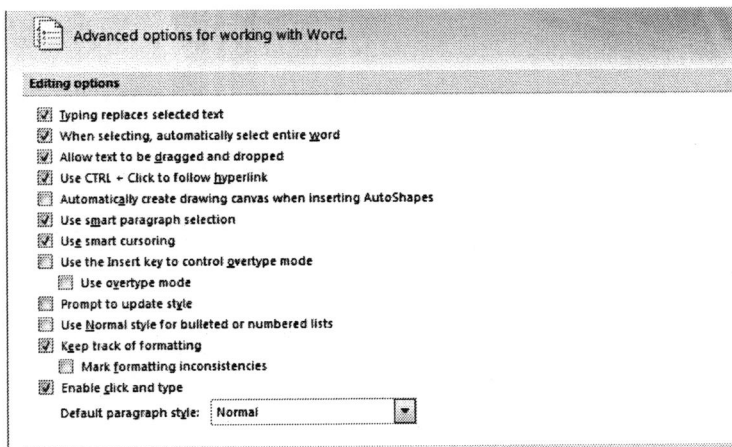

Advanced options for working with Word.

Editing options

- ☑ Typing replaces selected text
- ☑ When selecting, automatically select entire word
- ☑ Allow text to be dragged and dropped
- ☑ Use CTRL + Click to follow hyperlink
- ☐ Automatically create drawing canvas when inserting AutoShapes
- ☑ Use smart paragraph selection
- ☑ Use smart cursoring
- ☐ Use the Insert key to control overtype mode
    - ☐ Use overtype mode
- ☐ Prompt to update style
- ☐ Use Normal style for bulleted or numbered lists
- ☑ Keep track of formatting
    - ☐ Mark formatting inconsistencies
- ☑ Enable click and type
    - Default paragraph style: Normal

FIGURE 9.7

The second option is a little more helpful if you often find yourself wanting to select parts of a word and being frustrated that Word tries to be overly helpful and select the entire word. Clear that checkbox and your word selections can be a little more precise, but a little less efficient. I more often want to select entire words, rather than parts of words, so I leave it checked.

Word 2007 is increasingly smart in little ways. Smart paragraph selection makes sure that when you select a paragraph that the hidden paragraph mark (which is what holds the paragraph's formatting) is selected with it. That's good because if you select the paragraph to cut or copy it to somewhere else you'll probably want to cut or copy its formatting too.

Smart cursoring means that when you scroll through a document, for example by dragging the vertical scrollbar up and down, that the insertion point (i.e., the vertical bar that marks where you're typing) will jump to the page you're viewing if you touch an arrow key. To illustrate—if you drag the scroll bar several pages up or down, you will no longer see the insertion point. That's because it's still back at the last place you were editing. But if you press the left or right arrow key, the insertion point will suddenly jump to the page you're looking at. This saves you the extremely difficult task of using the mouse and actually clicking on the page you're looking at.

Wondering why the Insert key on your keyboard seems dead in Word? Probably because you have the "Use the Insert key to control overtype mode" option unchecked. That option was added because some users would inadvertently toggle on Overtype mode by hitting the Insert key on their keyboard accidentally.

If you change the formatting of text that has been formatted with a particular Style, Word can ask you if you want to update the style to match that new bit of formatting. The assumption being that maybe you want *all* of the text in that style to have this new formatting. The checkbox "Prompt to update style" is what you check if you want Word to ask you about that. It can be a quick way to update your styles with custom formatting; but I find it fairly annoying to be asked every time I apply a little direct formatting (remember Chapter 4?) and so I leave it turned off.

Speaking of formatting and styles, the next options of interest are the "Keep Track of Formatting" and "Mark formatting inconsistencies" options. What these do is that if you apply a style to some text in your document, let's say you use Heading 2, and then later you use direct formatting (font size, font attributes like Bold, etc.) to format some other text in a very similar way, Word will underscore that text with a blue wavy line to indicate that you appear to be formatting two pieces of text in a similar way but with inconsistent methods. That's to suggest that you should use the same style for both. The idea is to help you create documents where you're using styles, consistently, throughout. Rather than formatting different paragraphs with different methods—which can lead to some interesting issues later.

The final option of the editing options section is the rather handy "Enable click and type." The default is "enable" and that's the right way to go. This is what lets you basically click anywhere on the page with your mouse and just start typing. Gone are the days of having to manually insert a bunch of tabs or spaces if you want to start typing 1/3 of the way across a page.

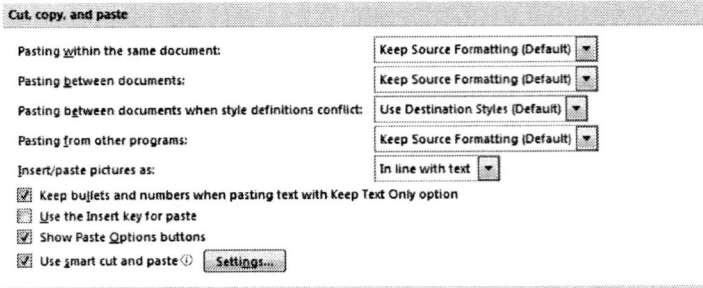

FIGURE 9.8

The next set of options are for Cut, copy and paste as you can see in Figure 9.8 above. They let you configure how Word will behave when you make use of the clipboard.

The first four settings let you configure the default behavior for various kinds of copy/paste operations and for those you have three basic choices:

- Keep Source Formatting—this will paste the text and whatever formatting came with the text. If the original text in the other document was 24 point and green, then it will be 24 point and green when you paste it regardless of what the document you're pasting it into looks like.
- Use Destination Styles—This will bring over the text and any style definition associated with it but it will apply the characteristics of the matching style (if there is one) in the destination document. For example, let's say you copy some text formatted for Heading 3 in a source document and in that document Heading 3 text is Bold, Italics, and Red. You paste it into your destination document where Heading 3 is Bold, Underline, and Blue. The text will come over but the formatting will be changed to Bold, Underline, and Blue.
- Keep Text Only—This is sort of similar to the last option except that *no* formatting information will be brought over. Just the pure text. If you're having problems with formatting after pasting in some text, try using this option to eliminate any odd formatting elements that might have been brought over in the paste operation.

One exception to this is found in the first of the four checkboxes at the bottom of this group: *Keep bullets and numbers when pasting text with Keep Text Only option.* The description is fairly self-explanatory. Word won't bring over formatting, *however*, if the source text was in a bulleted or numbered list, Word will preserve that formatting element.

The next checkbox I want to mention is the "Show Paste Options" checkbox. Have you ever pasted something into an Office application, like Word, and seen the little clipboard icon that appears immediately alongside your freshly pasted content? That's the Paste Options icon. It has a drop-down menu that gives you a few options (mostly what I've described previously about keeping source formatting, etc.) for how you want to handle the pasted text. It lets you override the defaults you specified just above on a case-by-case basis.

Finally, you have a checkbox that asks if you want to "Use smart cut and paste" followed by a Settings button that lets you specify a myriad of granular configuration options for how cut and paste will work. Honestly . . . stick with the defaults here. These settings mostly concern merging lists, spacing and alignment of pasted items, and the defaults generally work just fine. If you're really having problems with how pasted items space or align, then you might want to tweak these settings. I have yet to meet an lawyer who did.

▼

If you're running Word 2007 on an old workhorse of a computer that is really gasping and wheezing to get the job done . . . well, then you probably need to buy a better machine. Until your new machine arrives, however, you might disable the Smart Cut and Paste and Show Paste Options features. That might get you a barely perceptible performance improvement.

The next section, Show document content, lets you control how Word displays certain bits of custom document content. (See Figure 9.9.) There isn't really much here that is of interest to us, but do be aware of the "Font Substitution" settings because if you receive a document that

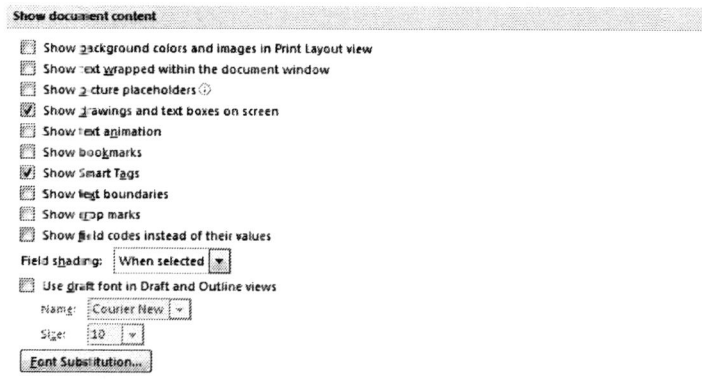

Show document content

☐ Show background colors and images in Print Layout view
☐ Show text wrapped within the document window
☐ Show picture placeholders ⓘ
☑ Show drawings and text boxes on screen
☐ Show text animation
☐ Show bookmarks
☑ Show Smart Tags
☐ Show text boundaries
☐ Show crop marks
☐ Show field codes instead of their values
Field shading: [When selected ▾]
☐ Use draft font in Draft and Outline views
  Name: [Courier New ▾]
  Size: [10 ▾]
[Font Substitution...]

FIGURE 9.9

was created with a font you don't have, then Font Substitution is how Word tries to imitate the original font using a font that you *do* have. This is usually not an issue but when it *is* an issue . . . it really is an issue. Font substitution can be one of the bigger headaches in troubleshooting why documents don't look right when transferred between different machines.

The other setting on the Show document content group I want to mention is Show Smart Tags. Smart Tags are a feature that debuted with Microsoft Office XP (AKA Office 2002) in which Office applications can recognize certain bits of text, such as a date or a phone number or an address and provide you some options. For example, a Smart Tag might recognize that you've typed in a street address and underline that address with a purple dotted underline. If you hover your cursor over that text, a Smart Tag Actions button will appear (it looks like an "i" in a purple circle). Click on the down-arrow next to it for a menu of actions of what you can do with that text, as you see in Figure 9.10. With an address, you may have the option to display a map to that address, add it to your Contacts folder in Outlook, display driving directions . . . all sorts of things. Smart Tags are powerful however.

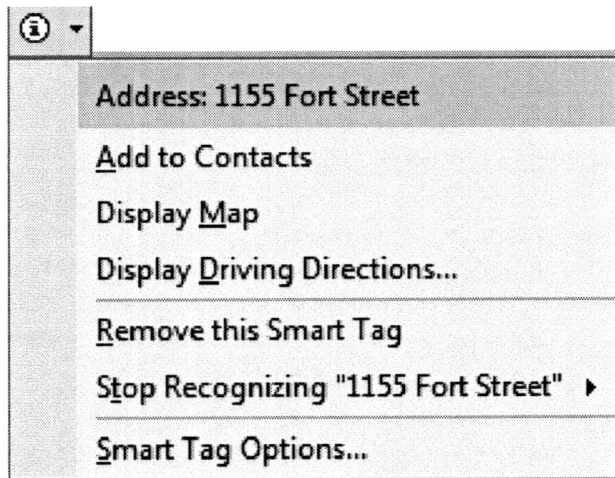

FIGURE 9.10

1. They do take up a bit of additional resources so most people have them disabled by default.
2. They're only useful on the electronic copies of the document. Obviously, a printed document has no use for Smart Tags.
3. Powerful though they may be, you might not really have much use for them yourself. They're often a solution in search of a problem. I've never asked Word to give me driving directions to an address I had in a Word document.

If you find that Smart Tags aren't working for you, it may be that they're just disabled. In addition to clicking the check box we talked about earlier, you also need to enable them in the Add-ins section. Under Word Options, go to the Add-Ins page, select "Smart Tags" on the Manage pick list at the bottom of the page, and click Go. Figure 9.11 shows what you'll get. Make sure the "Label text with smart tags" option is enabled—it's often disabled. Then check the kinds of smart tags you want to use.

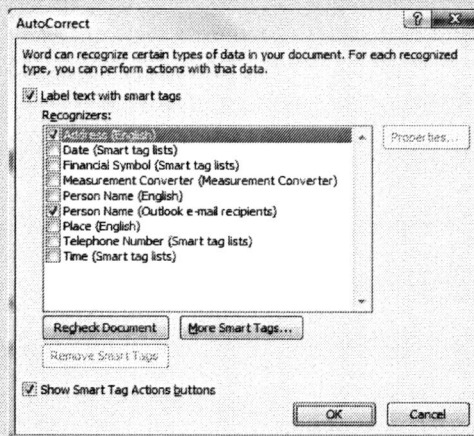

FIGURE 9.11

The More Smart Tags button should take you to a useful place to add additional Smart Tags, but in reality it just takes you to a Microsoft Web Site that vaguely promises a collection of Smart Tags developed by Microsoft and third parties and makes it rather difficult to find any actual Tags.

If you're a LexisNexis subscriber, you can get LexisNexis Smart Tags that let you access Lexis research services through a person, address, or case name typed into a Word document. This feature is currently downloadable from: http://support.lexisnexis.com/lndown load/record.asp?ArticleID=Download_SmartTags.

The next section is the Display section and that controls some of the more general display elements of Word. (See Figure 9.12.)

The first option lets you control how many Recent Documents will appear when you click the Office button. Seventeen is the default, but you can set it as high as 50. Of course, your screen size/resolution might not support *displaying* 50 files in that area, but you can give it a try if you really want to.

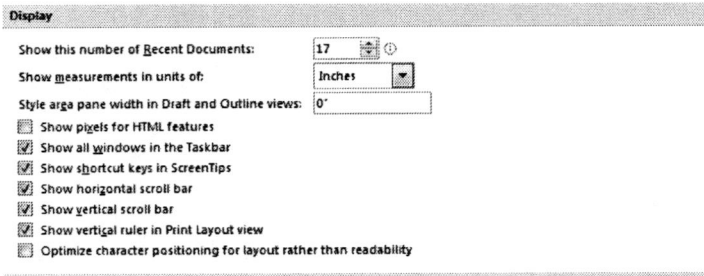

FIGURE 9.12

If you prefer to work metrically rather than imperially, you can change from displaying measurements in inches to display them in centimeters (or millimeters). You could also choose Points or Picas if you are so graphically inclined.

If you have more than one Word document open at a time, you may notice that you end up with multiple "instances" of Word on your Windows Taskbar. This is handy for switching between them, but if you're uncomfortable with the amount of Taskbar real estate it occupies, you can uncheck the "Show all windows in the Taskbar" option and that will consolidate all of your Word documents into a single window. It's a little harder to switch between them that way (you need to go to View | Switch Windows), but it does result in making Windows look a little cleaner I suppose.

The only other setting in this group worth mentioning is the ability to turn on or off the scroll bars.

The Print group offers a couple of useful options too. (See Figure 9.13.)

"Use draft quality" is handy on slower printers or if you're printing large documents and want to reduce the amount of ink/toner you're using. Great for documents you're printing for internal use and don't intend to show a client.

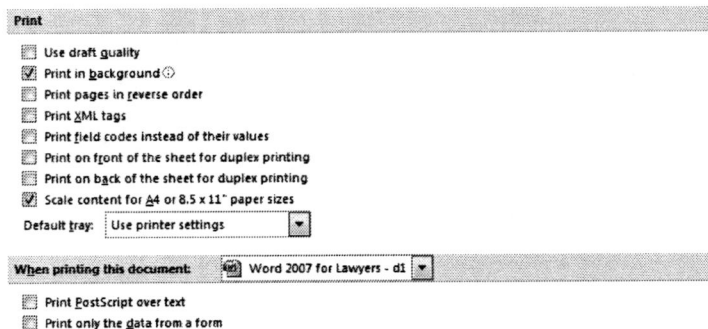

FIGURE 9.13

"Print in background" speeds your "RTA" (Return to Application) time by letting Word return to editing while the printing occurs in the background. If your machine is low on resources, this might not work that well, but most modern systems can handle printing in the background while you get back to editing.

The last settings I'll mention here, but won't go into detail on, control printing pages in reverse order (in other words printing the last page first) and printing on the front/back for duplex printing. Those are little-used but occasionally handy options for dealing with certain kinds of printers. If your pages come out of your printer face up instead of face down, you might want to have Word print in reverse order so that they are already in order when you take them off the printer.

In the Save group (see Figure 9.14 below), there are some options we should look at.

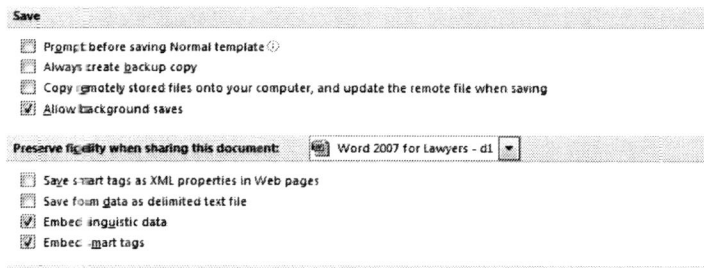

FIGURE 9.14

"Prompt before saving Normal template" is a safety feature. A lot of Word malware attempts to infect the Normal template. Prompting before saving causes Word to warn you that changes have been made to Normal.dotm, which might alert you to something unfortunate before it can cause any problems. If you get prompted to save changes to the Normal template but didn't intend to make any, you should click "No" just as a precaution.

"Always create backup copy" will give you primitive document versioning. When you go to save your document, the prior version that was saved is renamed to "Backup copy of *filename*.wbk" and saved in the same folder as the document you're saving. That way if you realize you made a bad change it's easy to restore the backup copy. Each time you save the document, the backup is replaced with the most recent prior save so you only have one version back.

To restore a backup, just click Office Button | Open, set the "File of Type" field to "All files," then locate and open the appropriate .wbk file.

Once it's open, you can Office Button | Save As to save it as a regular Word document again, including re-saving it over the bad copy of the document (which will then itself get saved as a backup).

The "Copy remotely stored files onto your computer, and update the remote file when saving" option is not only long-winded but also sort of useful. With this option enabled, if you open a document from a network location, Word will create a temporary copy of the document on your local hard drive and work from that temporary copy. That gives you better performance than trying to work off the original remote copy of the document and also protects you in case you lose network connectivity in the middle of editing the document. When you do a Save of the document, Word will save your changes to the remote location.

"Allow background saves" is another performance enhancing effort. When you do a Save, Word 2007 will do the save operation in the background so that you can continue editing. If you're saving a five page document, it probably doesn't matter. When you're saving a 205 page document, it can matter a lot in terms of your RTA (Return to Application) time. With this option turned off, Word will stop to save the document and not let you do anything else (in Word) until the save is complete.

In the General group, there are a few options that cover things they couldn't fit anywhere else.

I always uncheck "Provide Feedback with Sound" because I get tired of Word chirping at me as I work to notify me of things.

The only other option in here that I think you might care about is the one that lets you enter your mailing address. That's the address Word is going to use, by default, in places like the envelopes where it asks for your mailing address.

Near the bottom of the General tab are three buttons. (See Figure 9.15.) Two of them: Web Options and Service Options are things you prob-

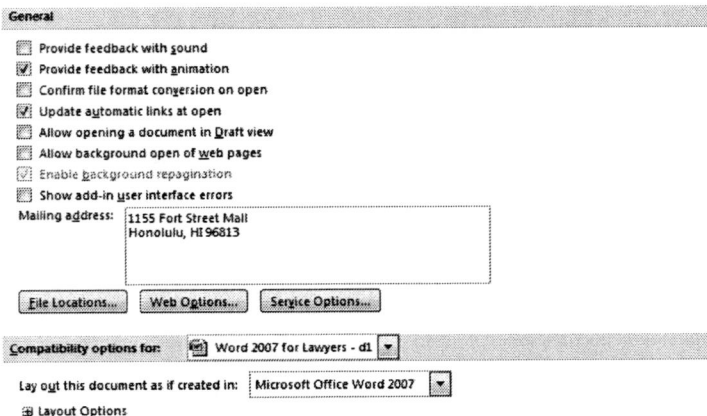

FIGURE 9.15

ably don't care about. Web options are used if you're creating web documents with Word 2007, which I generally discourage and Service options regard how Word and SharePoint operate and are really best configured with the assistance of your SharePoint administrator (if you have one).

The File Locations button, on the other hand, is occasionally useful. Click that button to get the File Locations dialog you see in Figure 9.16. Here you can specify the locations of key Word directories—from where User templates are located to where AutoRecover files will be stored to where the Startup folder is. Most of this you don't need to change, but if you want to find (or change) them, here's where you can do that.

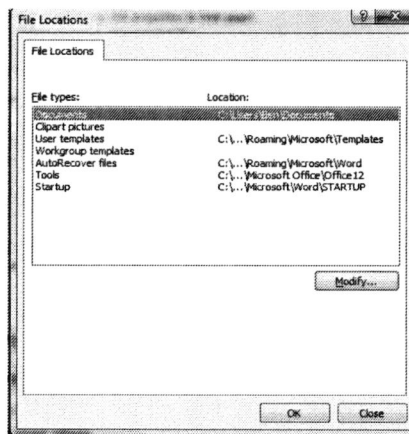

FIGURE 9.16

Customize

Below the separator in Word Options you'll find the Customize page. (See Figure 9.17.) This page is primarily about customizing the QAT

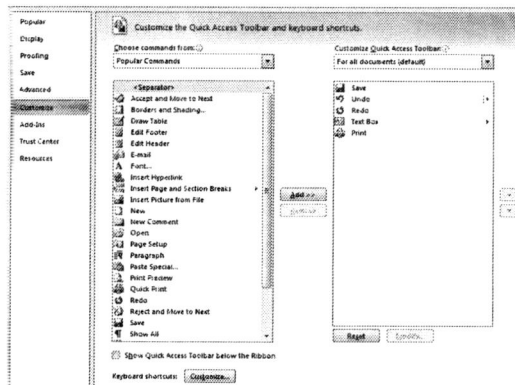

FIGURE 9.17

(Quick Access Toolbar), which you will probably want to do. It's fairly self explanatory. You select commands from the left side and then click "Add" to add them to the Quick Access Toolbar.

Quietly hidden on this page is the button to customize the keyboard shortcuts. Click it and you'll get the dialog box you see in Figure 9.18. You can choose a category from the field on the left and then a command from that category from the field on the right. If there is already a keyboard shortcut for that command, it will appear in the "Current keys" window once you have the command selected. Otherwise (or even so), you can click in the "Press New Shortcut Key" field and press a hotkey combination that you would like to assign to that command.

Tricks of the Pros

A lot of hotkey combinations are already taken. Things like CTRL+B or ALT+P are well-used already. But combinations involving the symbol keys like "ALT+`" are often unassigned.

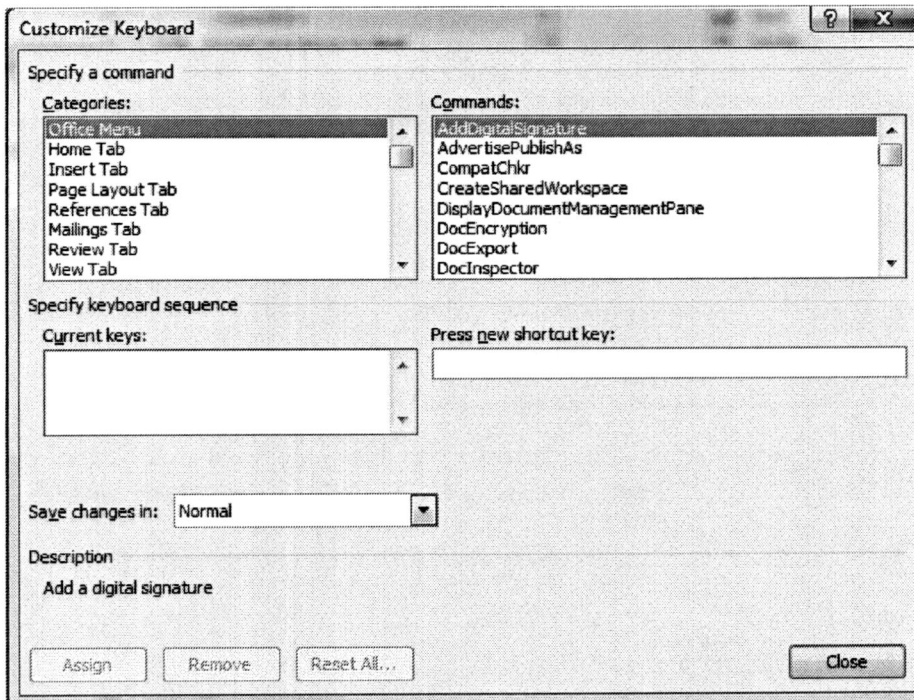

FIGURE 9.18

If the combination you select is already assigned to something, it will show up under the Current Keys field on the left. Otherwise, it will say "[unassigned]," which means it's available for use. If you select something that is already assigned and click the "Assign" button, it will re-assign it to your new command. That means you can remap the current Word hotkeys if you want to.

When you have the shortcut key you want, just click "Assign" to make it so.

If you later decide you'd like to undo those custom assignments (and restore the default assignments), you can do that in one move with the "Reset All" button at the bottom.

Add-Ins

The Add-ins group (see Figure 9.19) lets you control the helper programs that are running with Word. Honestly not only will you rarely need to use this, but you really *shouldn't* mess around in here too much if you don't know what you're doing. The most common things you would do here would be to disable certain add-ins for the purpose of troubleshooting issues or use the "Manage" tool at the bottom of the window to do things like add/remove Smart Tags (see above).

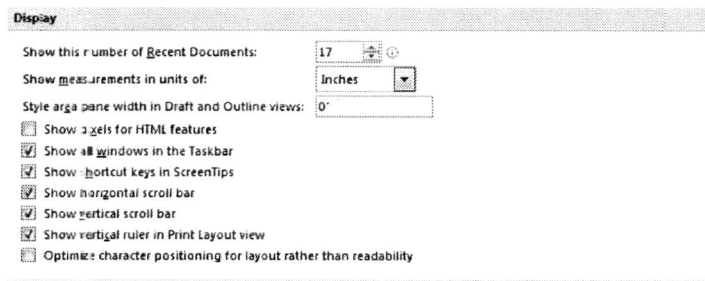

FIGURE 9.19

The initial screen you see in Figure 9.19 only displays the add-ins. To actually manage them, you need to click the "Go" button at the bottom of the page.

Trust Center

The Trust Center is where you control the security settings of the application, and in Microsoft Word 2007, it's pretty basic primarily concerned with privacy and how macros are handled. I wouldn't change any of the settings in here unless you know exactly what you're doing or you have the guidance of a good technical support person. There are two features of the Trust Center that I do want to highlight for you though.

Trusted Locations

One common complaint with Office has been the security features added to the more recent versions. You open a document and have to click thru a variety of warnings just to open your own documents! Well, Office 2007 gives you a way around that—you can specify folders on your computer (or on your network) which are automatically trusted. (See Figure 9.20.) Documents you open from those locations won't prompt you. If you add a trusted location on your network, you'll need to check the box that says "Allow trusted locations on my network" in order for it to work. If you're particularly paranoid, you can disable all trusted locations. Unless you're particularly fond of dialog boxes, I wouldn't do that as you'll be prompted nearly every time you open any kind of document.

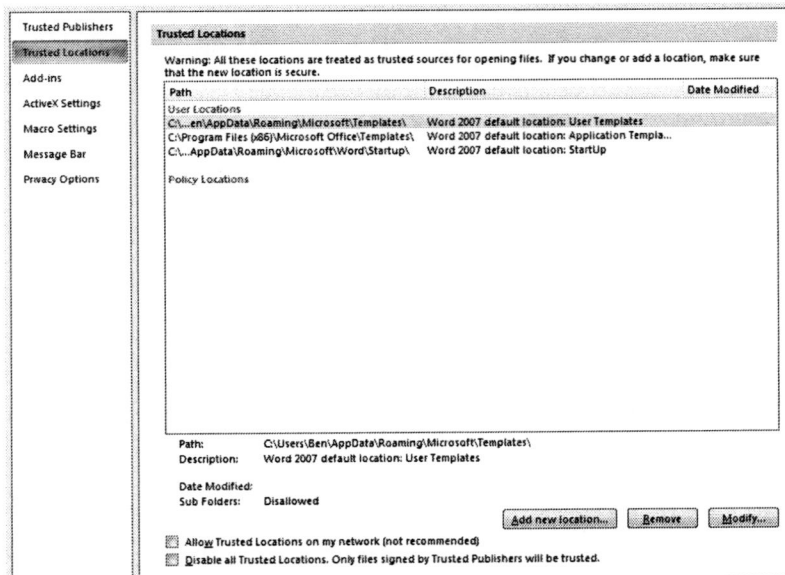

FIGURE 9.20

Privacy Options

In the Privacy Options window (see Figure 9.21), you can tell Word how paranoid you want to be. If you don't want Word to search Office Online for help content when you're connected, you can turn that off here (though honestly you really should use it; it's good).

If you've decided that you don't want to participate in the Customer Experience Improvement Program, you can opt back out (since you had to

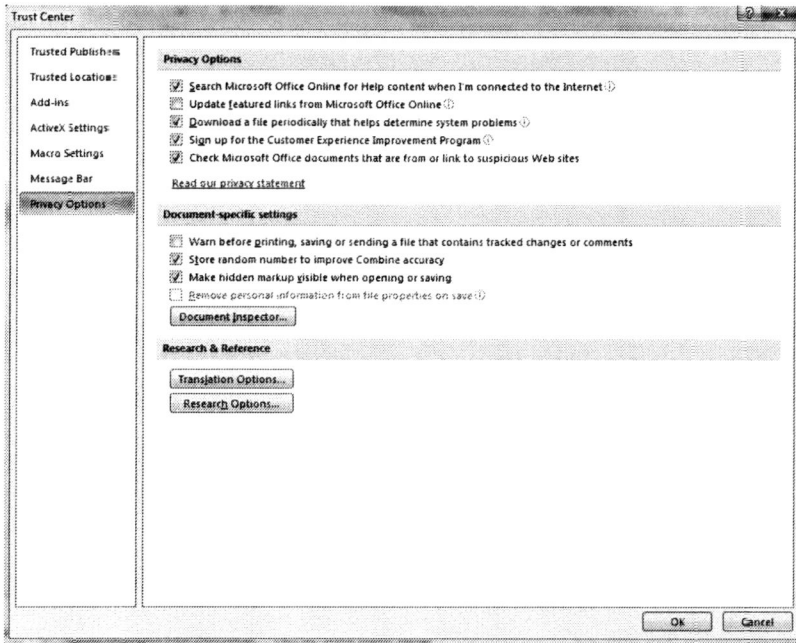

FIGURE 9.21

opt-in to begin with) here. Again, this is a really useful program so I encourage you to participate and assure you that there's no good privacy reason not to . . . but if you'd really rather not, then here's where you can say so.

The final setting in here that I want to point out is the "Warn before printing, saving or sending a file that contains tracked changes or comments." It's probably a good idea to turn this option ON, just to minimize the chances that you might inadvertently distribute a document with embarrassing metadata in it. See Chapter 11 for more on that subject.

Resources

The final page in Word Options is the Resources page. (See Figure 9.22.) This looks a little more like a web page than the rest and includes just a few fairly simple buttons.

- Check for Updates—Microsoft periodically releases updates to their products, and if you don't have Automatic Update turned on (or Windows Software Update Services or any of a number of other patch management tools), you might not have all of them installed yet. Click the "Check for Updates" button to connect to Microsoft's Office Update site and see if there are new patches/

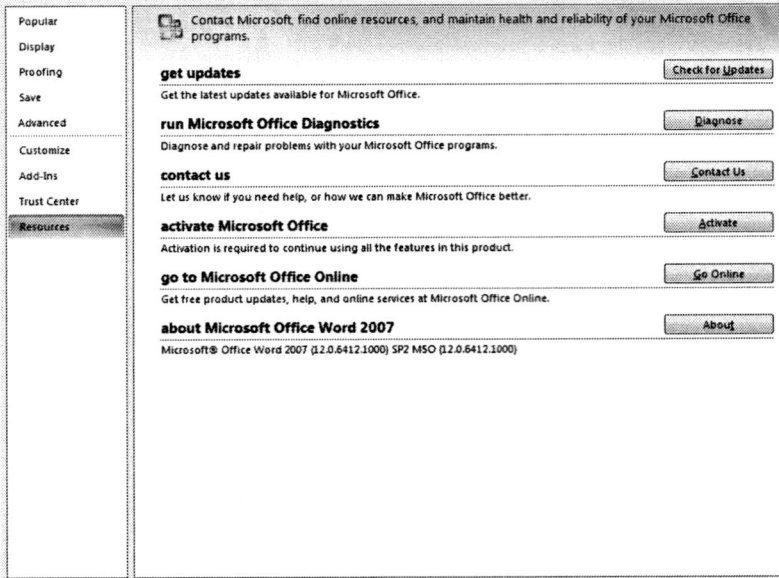

FIGURE 9.22

fixes for Word 2007. Don't worry, if there are some, they'll be free and easy to download and install.

- Diagnose—Runs Microsoft Office diagnostics, which checks for problems with Microsoft Office and (sometimes) offers to repair them.
- Contact Us—Is not really as useful as it sounds. It just loads the Microsoft Support page that has links to different options for technical support. Perhaps the best one of the bunch is the Office Discussion Groups, which lets you see questions and answers posted by other users and peer support folks like Microsoft MVPs.

▼ ▼ ▼ ▼ ▼

What's a Microsoft MVP?

A Microsoft MVP or "Most Valuable Professional" is a volunteer who has been recognized by Microsoft as an expert in one or more particular products. Anybody can be an MVP if they demonstrate a level of expertise and a willingness to help support that product. MVPs are not Microsoft employees and aren't paid for their efforts. For more information, visit http://support.microsoft.com/mvp.

- Activate Microsoft Office—If you're not seeing all of the features you expect to see, especially if the product is pretty new, you probably haven't activated it yet. Click the button to Activate. Yes . . . activation is a clever way for Microsoft to try and limit pirated copies of the software.
- Go to Microsoft Office Online—loads the Microsoft Office website. The site is actually quite useful, full of tips, instructional materials, downloads (free and otherwise) and other support resources. You can get there by going to http://www.microsoft.com/office or you can go to Word Options | Resources and click the button. Whichever makes you smile.
- About—Finally, the venerable About button that tells you the more intimate details about the exact version of the product you're using. If you ever call or e-mail for support, it is very helpful to have this information as the support person you're dealing with will probably want to know it.

Hidden under the About button is actually one of the more useful and lesser known Microsoft Office troubleshooting features: System Information. (See Figure 9.23.) System information loads up a little utility that can tell you (and by extension your support person) all about your com-

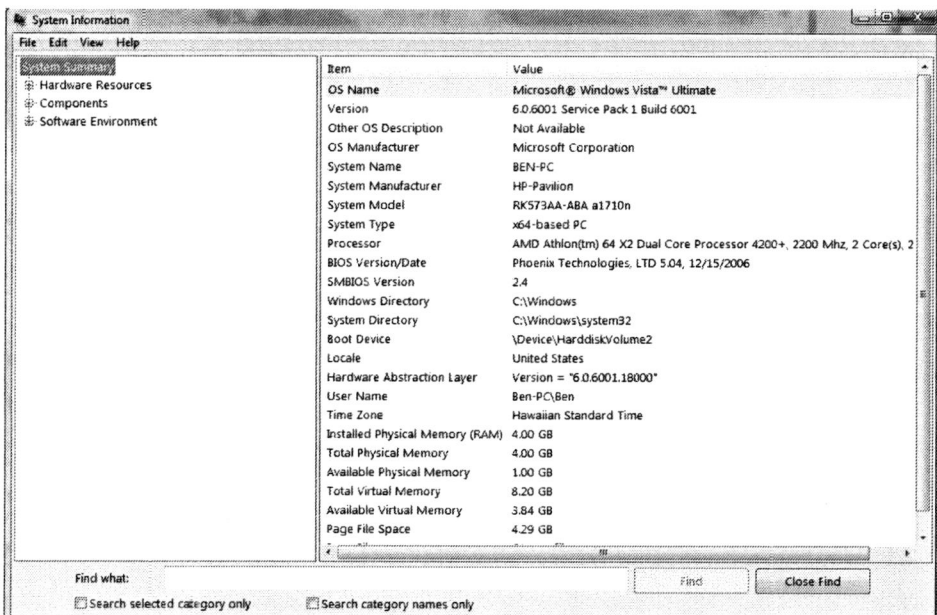

FIGURE 9.23

puter. What kind of operating system you're using, how much RAM you have, where your Windows directory is . . . all sorts of stuff that is really handy to know. And by clicking File | Save, you can create a .NFO file to e-mail to your support person if they need to look at it themselves. They won't have to ask you a lot of questions you might not know the answers to. Very handy stuff when you're trying to get help with your system. Which brings us to . . .

Getting Help

Microsoft Word 2007 is a remarkably well-understood and well-documented application. There are a plethora of forums, web sites, books, classes, and other resources out there to help you get the most out of Word 2007.

In the old days, you used to get a big thick manual with your software. It explained all of the features and capabilities in language that was rather dry but made up for it by being poorly organized. Software publishers quickly found out, mostly via calls to their support lines, that most users didn't bother to read the printed documentation. So these days they save a lot of money on printing, paper, and shipping and just include that content, occasionally better written, as either online or digital content in the help system. Office 2007 is no different. On the right end of the Ribbon, on the same row with the ribbon tabs, you'll find a small blue question mark in a circle like what you see in Figure 9.24.

FIGURE 9.24

Clicking that will launch Word help, and if you're lucky, and connected to the Internet, it can be a powerful and rich tool. Without Internet connectivity you *still* get the off-line help, but that system is not quite as robust.

At the bottom of each help topic in Word 2007 (when you're connected), you'll find something surprising . . . comments, left by other users! These are tips and tricks that other users have that they've chosen to add to the help system and sometimes you find some real gems in there! Just pick a help topic and scroll to the bottom to read the comments. And . . . you'll get the chance to leave your own comment if you want to.

The other thing I encourage you to use is the "Was this information helpful" feedback tool. The Microsoft Office documentation teams *do* look at that feedback and it really does help them to craft better articles for you. So please, take a moment to click "Yes," "No," or "I don't know" to express your opinion on the article.

▼ ▼ ▼ ▼ ▼

It Looks Like You're Writing a Eulogy. Would You Like Help?

One thing you won't find in Office 2007 is Clippy (see Figure 9.25), the persistently helpful Office Assistant whose popularity was so low even Congress thought he was unpopular. Although you didn't have to use the paper clip—other Office Assistants like an Einstein-esque professor, a curious cat, or a cute little dog were readily available—the annoying tendency to use up screen space and constantly offer help caused most people to turn it off within hours of installing the application. A feature of every version of Office since Office 97. It was mercifully removed from Office 2007.

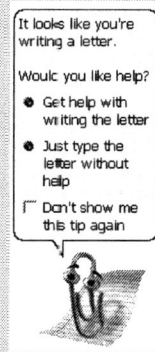

It looks like you're writing a letter.

Would you like help?

● Get help with writing the letter

● Just type the letter without help

☐ Don't show me this tip again

FIGURE 9.25

Get Updates

Keeping Microsoft Office 2007 updated is a good way to keep it running smoothly. The first option under the Resources section is to "Get Updates," which will tell Office to connect to Office Update (Microsoft's free update site) and check for and download if necessary any new updates to the applications. Those updates can be security updates, bug fixes, or even service packs. On rare occasion there might be new features but that's pretty unusual so don't count on that.

Summary

For such a simple seeming product, Microsoft Word 2007 can be configured and personalized in a lot of different ways. Some of these features are really useful to tweak; most of them you're better off leaving alone.

Among the features that you'll probably want to pay some attention to are the proofing tools and the way Word is going to display the documents you enter. It can make a big difference if the proofing tools are working for you, rather than against you, and if you're comfortable with how the document editor actually *looks*.

Troubleshooting **10**

Word 2007 is probably the most robust and resilient version of Word Microsoft has ever created. That doesn't mean that nothing ever goes wrong with it though, so in this chapter we'll take a look at a few of the common problems and how to resolve them.

Activating

If you find that certain features of the product don't seem to be available or if you get an error message telling you that a certain selection is "blocked," it may be that you either haven't activated the product yet or that you're using a trial version of the product that has expired. A lot of computers come from the manufacturer with only trial versions of Office installed and those will expire in approximately 60 days. If you go out and buy the full version, you can install over your trial and all of your data and documents will be just fine. It's easy.

If you're sure you have a full version, just go to the Office Button, click Word Options and go to the Resources group to get what you see in Figure 10.1.

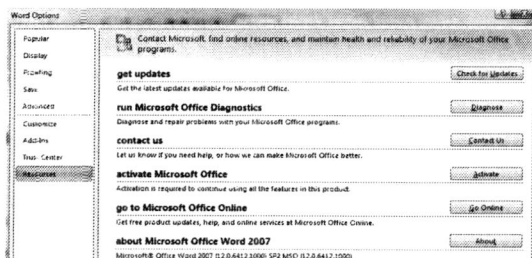

FIGURE 10.1

The "Activate" button is the fourth selection down on the right and it will appear available even if you've already activated (like mine does in that image). If you click it and you've already activated, you'll just get a helpful message box informing you that you've already activated, so no harm done.

Office Diagnostics

One of the easiest things to do when Word starts acting oddly, freezing up or corrupting documents is to run the Office Diagnostics. (See Figure 10.2.)

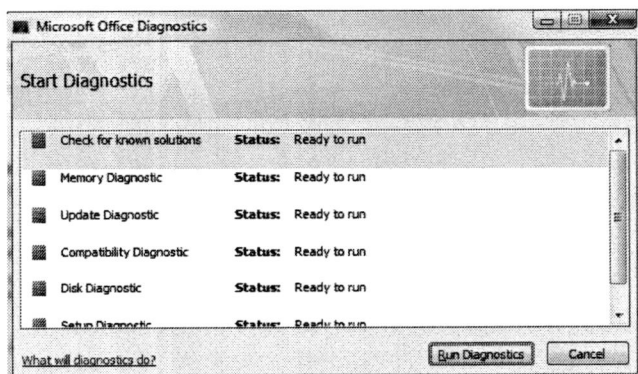

FIGURE 10.2

Office Diagnostics will run on your system and try to identify (and correct, if possible) any known problems. One of the most useful things it will do is check your Office application files to see if any of them are corrupted. If one is, Office Diagnostics will reload that file from the setup files that are still located on your hard drive (remember, that's why the hard drive requirements for Office 2007 are so high).

Office Diagnostics will *not* delete any of your data files so no worries there. Depending upon how fast your system is, Office Diagnostics may take a little time (10 minutes or more) to complete, but it's a painless thing to try if your Office applications are misbehaving.

You can also launch Office Diagnostics by going to Start | All Programs | Microsoft Office | Microsoft Office Tools.

Safe Mode

Word 2007, like all Office 2007 applications, has a safe mode it can start in. Safe mode basically means that the program opens without any add-ins, customizations, or advanced features running. It's a quick way to find out if the problem is the result of a faulty add-in or something else. To start Word 2007 in Safe mode, just hold down the CTRL key when you start Microsoft Word (or any other Office 2007 application for that matter). If you don't see the problem you're troubleshooting when Word is in Safe mode, then try disabling add-ins by going to the Office Button | Word Options | Add-ins section, as you can see in Figure 10.3. As I mentioned in the previous chapter, the Add-ins tool can help you manage Word Add-ins. Click the "Go" button at the bottom of the screen to get into the tool that lets you enable or disable add-ins.

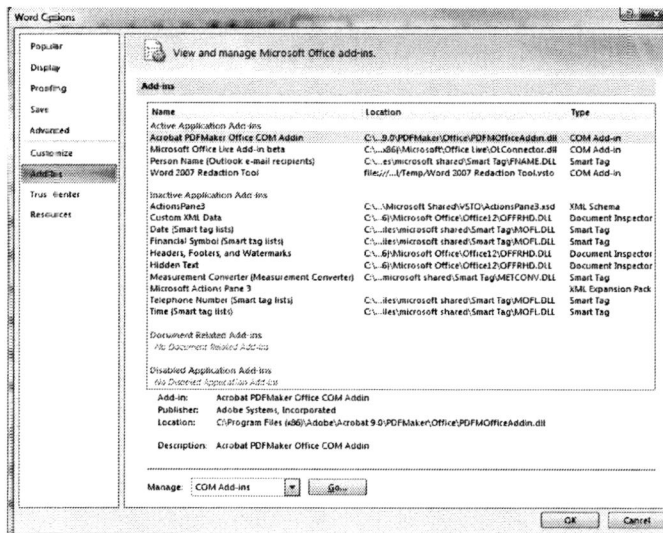

FIGURE 10.3

Recovering from Word Crashes

If just starting Microsoft Word 2007 with a blank document causes it to crash or behave oddly, it could be that there is some corruption in your normal.dotm, which is the standard template Word 2007 loads when it first starts up. Luckily this is very easy to recover from. With Word 2007 closed, locate the normal.dotm file (which should be located under C:\Users\[your profile name]\AppData\Roaming\Microsoft in Vista or C:\Documents and Settings\[Your profile name]\Application Data\Microsoft\Templates in Windows XP) and rename it to something like "normal.old." Then start Word 2007 normally. Word will detect that it can't find the normal dotm file as it expected and it will just automatically create a new one for you. If Word starts and runs normally, then you can be pretty sure that the problem was some kind of corruption in your old normal.dotm file.

If that doesn't resolve the issue, then you may need to get down and dirty with your registry. This is the time when I need to offer you the standard disclaimer that editing the registry is really not something I encourage regular users to do. If you change the wrong thing in the registry, you can do really bad things to your computer, so before you embark on this make sure that you have a good backup of your system and *really* want to do this yourself rather than ask a computer professional to take on this task for you. Assuming you really do want to proceed, and I have to make that assumption to continue this chapter, exit all Microsoft Office programs (including Outlook) then click Start, Click Run, and type REGEDIT in the provided command box. Click OK or press ENTER.

Within the registry find this subkey:

HKEY_CURRENT_USER\Software\Microsoft Office\12.0\Word\Data

With that subkey selected, click the File menu in Regedit and choose Export. Save the file to your desktop in a file named something like "Word Data Key.reg." The reason we're doing this is because most of the Word customizations found under the Office Button | Word Options button are saved in the Data key of the registry (and yes, that includes the Recently Used Files list from the Office Button). What we're about to do will wipe out those customizations, and if that doesn't fix the problem, you may want to be able to restore those customizations. Hence the exported .reg file.

Once you've exported your Data key to the .reg file for safekeeping, delete the Data key from the registry. Exit the Registry Editor and start Word. When Word 2007 starts up, it will notice that the Data key is gone and it will automatically create a new one for you using the factory default settings. If your problem is solved, then you're good to go from there. If not, you can either continue with this new setup or you can close Word, go to your Windows desktop and double-click that "Word Data Key.reg" file we made and put your customizations back in.

Corrupted Documents

Occasionally with Word documents, they will get corrupted or otherwise damaged. That can happen for a number of reasons—malware, hardware problems, power failures . . . or just darned bad luck. Corruption in a document isn't always obvious either, such as a document that won't load or text that is completely ruined (though that would do it too). Sometimes it's more subtle like odd behavior in the document, such as page breaks moving around on their own, strange page renumbering, or other odd behaviors. If that happens, the first thing to do is confirm that the strange behavior is limited to that one document. Open another document and see if the problem exists there as well. If it does, then you have some other issue with your system that you need to address. Then the afore-mentioned Office Diagnostics may come in handy.

If the problem is limited to the document, then the first thing to do is find out which template is used by the document. With the document open in Word, click the Office Button and then Word Options. Click Add-Ins. Click the drop arrow on the Manage box (see Figure 10.4 below), then click Templates from that list.

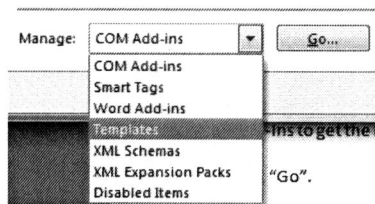

FIGURE 10.4

Finally click "Go" to launch the Templates and Add-ins dialog box you see in Figure 10.5 below.

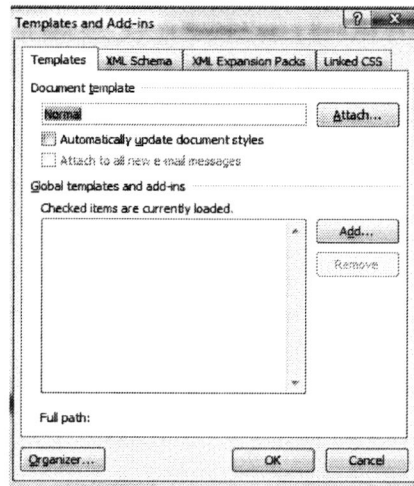

FIGURE 10.5

From this dialog box, you can quickly see what the Document tem-plate is. In Figure 10.5, you can see that the current document template is "Normal," which is the default Word Template. That's good news for your troubleshooting because you can rename (or delete, if you're feel-ing brave) the Normal.dotm global template and the next time you start

Word 2007 it will automatically recreate it for you (hopefully without the corruption that caused your problems). The only downside to deleting normal.dotm, honestly, is if you've customized the Normal template in some way and you don't want to lose those customizations. Chances are good that, like most lawyers, you haven't customized normal.dotm (at least not intentionally) so deleting it is just fine. Again, Word 2007 will quietly recreate it for you the next time you start up.

Finding and Fixing Formatting Mysteries

One of the more perplexing issues lawyers and law firms have to deal with tends to be Formatting problems. "Why the heck is that italicized?!" is a common refrain. In the good 'ole days of Word Perfect, we'd just open the Reveal Codes pane, track down the offending code, and remove it. But Word doesn't use codes that way so tracking down an errant bit of formatting can be a little more challenging. (That's why you want to use styles as often as possible and as little direct formatting as you can.)

There are two common scenarios where you may have to troubleshoot some curious formatting.

Documents You Created

If it's a document that you created, the chances are good that you have an unfortunate combination of direct and indirect formatting. You may want to re-read Chapter 4 and pay particular attention to the information on Styles. The other thing you might want to do is go into Word Options (review Chapter 9) | Advanced and make sure that "Keep Track of Formatting" and "Mark formatting inconsistencies" checkboxes are enabled. Then Word will help you to locate, and fix, places where you may have inconsistent use of styles and direct formatting.

Documents from Somebody Else

Sometimes if you receive a document from somebody else there may be formatting issues, especially if they are using a different word processor, even a different version of Word. A common cause of that issue is the fonts that they have installed on their machine versus the fonts you have installed. For example, they may be using Word for Mac and have older, non-unicode, fonts on their machine that you don't have installed on your machine. Generally, if the differences are minor, you can solve it by just reformatting the text with your own font and minimal disruption. If, on the other hand, the differences are substantial and the formatting is unusable on your machine, you may have to go back to the originator of the document and ask them to reformat the document using a more common, or updated, font and then resend it to you.

Printing Issues

There are two basic kinds of printing issues with Word: documents that don't print the way you expect them to and documents that don't print at all. The first kind are a little harder to troubleshoot because there are so many variables.

Document Doesn't Print As Expected

The first thing to check if a document doesn't print the way you expect it to is to run a Print Preview and see if it looks correct on screen. If it looks fine on the screen but doesn't look the same when the print actually hits the paper, then the problem may be with your printer.

The next thing to check is the font you've used in the document. If the text that doesn't print right is in an unusual font, it may be that you've chosen a font your printer doesn't support. In some cases, you can add the font to the printer, but in most cases, it's a lot easier to just select a more standard font. There are a lot of PostScript fonts available and all modern printers should support PostScript. In some really unusual cases, you may be able to have your printer print the font as an image instead of text, or download the font from the computer to use. You'll just have to decide how committed to that esoteric font you really are, I guess, to determine how much effort you want to go to in order to make it work.

> **Tricks of the Pros**
>
> One trick I sometimes use if I have a document/printer combination that just doesn't want to print correctly is to save the document as an Adobe PDF file. If it looks right there, then I can print the PDF file.

If none of this has resolved your issue, then keep reading . . .

Document Doesn't Print at All

Not surprisingly most printing issues are the result of problems with the printer. Before you get involved in any complex troubleshooting try a few basics. Make sure the printer has paper, toner (or ink as the case may be), and is turned on and connected to the computer (or network) that it's supposed to be connected to.

If that all checks out ok, try powering the printer off and powering it back on. That will clear the memory of the printer and cause it to try and reestablish connection with your computer and/or the network.

The final thing to try, before seeking professional assistance, is to reboot your computer in case your print queue is jammed up.

If none of those remedies get the printer to work, then your problem is more than casual and you should contact your tech support person for further guidance.

▼ ▼ ▼ ▼ ▼

WARNING: GEEK CONTENT

The Print Spooler. Put simply, the print spooler is a software process that resides on both the client computer (i.e., the workstation you're using) and the print server (which may also be the workstation you're using if the printer is directly attached) and handles the processing of the print jobs. The spooler handles the final rendering of the print job. If the print spooler stops for any reason, your print jobs will back up and never make it to the printer. You can restart the service if you know how, but it's probably easier to just restart the computer. If the problem persists, then you should contact your tech support person—if it stops once that could be a fluke. If it keeps stopping, that's a problem.

An Extra Page Prints at the End

Another common printing issue is that an extra blank page may print at the end of your document. Usually that's because you actually have a few extra lines at the end of the document you didn't know about and couldn't see. Go to the end of your document and turn on "Show Paragraph Marks" by clicking the Show/Hide Paragraph Marks button in the Paragraph group of the home tab (it looks like this: ¶). You'll probably discover a couple of extra paragraph marks at the end of your document . . . delete them, then check Print Preview to make sure that your blank page is gone.

▼

The ¶ symbol is called a "Pilcrow" mark. It is also sometimes referred to as the "alinea" from the latin meaning "off the line."

Word May Seem to Hang When You Try to Insert a Building Block

Sometimes when you go to insert a building block Word might appear to freeze up and the problem seems to get worse when you add more and more items to your Building Blocks list. That seems sort of obvious when you think about it, but the issue really is with how long it takes Word to build the Building Blocks gallery. Word isn't really frozen, it's just struggling to get the galleries populated. The faster and more powerful your machine is the less problem you'll have with this. So there are two basic solutions: either upgrade your computer or remove some unneeded building blocks from the template so that Word doesn't have to work so hard to get those Galleries built.

You're Seeing a Lot of Oddly Named Files

If your folders are filling up with files whose names start with a tilde ("~"), you may have a problem with Word not shutting down properly. Those files are temporary files that Word should clean up when it shuts down normally. While Word is running, you'll see those files from time to time and that's fine. If Word is closed or if you're seeing growing numbers of those files, that may indicate a faulty add-in or other problem that is preventing Word from shutting down normally.

You See a Lot of Odd Text in Brackets

What you're seeing are field codes and they are often used in complex documents, especially documents that make use of document assembly. Word is supposed to substitute data for the field code, such as the path name to the document, author name, current date or time, merge data, and so forth. If you're seeing the codes instead of the data, chances are you just have "Display Field Codes" turned on. To turn them off, press ALT+F9.

You See a Lot of Curious Marks in Your Document . . .

. . . like dots where the spaces should be and pilcrows at the end of every paragraph? You've just got the formatting marks displayed. You have several options to turn that off (and back on) but the easy ways are either to click the Show/Hide button (looks like a Pilcrow) on the Home tab of the Ribbon or press CTRL+SHIFT+8 on your keyboard. If you want to display some of the formatting marks but not all of them, you can configure that under the Office Button | Word Options | Display.

Performance Problems

If Word 2007 isn't performing very well, there are a few things you can do to improve it, other than adding more RAM to your system, which is almost always a good idea.

1. Use fewer fonts in your document. If you have a lot of fonts, that can suck up system resources.
2. Store your documents on a local hard drive. You may not be able to do this due to policy issues at your firm, but if you *are* able to, you may find that Word operates faster on documents that are located on a local hard drive instead of a network drive. This is a good example of where enabling "Copy remotely stored files onto your computer and update the remote file when saving" can really help. Go back to Chapter 9 if you don't recall how to enable it. Go ahead, we'll wait.

   ▼

   If you're one of that dwindling percentage of folks who still has a floppy drive in your computer, *never* edit Word documents that are located on the floppy drive. Copy the document to the hard drive first, edit it there, then copy it back. You're welcome.

3. Disable the automatic spelling and grammar checks. These features require a little bit of system attention to operate and turning them off can optimize Word performance a bit. See Chapter 9 for details on how to turn them off.

Summary

Microsoft Word 2007 is the most robust and recoverable version of Microsoft Word yet. But that doesn't mean you'll never have problems with it. Office Diagnostics and Detect & Repair will fix most things that go wrong with the program itself but often the problem in Word may be a corrupted template or a misbehaving add-in. Be very reluctant to add even more add-ins to Word, especially if you're not sure what they are or why. More add-ins is not better. The best installation of Word is tight and fast with only the add-ins you actually need and use.

Mistakes Lawyers Make with Microsoft Word   **11**

Over the last 20 years, I've seen lawyers make a lot of mistakes with word processors. As the systems have gotten more powerful and easier to use, the mistakes have become easier to make. Let's take a few minutes to look at some of the most common mistakes and how you can avoid them. Remember: the first step to recovery is admitting it!

> **"**
> I never make stupid mistakes. Only very, very clever ones.
> —*John Peel*
> **"**

Inconsistent Use of Styles

Styles are a powerful tool to standardize how paragraphs and text are formatted in Word. Sadly, most lawyers don't take advantage of their full potential. Too many lawyers rely on direct formatting instead of a well thought out set of styles. In Chapter 4, we explored styles in more detail. If you only read one chapter in this book, well then you've spent a lot of money for just one chapter. If you want to get the most for your money, choose Chapter 4.

Document Naming

As discussed in Chapter 6, lawyers and staff are often in a hurry when they create documents, so much so that when it comes time to saving and exiting the document, they occasionally name the document "Memo" or "Letter" or some other quick thing they can type. The problem is that with a title like that it's almost impossible to find this document later or figure out what it's supposed to be. Worse yet, if you don't have a good document management system, you could end up with a folder full of documents called "Memo.docx," "Memo1.docx," "Memo2.docx," and that just doesn't help anybody. Word supports long file names like "Memo to Dr Sanders regarding Bruha claim.docx." Take the time to really name your documents and you'll be a lot happier and save a lot of time in the long run.

Saving Over Old Documents

One thing most lawyers do is reuse old documents. The Smith will was so good that when Mr. Jones needs a will you just open the Smith will, make the necessary changes, and save as Mr. Jones's will. One problem with that arises when you open the Smith will, make your changes, then just click "Save" . . . and you've just saved over Mr. Smith's will with Mr. Jones's will. Oops.

> We get two to four calls per month from law firms who need us to help them retrieve a previous version of a document because somebody saved over the old one with an incorrect version. Fortunately, most of them have backup systems that allow us to retrieve the old version. In the case that happens to you, however, don't delay. Backups are in a constant state of change. Every night (hopefully) a new backup is done and in many cases it overwrites a previous backup. If you wait too long to request a restoral, the correct file may be overwritten by the erroneously edited one. Let your IT staff know as soon as you realize the error—that will maximize your chances to get it fixed.

There are a couple of ways to prevent this. One is that when you open Mr. Smith's will, but before you make any changes to it, click the Office Button and do a Save As to save a copy of the document with a new filename (if you prefer the keyboard, press F12). Then you're working with that new document and Mr. Smith's original will is untouched.

A second way, and we'll talk about it in more detail a little later in this chapter, is that after you open Mr. Smith's will, select all of the text by pressing CTRL+A, copy that text to the clipboard with a deft CTRL+C, then click the Office Button and start a new, blank document. CTRL+V pastes that text into the blank, new document and CTRL+S lets you save that now not-so-blank new document with a new filename and location if desired. You may then tap the CTRL key however many times you like to make yourself grin at how clever you were to not only preserve Mr. Smith's will but probably significantly reduce your metadata issues in one (well, four or five) swift strokes.

Not Saving Documents

Saving over old documents is one mistake with save. Another mistake is not saving often enough. I can't tell you how many times I've gotten calls from folks who lost a document (or at least part of one) because something bad happened and they'd forgotten to save during the last one or two hours.

▼ ▼ ▼ ▼ ▼

Tales from the field . . .

A few years ago I got a call from a client late on a Thursday afternoon. She had spent the better part of the day working on a brief for a case and at the end of the day she went to close her word processor (in fairness it wasn't Microsoft Word, but for our purposes the story is the same). It asked her if she wanted to save the document. In her haste she accidentally clicked "No" and her word processor quickly and dutifully closed down . . . discarding hours of her work in the process. She immediately realized her mistake and grabbed her phone to call me. After she explained her predicament, the call went something like this:

> *Me:* OK, well, how long ago did you last save the document?
> *Her:* <long pause> I didn't.
> *Me:* You didn't save it *at all* today?
> *Her:* I know, I know. <sigh>
> *Me:* OK, well, did you e-mail a copy of it to anybody?
> *Her:* No.
> *Me:* Did you print a copy?
> *Her:* No. Is it gone?
> *Me:* <long pause> Maybe not. I'll be there in 10 minutes. DON'T TOUCH ANYTHING!

Pondering her problem I remembered that her word processor, like Microsoft Word, makes automatic backup copies every few minutes in the background. Those are there in the event that your computer (or even just your word processor) has an unexpected shut down. These can be due to power failure, system error, foot/dog/cat/child/spouse brushing up against the power switch . . . you name it. If that kind of unexpected shutdown happens, the next time the word processor starts it detects that the backup files are there and offers to let you recover them. That can be quite a relief in those instances when you really need them.

However, when you close the document normally (such as by closing the word processor and answering "No" to the "Do you want to save?" question), the word processor is a good computer citizen and cleans up after itself, which includes deleting all of those apparently unnecessary backup copies. It occurred to me in pondering her problem that perhaps there was a way to recover one of those deleted files.

A computer deleting files is not really as thorough as you might imagine. All the computer really does in those instances is mark that space as available. It doesn't actually clean off the bits on the hard drive that previously stored that file. It leaves them as is, but just indicates that the space is available to be used by the next piece of data that needs to be stored. If I could get to her computer before any further data was written to that space on the hard drive, I just might be able to get it back.

When I arrived at her office she was in a bad way . . . she was sure that all was lost and she was going to have to spend all night recreating hours worth of work. "It's impossible, isn't it?" she said with a pained voice. "It's unlikely." I responded "But don't give up just yet."

I fired up my handy undelete program (there are a number of them available from various vendors) and set to work browsing to see if I could find the deleted backup files. Sure enough, I found several files that were of the type we were seeking and by comparing the date and time stamps I identified one or two likely suspects. I restored them to her hard drive and started her word processor, which correctly recognized the presence of the backup files, assumed it had crashed, and offered to recover them. She jumped up and down with glee when she recognized the first page of her lost document. Sure enough, she had lost only about the last 5 minutes of her work that amounted to a couple of minor edits she was able to easily redo. To say she was happy is an understatement and our firm earned our unofficial slogan: "We Make The Impossible Unlikely."

Fortunately modern technology has largely, but not entirely, minimized this problem. I have my computer plugged into an uninterruptible power supply so that if my electricity blinks momentarily my computer won't notice. AutoRecover means that Word has frequent backup files, so that if Word happens to crash for some reason, I have a good shot to be presented with a recovery file the next time I start Word and I'll only lose a couple of minutes worth of work.

But honestly, how hard is it to press CTRL+S to save your document? Watch, I'll do it right now. There, wasn't that satisfying? Even though I know intellectually that the odds of losing my document (currently well into the 11th chapter of it) are increasingly slim, I've been in this business long enough to remember when it was a regular occurrence. And I'm in the good habit of frequently saving my work as I go, so that just in case the cat jumps on my keyboard at the wrong moment I still have a recently saved copy I can re-open. Right after I figure out whose cat that is.

Is it annoying or difficult to press CTRL+S every few minutes? Not at all. Look, I'll do it again.

Metadata

Metadata is data about data. Simple as that. The text of your document is data. The *title* of your document is metadata. The date the document was created, the name of the author, the number of words or characters within the document, any comments or tracked changes within the document . . . these are all metadata.

It's a popular misconception that metadata is strictly a Microsoft problem. In fact, virtually all office productivity applications, including Corel's WordPerfect, use metadata and face potential issues with it. That's why Corel included a metadata checker/cleaner in WordPerfect X3.

What's the Matta with Metadata?

Other than being a sort of cheesy section heading, the "matta with metadata" is that there may very well be information contained therein that would be damaging to your case, your client, and perhaps your career if it should be leaked outside your firm.

For example, let's say you have a Word document and you have Track Changes turned on. (Go back to Chapter 6 if you're not sure what Track Changes does.) This Word document is going to be a settlement offer to opposing counsel. You decide that you will offer the other party

$500,000 to settle the matter. Before sending the offer and after discussion with your client you decide to reduce the offer to $350,000. So you open your Word document, change "$500,000" to "350,000," save the document, and promptly e-mail it to opposing counsel. Opposing counsel opens the document in Word, makes sure that they have Track Changes turned on as well, clicks the Review tab on the Ribbon, and changes their view to "Final Showing Markup." At which point they discover that you had originally intended to offer $500,000 but later revised that figure down. Do you suppose that might affect your negotiating position?

Does it make your situation better or worse if you and the client collaborated on the document and used the comments feature of the document to discuss your settlement strategy as you prepared the offer letter?

Another scenario: You're assisting a client with a press release for a pending acquisition. It's all very hush-hush and not finalized yet so you're just holding on to the draft of the release. In the meantime that client also wants your help with a press release for their new bond offer. Since you like the press release you did for the acquisition and it already has all of the client's contact information in it, you decide to reuse the pending acquisition release and just change the relevant bits. You've already read the bit I wrote about not saving over old documents so you know that you should open your original document and do a "Save As" to save the new version with a new name. You change the names, dates, and amounts to reflect the bond offer and once you're satisfied that's all done you helpfully send it off to the local business press. The next day the front page of the local paper reads "BIGCO Inc. to Acquire SmallCo, LLC for $5 million!" Oops.

How Do You Discover Metadata

There are a number of tools available to discover Metadata but the simplest is Word itself. With a Word document open and Track Changes turned on, go to the Review tab and make sure under Tracking that you have "Final Showing Markup" selected in the Display for Review field. (See Figure 11.1.) Then you should be able to see the edits and changes made, if any were preserved in the document.

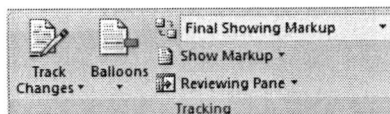

FIGURE 11.1

Alternatively, you can use third party tools like Metadata Assistant or Doc Scrubber (see Figure 11.2) to analyze your document (and remove potentially damaging metadata).

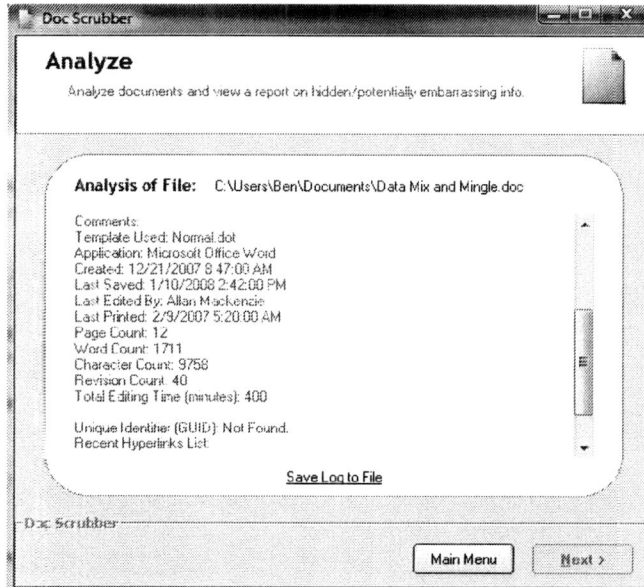

FIGURE 11.2

How Do You Clean/Prevent It

There are a number of methods available to clean Metadata out of a Word document and a few ways to prevent it in the first place. The method you use to clean it should depend upon what the document is ultimately intended to do.

If the intention is to print the document and provide it in hardcopy, then your metadata worries are few. Very little metadata would appear in a printout—in fact you would have to deliberately set the print options *to* print the metadata (such as comments and other markup) for it to appear. (See Figure 11.3.)

So if your intent is to print the document and only provide it via hardcopy, then don't worry about the metadata. Print your document, proofread it, then rest assured that they aren't getting anything you didn't intend to give them (unless they're going to be testing your printout for incriminating fingerprints or DNA).

If the intent is to send the document electronically, as it so often is these days, then you have to make another determination before you proceed. Do they need to edit it? If the party you're sending to doesn't need

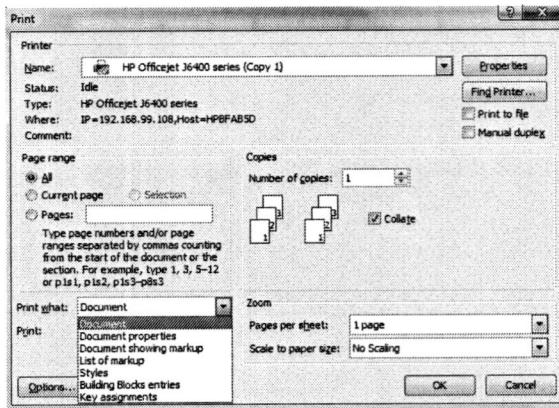

FIGURE 11.3

to edit the document, then the preferred way to send the document—and
for them to receive it in many cases—is as an Adobe PDF file. PDF has a
number of advantages:

1. First, the formatting is going to be consistent. The way the PDF
   looks on your computer is how it looks on their computer and
   how it looks on their printer. No questions about whether they
   have the right fonts or what version of WordPerfect they're using.
   A PDF is a PDF is a PDF. It's electronic paper. All they need is a
   compatible version of Acrobat Reader and they can get that from
   Adobe for free.

2. Second, it's portable. This relates a bit to #1 but there are PDF
   readers for nearly every platform. So if you're dealing with an
   lawyer who is still running Windows 98 or an lawyer who has gone
   over to the Mac or a real propeller-head who insists that Linux is
   the only true operating system . . . it doesn't matter. They can
   read and print PDF files you send them. Heck most mobile devices
   like Blackberries, iPhones, and Treos can read PDF files now too.

3. Third, and most importantly for the purposes of Chapter 11 in this
   book, almost no interesting metadata goes with a PDF file. When
   you send a Word document to PDF, you're effectively printing it
   and that means the same rules apply . . . unless you have explic-
   itly told Word to include things like comments, tracked changes,
   or other markup in the PDF file, it won't. The worst you're likely to
   see in a PDF file is the document title, author, and perhaps some
   keywords. You have to try pretty hard to get metadata into a PDF
   file.

That said, Adobe does create just a little bit of its own metadata, like
all files on a computer it will have an associated creation date for exam-

ple. But I'd suggest that if you're really concerned with the simple creation date of the document you may want to reexamine the ethical issues of the matter.

So, let's examine the scenario where you need to send a document out that they *do* need to be able to edit or where you are, for some reason, required to send it in Microsoft Word format.

Document Reuse

One thing that lawyers *love* to do, and we talk about it a little in Chapters 11 and 12, is reuse existing documents. It's a big time saver and can help to maintain a high standard of quality. If you already know a document is good, why not use it as the basis for a future document? Well, the answer to that question can be found in Chapter 8. You're really better off using templates and/or document assembly software and building a fresh new document with those tools rather than using an existing, completed, work product as the basis for a new one. Unfortunately the practice of document reuse is widespread and old habits are hard to break. When you reuse that old document, you risk also reusing the metadata from that document. So, in our scenario where you *have* to send a Word document and you've succumbed to the pressure to reuse an old document, then you want to try and minimize the chances that any metadata is transferred from the original document.

To do that, open your old document and the very first thing you want to do is make sure Track Changes is turned ON in that document. Then go to the Office Button and click New to start a new, blank document. In that document, make sure that Track Changes is turned OFF. (Yes, OFF.) Now go back to your original document (sometimes referred to as the "Donor Document") and press CTRL+A to select all of the text. Go to the new document (sometimes referred to as the "Recipient Document") and press CTRL+V to paste that text in. Now save that new document with a new file name. Close the old, or donor, document. Now you can go through and make any edits or changes you need to make to the new document. When you have it finished, go to the Office Button, click Prepare, and let Word's built-in Metadata Inspector take a look at your document.

If you haven't saved it lately, the metadata inspector will prompt you to save. That's a smart move. Then it will ask you what data to check for. (See Figure 11.4.) Generally speaking, I would just let it check for everything. Except perhaps for Headers, Footers, and Watermarks, there probably isn't any other data that your recipient should have. Besides, the metadata inspector will ask you before it removes anything so I'd just leave them all checked.

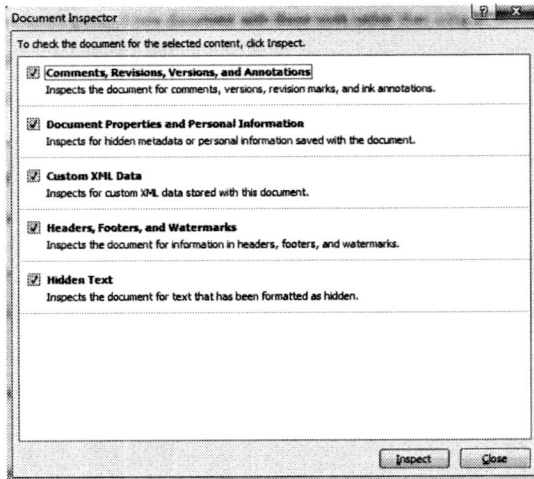

FIGURE 11.4

After it's done inspecting you'll get a report, like in Figure 11.5. You can see here in our example that there were comments, personal information, and custom XML data found. Word's tool is reasonably primitive in two respects:

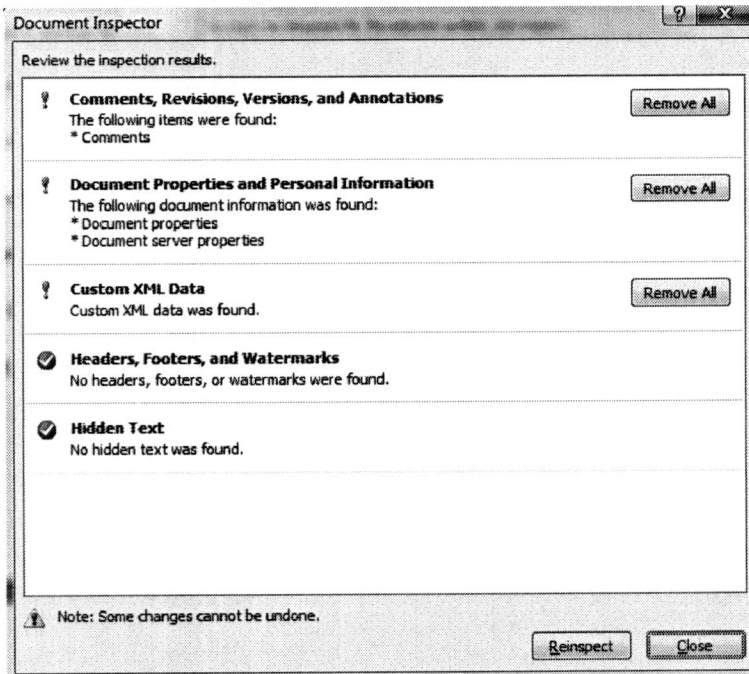

FIGURE 11.5

1. It's not going to show you the specifics of what it found. It just tells you it exists, that's all.

2. It doesn't let you selectively remove it. If you have Word remove comments, for example, it's going to remove all of them. If you want to selectively remove some, you'll have to go back through the document yourself and delete just those comments you don't want to retain.

Configure Word to Warn You

If you use Track Changes a lot, then you might want to have Word warn you if you go to save or send a file that has tracked changes in it—if nothing else it's a good reminder to run the built-in metadata inspector. To enable that, just go to the Office Button | Word Options | Trust Center and click Trust Center Settings. Halfway down the page you'll see what I have in Figure 11.6.

If you're collaborating on a document with others, you may not even realize that a document has track changes turned on. It's possible that somebody else has enabled track changes without your knowledge—or even theirs. Better safe than sorry.

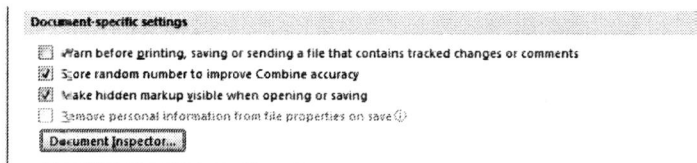

FIGURE 11.6

The very first option lets you turn on the warnings that you want and I encourage you to enable it; again just to be on the safe side.

Summary

Word seems like a pretty simple tool, but it's a powerful one as well. As any first semester law student can tell you, documents are a critical part of the practice of law and the word processor is an important tool for the law firm. There are a number of mistakes that lawyers and staff can make with Word, some of them merely efficiency issues but others can be very serious. Leak the wrong metadata to the wrong person and the consequences could be as severe as disbarment. And that's really not the way to move your practice forward.

Tricks to Impress Your Law School Classmates With 12

Word 2007 has a surprising number of great tricks that can be used to improve your productivity, and considering that law is such a document-intensive field anything that helps improve your effectiveness in this product can directly translate into your practice. In this chapter, we'll take a look at some of those nifty tricks you can use to get even more out of Word 2007.

Minimize the Ribbon

One of the first comments folks have when they see the Ribbon is that it takes up a fair bit of screen real estate at the top of the screen. If you'd like to minimize it to give yourself more room to work, just right-click anywhere on the tab line and choose "Minimize the Ribbon." To get it back . . . repeat that process. Alternatively, you can double-click any of the Ribbon tab labels to minimize, and subsequently restore, the Ribbon.

Publishing to PDF

Lawyers love to save and send PDF files. There are some good reasons for that:

1. PDF files are difficult to surreptitiously modify. Saving to PDF effectively "finalizes" the document.

2. PDF files contain only minor amounts of relatively harmless meta-data and thus are safer to send to clients or opposing counsel.
3. PDF is a nearly universal format. Virtually everybody has the ability to read and or print PDF files.

Office 2007 has a free add-in you can download and install that will let you save your documents as PDF files without having to purchase and install Adobe's Acrobat program. Of course the PDF files you can create with this are fairly basic—you don't get the advanced features of Acrobat—but for most users that's perfectly sufficient.

▼

Want to know more about Adobe Acrobat? Pick up a copy of David Master's book, *The Lawyer's Guide to Adobe Acrobat*, Third Edition (ABA, 2008).

To Install the PDF Add-in . . .

If you go to the Office Button and choose Save As, you'll see "PDF or XPS" listed. (XPS is Microsoft's version of a portable digital document format.) If you don't already have the PDF add-in installed, Word will tell you so and give you a link to click to download and install it. It's just about as simple as that—in moments Word will have downloaded and installed the add-in for you and you'll be ready to go. You only need to do that once, per machine, by the way. Once you've downloaded and installed it, you have it.

▼

If you're in a firm with an IT department, you should always check with your IT department before downloading and installing any add-ins of this type. The IT department may have a reason for not already installing it or they may already be planning a structured roll-out of a solution like that. Best not to step on their toes or cause any headaches.

Saving to PDF Format

Saving to PDF is simplicity itself. With your document open, click the Office Button, choose Save As, and then PDF from the menu that appears. If you just want to keep it simple, you can just click the "Publish" button on the next dialog box. There are a few options you can configure, if you like:

- Open File After Publishing: Checking this box will open your document in Adobe Reader after your save completes.
- Optimize For—Standard: This creates a larger but better quality PDF file.
- Optimize For—Online publishing: This creates a smaller, tighter file, but sacrifices a bit of quality.

Once you've set your options, just choose a file location to save to, give it a file name, and save it. Voila!

Outlining

Outlines are a powerful way to create new documents (it's how I started this book for instance) as well has a handy way to organize your thoughts. Word is a very good outlining tool, even if you never take your outline all the way to a full document. Word is even smart enough to recognize an outline when you start one. Just type an "I" (like a roman numeral 1) and followed by a period and then your first heading. Word will automatically jump into Outline mode for the succeeding text.

Use Tab (and Shift-TAB) to move items up and down levels (left and right), but you can also use your mouse to drag items up and down within your outline.

Generally, I'll start with my major level items (I., II., etc.), then go back thru and fill in the second-level items, then go back thru and flesh those out with third and fourth level items and . . . next thing you know I have a fairly detailed outline. From there, I can start writing the actual text to explain each of the items.

▼

As I mentioned in Chapter 7, I will often do my outlining in Microsoft OneNote and then send that nearly completed outline to Word to finish the document. If you haven't looked at OneNote yet, you really should check it out. Great stuff for lawyers; it does a lot more than just outlining and note taking.

AutoCorrect

AutoCorrect is great for correcting spelling errors but did you know you can also use it to speed up your typing? Create custom AutoCorrect entries that replace shorthand acronyms with full text. We talked about that a bit in Chapter 8 under automating Word.

Document Map

When you're creating a lengthy and extensive document, like a book on Microsoft Word 2007 for example, it can often be handy to be able to see all of your headings in the style of a table of contents so that you can make sure that your content is complete and in a logical order. (See Figure 12.1.) The document map shows you the headings in your document and provides for an easy way to navigate up and down in the document. This is especially important when your document is more than 200 pages long and your Page Up button is getting a bit worn down.

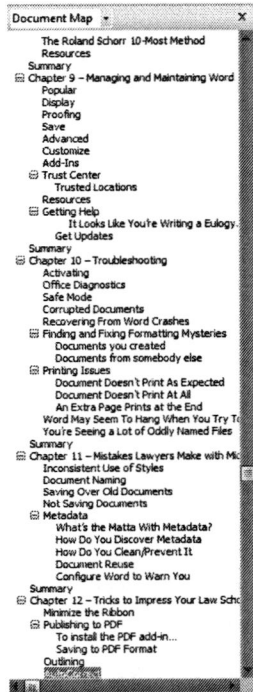

FIGURE 12.1

Encrypt Document

There may come times when you'll want to protect the content of your document—perhaps you're collaborating with co-counsel and you want to use Information Rights Management (see Chapter 6) to control who can access your document and what they can do with it.

Digital Signatures

You can use a digital signature in much the same way you use a printed signature—to lend authenticity to your document. Digitally signing a document is not a new feature in Word 2007 but it's a lot easier in 2007 than it was in previous versions. Digitally signing a document requires a digital certificate that verifies your identity. There are two basic classes of digital certificate:

1. Third party certificates: These are certificates that you obtain from a trusted certificate authority like Verisign, Thawte, or others.
2. Self-signed certificates: These are certificates that you generate yourself.

The self-signed certificate has several big advantages and only one real drawback. On the plus side, it's free and you can generate one and use it immediately. You know who provided the certificate, you don't have to jump through very many hoops to create one, you don't have to break out your credit card, and you can start to use your certificate right away. The only real downside is that it's almost useless.

Self-certifying a certificate is like letting people print their own driver's licenses. Without an independent authority, there's almost no way to confirm that a signature is authentic or that the sender is who they say they are. What stops me from creating a self-signed certificate that claims that I'm you? Nothing.

The only thing self-signed digital signatures will do for you is confirm that the version of the document they've received hasn't changed since it was signed. If a signed document is changed, the signature is invalidated. Of course, if somebody intercepts your document and changes it, there's nothing to stop them from RE-signing your document with a forged digital signature. Again, if you're self-signing.

To do digital signatures correctly you need to get a real certificate from a third-party authority. It's not hard to do, when you go to digitally sign your document for the first time (Office Button | Prepare | Add a Digital Signature), you'll be offered a button that will take you to the Office Marketplace online where you can get a digital signature from one of a variety of digital signature providers. If you already have one, then you can just use that, of course.

Either way, if you're self-signing or using a third party certificate, you'll get the Sign dialog box that you see in Figure 12.2. You have an op-

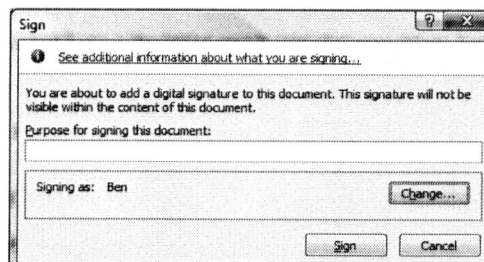

FIGURE 12.2

tional field that asks for the reason you're choosing to sign the document and you'll have a chance to choose which certificate (if you have more than one) to sign with. Assuming it's already signing with the certificate you want to use you can just click the "Sign" button and your digital signature will be affixed.

If you're using a third-party signature, then when you send this document to others and they open it in Word, Word will verify, in the background, that the signature is authentic by contacting the third-party provider—and yes, they will have to be connected to the Internet to do that verification. If you're using a self-signed signature, then it will just tell them that there isn't any way to verify the signature.

Research Tools

Most people seem to think that the pinnacle of Word document creation assistance is the real-time spell checker that puts a red squiggly line under words it thinks you've misspelled. Actually, Word offers a far richer set of tools than just that. If you're like me, you probably are used to having a dictionary and maybe a thesaurus close at hand when you work. You just may not have realized quite how close at hand. Select any word you've typed, right-click it, and choose "Look Up." The Research Pane will appear on the right side of your screen offering you dictionary, thesaurus, encyclopedia, even a translator that will translate the word to and from about 14 different languages.

> **Tip**
> Some of these features, like the Thesaurus, will work even when you're disconnected but most of them will require you to be connected to the Internet.

Legal Research

The folks at LexisNexis have even gotten on the bandwagon. If you go to http://www.lexisnexis.com/ms office, you can download a free research pane tool that connects to LexisNexis so you can Shepardize cases, access the LexisNexis Bookstore, and even LexisONE (if you're a LexisONE user).

> **Note**
> The research pane tool is free and some of the LexisONE services are, as of this writing, free. I can't say for sure if everything accessible through the LexisNexis research pane tool is free but if you're already a LexisNexis user then it makes sense for you to add this research pane tool to your arsenal.

Watermarks

One of those features that many users didn't realize Word has had for quite a while is the ability to add a watermark to your document. A watermark is a bit of text or image that is in the background, behind your text. It's a fairly subtle effect—subtle enough that I can't even screen capture it and have it look decent for this book. It can say or be just about anything you want and is a really handy way to mark a printed document with an indication of the document status—for instance "Draft" or "Confidential" or "Client Copy." To use the Watermark feature, just go to the Page Layout tab and click the Watermark tool. (See Figure 12.3.) You'll get the Watermark gallery, which has twelve sample watermarks you can use. If you don't like any of those, you can create your own by clicking the "Custom Watermark"

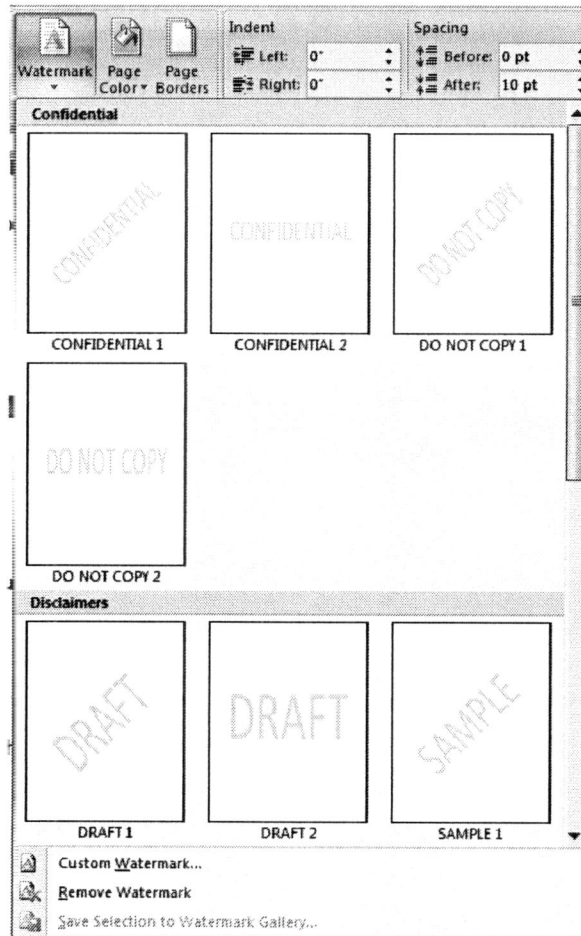

FIGURE 12.3

command you see toward the bottom of the gallery. Clicking that will get you the Printed Watermark dialog box that you see in Figure 12.4 below.

FIGURE 12.4

In the Printed Watermark dialog box, you can create a picture watermark by selecting that radio button, then selecting the image you want to use. Word will automatically scale the picture so that it aligns on the page properly, but you can customize that if you like.

If you don't want to use a picture watermark, you can type your own custom text, complete with custom layout, color, font, and everything. Watermarks can be a nice way to add a stylish and functional element to your printed or PDF'd documents.

Full Text Search

One of the big trends in desktop computing in recent years is the move toward powerful full-text search engines. Google Desktop, Copernic Desktop and, of course, Windows Desktop Search all let you index your workstation, server, and even external hard drives to make searching for files and documents faster and easier. If you're not using a Full Text Search tool, you really should be. It can help you find documents and files, including documents and files you might not have thought about. The thing with full text search that makes it different from what you may be used to is that it searches the *content* of the document, not just the name. Any words or phrases you've got will be found. And the full text search tool will not just search Word documents, but PowerPoint, Excel, Outlook e-mails . . . all sorts of documents.

Run a full text search for a particular citation and you may discover other documents in your document library that refer to it that you hadn't thought of. Doing conflict checks? How about a quick full text search on the name; who knows what you might discover?

Windows Desktop Search is built into Vista. Just hit the start button and start typing in the search box and Windows Desktop Search will do the rest. It's also available for Windows XP, though you'll have to download it and install it. Google Desktop and Copernic Deskop are the same—available for XP or Vista. As of this writing all of these tools are free. If you have an version of Windows older than Windows XP . . . well, then you're not running Office 2007 anyhow so you've probably bought the wrong book (but thanks!).

Redaction

Every now and then you may want to send out a document with parts of that document blacked out, to obscure particular facts the other party (or the public) shouldn't read. As you probably know, that's called "Redaction" and there are a couple of ways to do that in Word.

First off it once again comes back to knowing the medium in which your document is going to be transmitted. If it's going to be printed or sent as a PDF file, then you could just select the text you want to redact and use the highlighter tool in Word to redact those words you want hidden (see Figure 12.5) by highlighting the black text with black highlighter.

transmitted. If it's going to be printed or sent as a PDF file then you could just select the text you want

to redact and use the highlighter tool in Word to redact ████████████████████

FIGURE 12.5

That works fine if you're transmitting in a format where the end user can't access the actual document data. Where you can't use that is if you're going to be transmitting the document as a Word document—because the recipient could just turn off the highlighting. If you're PDFing the document as an IMAGE (not a searchable file), then all the recipient is going to get is a picture of the text and it will be obscured. If you're going to print the document, then the printer will just print your redactions and that will work ok.

There are some other creative ways to redact text but really . . . if it's text that needs to be redacted, then it's probably important that it be done right. If you go to http://www.codeplex.com/redaction, you can find the Word 2007 Redaction

As with any URL I give you in this book, I can only vouch for its accuracy as of this printing. The Internet is sort of like a river, you step in the river but the water has moved on. If you try one of the URLs I've posted and it doesn't work, then I would suggest Googling for the content . . . perhaps it has merely moved somewhere else.

tool. It's made by the team at Microsoft but not officially supported by Microsoft.

When you install it, which can take quite a while by the way so be sure you don't wait until five minutes before the document is due, it adds a "Redact" group to the Review tab of the Ribbon. To use the tool, then you just go through your document marking text that you want redacted. (See Figure 12.6.) When you've marked everything you want to redact, you can click the down arrow on the Mark button and have it redact the entire document. Figure 12.7 shows you that menu. The redaction tool will then go thru your entire document and replace all marked text with black bars.

> **Caution!**
>
> This can't be undone. I strongly suggest that you save a copy of your document UNredacted first, then do your redaction. That way if it turns out that you inadvertently redacted something, you can go back to the pre-redaction copy. After you finish the redaction, the tool will suggest that you run Word's metadata inspector (remember Chapter 11?), which is a good idea.

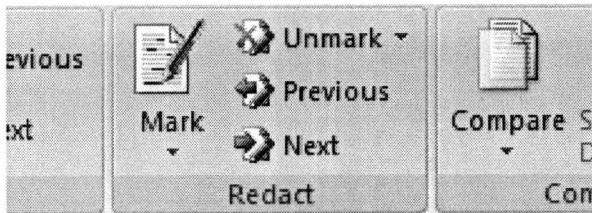

FIGURE 12.6

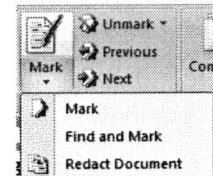

FIGURE 12.7

One other thing you'll notice on the menu in Figure 12.7 is a "Find and Mark" command. That lets you search the document for all instances of a string (a client's name for example) and have all of those instances marked for redaction automatically . . . so you don't have to search it manually.

Publishing to the Web

These days it's all about the web, of course. Microsoft Word has long been "capable" of generating web content, allowing you to put together a basic web page and have it generate the HTML (HyperText Markup Language) for that page. Did it look ok? Sure. But there's a reason why professional web designers don't use Microsoft Word for that task. The HTML code it generated was widely derided as being fairly sloppy. Still, if you just need a quick and simple page and Word is the tool that you're com-

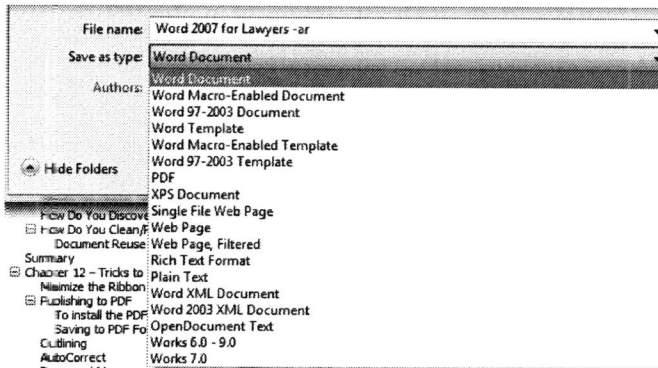

FIGURE 12.8

fortable with . . . you can use it for that purpose. Just lay out your page, do a Office Button | Save As, and choose "Web Page" to save your document in the right format. (See Figure 12.8.) Upload it to your web site and you've got a basic web document.

The more interesting new feature in Word, however, is the ability to use it as a blogging client. Blogging has really taken off in the last year or two not only as a way to get information but also as a marketing tool for lawyers. More lawyers have blogs today than ever before. Word is a powerful tool for creating text so there's no reason why you shouldn't use it to author your blogs as well.

To get started, go ahead and create your first article. Go to the Office Button, click New, and one of the options on the New Document dialog box is "New Blog Post." (See Figure 12.9.)

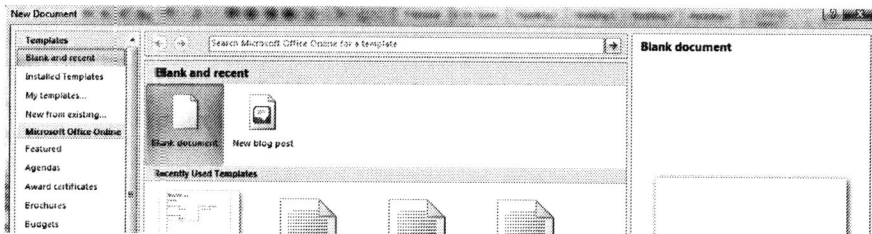

FIGURE 12.9

The first time you select that template you will have to register your Blog with Word . . . which tells Word where and how to send the content. You'll be prompted to register your blog, as in Figure 12.10. Click the down-arrow next to Blog and choose your blog provider. Chances are pretty good that it's one of the ones listed there, but if it's not, you may still have some hope.

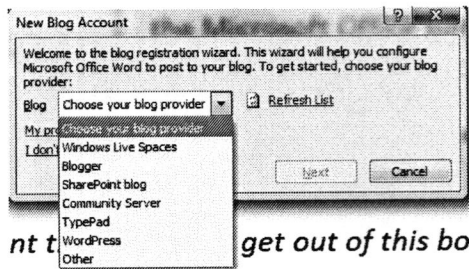

FIGURE 12.10

Select your blog provider from the list and click Next. Word will then lead you though a short wizard that asks you to give it the URL, username (if applicable), and password for posting to your blog. Depending upon your provider, it may ask you for one or two other bits of information, or instruct you as to one or two minor adjustments you have to make in your blog configuration (such as configuring Live Spaces to accept E-mail publishing).

Once you have it set up though, posting new entries is as simple as starting a new blog post (Office Button | New | New Blog Post) and publishing it to your blog (Office Button | Publish | Blog).

The best blogs are the ones that are updated regularly. If you only post to your blog a couple of times a year, then you won't get many readers. Try to post at least once a week. Consider repurposing some of your other writings for your blog—maybe that great article you wrote for the local bar journal three years ago could be updated and posted as a blog entry? Or maybe it could be broken up and posted as a series of blog entries?

Speech Recognition

This is going to be one of the very few Vista-only tricks that I'll offer here. For years, lawyers have been asking for a good speech recognition application and many lawyers have spent a lot of money over the years trying various products with varying degrees of success. Vista offers a speech recognition module called Vista Voice (you may find it in the Programs list as Windows Speech Recognition), which is really pretty good (and it's included in Vista at no extra charge!). Can you use it to dictate text into Word 2007? Well, I'm dictating this sentence right here. Is it perfect? No. But it's good. Really I think it's better for voice control of your system. I can be working away and suddenly realize that I want to switch to another program on my system. I can just say "Switch to Inbox" and Outlook pops up with my Inbox displayed.

It's just another way to interact with your system but I think it's worth a shot.

	Tip	Get a good headset if you're going to give it a try.

Calculate

One of the most surprising features of Microsoft Word 2007 is a feature most people have no idea even exists: Calculate. I'm not talking about your run-of-the-mill, add-a-column kind of calculate. That's just so 1993. I'm talking about calculating off numbers in sentence format. Yes, it's a little primitive, but it's still pretty cool.

To use it, first you have to configure access to it. This feature isn't on any of the Ribbon tabs so you'll need to add it to the QAT. To do that, click the down-arrow to the right of the QAT and click "More Commands." Set the list of commands on the left side to "All Commands" and scroll down that list to find "Calculate." Click Add and then OK to close the customize dialog. You'll now see a curious green sphere on your QAT—that's the calculate button.

So, now that you can access it, what can you do with it? Type a sentence that has some numbers in it, such as "Carrie has 5 apples and Emily has 3." Then click the Calculate button. Nothing happened? Look at the status bar at the bottom left. This feature is still fairly primitive and it will tend to prefer addition, but if you use symbols such as "32,213-11,235," that will work for subtraction and other basic mathematical functions too.

Summary

Like any powerful program, Word 2007 has a lot of potential for tricks to improve its utility and efficiency. Heck, I have to admit at one point I had about 25 different sections in this chapter and I finally had to whittle it down a bit (though some of those tips found their ways into other chapters of the book).

Some of the tricks, like minimizing the Ribbon, using speech recognition, or using the document map are ways to make Word a more productive work environment. Others, like encryption or web publishing are about new ways to produce content that you might not have thought of before.

Getting the most out of Word requires constant learning—we've barely scratched the surface of what Word is capable of so far.

Keyboard Shortcuts 13

Like most of the Office 2007, Word has a number of great and useful keyboard shortcuts that can really help the fast typist who resents having to use the mouse to get things done.

One important thing to remember is that, despite the new Ribbon interface, the keyboard shortcuts that you learned for Word 2003 are still going to work in Word 2007. They may *look* a bit different, but they're still there.

Almost all of the commands on the Ribbon can be accessed via keyboard shortcuts, it's just that many of them are actually a sequence of keystrokes as opposed to a HotKey.

A hotkey is a single key or a combination of keys pressed at once to activate a command or feature. "Windows Key + S" is a hotkey. As opposed to a sequence of keys like "Windows Key, S" which wants you to press and release the Windows key then press and release the S key. If you see me type the plus sign ("+"), that means press this key AND that key at the same time by pressing the first key and holding it down while you press the next key. If I type a comma, that means press and release the first key, then press the next key.

To see the keyboard shortcuts to activate a command on the Ribbon, just press (and release) the ALT key.

In Figure 13.1, you can see that pressing the "F" will activate the Office Button, pressing numbers 1 thru 5 will activate the corresponding shortcut on the Quick Access Toolbar and you can see the letters that correspond to the tabs on the Ribbon. Pressing the "H" key to activate the Home tab gives you Figure 13.2.

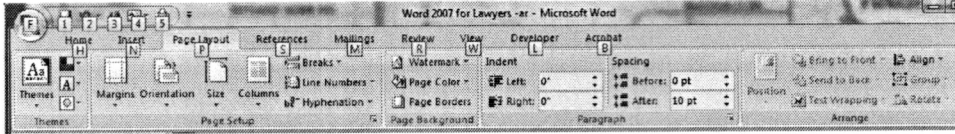

FIGURE 13.1

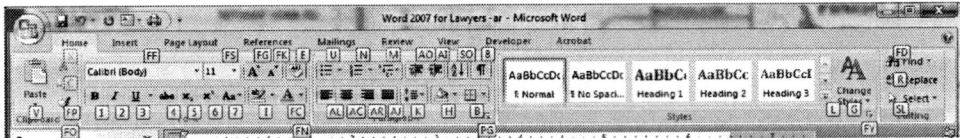

FIGURE 13.2

If we were to press ALT, followed by H (to activate Home), then the number 5 that would set the font of the selected text to Subscript. Alt, H, 7 activates the Change Case feature. ALT, H, A, R sets the alignment of the current paragraph to the right. And so forth . . .

Hotkeys in Office are almost always either Function Keys (F1-F12) or combination keys where you press and hold the SHIFT, ALT and/or CTRL ("Control") keys in combination with one or more Function Keys or letter keys.

For example: pressing F4 will repeat the last action. Need to type "I have no recollection of that at all, Senator." over and over again? Just type it once, then press F4 as many times as you need to.

Pressing and holding the CTRL +ALT + F1 (then you can let go of all of them) will launch a very handy tool most users never realized was there . . . System Information.

Those are both hotkeys. The first keyboard sequence I'm going to teach you here is to press F1 to launch the help system, and then type "Keyboard Shortcuts" in the search window. That will get you a list of articles and resources on the subject right on your own screen and you can readily find any shortcut in the program that way. In this chapter, I'm going to give you a few tricks to using keyboard shortcuts and highlight my favorite keyboard shortcuts and how you might use them. A full list of shortcuts would just be cheating on my page count and since I don't get paid by the page, I think I'll just be a little green here and not waste the paper with a simple list of shortcuts you can readily get elsewhere.

Navigating and Managing Word

First of all, there are a few good shortcuts for getting around in Word that you may like. I juggle dual monitors in the course of my work and I frequently find myself windowing and maximizing windows so that I can move them around my screens and then work with them.

ALT+TAB is a well-known keyboard shortcut that isn't really a Word 2007 shortcut but rather a Windows shortcut that launches the Task Switcher. It can be a quick way to switch between running programs, including multiple Microsoft Word 2007 instances. Hold down ALT, then press TAB. As long as you hold down the ALT key the list of applications will be displayed on screen as a set of icons or thumbnails. Each time you press TAB the focus will change to the next application on the list (clockwise). Let go of Alt and Windows will switch system focus to that application (in other words, put it in the foreground so you can work with it). **ALT+SHIFT+TAB** does the same thing but goes counter-clockwise through the list. As long as you don't let go of the ALT key, the list will stay up, so if you're a little dexterous you can go back and forth between ALT+TAB and ALT+SHIFT+TAB to move back and forth thru the list without having to start over.

If you happen to be a Vista user and have the Aero interface enabled (which most of you probably do), you can get the Flip 3D version of ALT+Tab. Press the **Windows Key + Tab** (or **Windows Key + Shift + Tab**) to see the fancy version and cycle thru (or backwards thru) the list of running applications. Functionally, it does exactly the same thing as ALT+TAB does . . . just does it prettier.

If you want to close your current Word 2007 window, you can press **CTRL+W** or **CTRL+F4**. This is one of those curious instances where the same command can be accessed from two different key combinations.

> It's handy to know that because it gives you an idea of a key combo you can remap to some other function if you want or need to. We talked about customizing the keyboard and 3rd party applications like AutoHotkey in Chapter 8.

Don't worry about hitting those keys accidentally and losing all of your data. If you press those keys while you have unsaved changes in your document, Word will pop up a dialog box prompting you to save, discard, or cancel like you see in Figure 13.3.

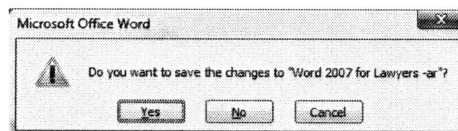

FIGURE 13.3

If you hit the key combo for close accidentally, just click "Cancel" and Word will return you to your document without any ill effects.

You can quickly window or maximize the current Word 2007 window just by pressing **ALT+F5** (to window it) or **CTRL+F10** (to Maximize it).

You probably already know that you can copy a picture of the screen to the Windows clipboard by pressing **Print Screen** (PRTSCN on many keyboards), but I'm going to show you two better ways to do it . . .

1. You usually don't want the *entire* screen, but rather a selected part of it. To capture just the active window to the clipboard, press **ALT+PRINT SCREEN**. That will crop off all of the other stuff on the screen and only grab the active window.
2. If you have Microsoft OneNote installed, it has a terrific screen grab tool in it. Just press **Windows Key + S** and you can select any part of your screen to copy to the clipboard, as big or small as you want. There are other 3rd party utilities that can do this as well, like SnagIt, but OneNote is one of the best I've seen and you might already have it installed.

If you want to open an existing document, you can get to the File Open dialog box by pressing **CTRL+F12** or **CTRL+O.** For a fast typist, this is a lot faster than mousing up to the Office Button, clicking that, then choosing Open, or pressing ALT, followed by F, followed by O.

If you want to create a new document **CTRL+N** gets you started on that.

Pressing **F12** will display the Save As dialog box. That, along with **CTRL+S** to save, is a hotkey you definitely want to know about.

For printing documents, **CTRL+P** launches the print dialog. **ALT+CTRL+I** will give you a print preview of the current document—handy for seeing what you're going to get before you use the paper.

CTRL+Left Arrow or **CTRL+Right Arrow** will move you one word left or right. **CTRL+Up** or **CTRL+Down** move one paragraph up or down. **CTRL+Home** or **CTRL+End** will take you to the beginning or the end of the document. **Home** and **End** go to the beginning or end of the current line. Use the **Shift** key in conjunction with any of those to select those things. **F8** is a handy tool for selecting as well. Pressing it twice selects a word, three times selects the current sentence, four times selects the current paragraph, and five times selects the entire document. (Easier to press **CTRL+A** to select the whole document I think.)

Speaking of selecting—this is actually a mouse trick—if you click once, you put your cursor on that spot to type. If you click twice, you select that word. Click three times to select the entire paragraph. Didn't see select the sentence in there did you? **CTRL+Click** does that.

The **F5** key will launch the GOTO dialog box—which you can then use to navigate to just about anywhere in the document. Handy if you want to go to a specific page number; or if you want to advance a certain number of pages. One feature of GOTO I also want to call to your atten-

▼ ▼ ▼ ▼ ▼

The Coolest Feature That Doesn't Actually Work

One of the niftier Word shortcut keys is one that is sort of broken in this version: **SHIFT+F5**. It returns you to the last place in the document you edited. In fact, it will step you back through the last three edit points if you continue pressing it. (Pressing it a fourth time will return you to where you started this exercise.) In older versions of Word, you could use that when you opened a document to quickly go to the place where you left off editing it. Unfortunately, in Word 2007 that functionality is broken. So, while you can still use SHIFT+F5 within an open document to go back to recent edit points, you can't use it on a freshly opened document to pick up where you left off. There is optimism that this bug will be fixed in the next version of Word.

tion (you have to scroll down to find it) is the Table option. If you press F5, then pick table in the left hand pane, you can have Word automatically take you to the next table in the document. Handy if you have quite a few and you want to step from one to the next.

The last operational hotkey I want to bring to your attention is one you may find yourself using a lot: **CTRL+Z.** Undo. It will undo whatever your last action was, at least within some reason. If you deleted some text and didn't mean to, CTRL+Z is your hero. If you lent your car to a teenager CTRL-Z doesn't really help.

Working with Text

There are several hotkeys available for setting the format of your text. Some of them you may be familiar with already, like **CTRL+B** to turn on boldface, **CTRL+I** for italics or **CTRL+U** to underline. Others may be a pleasant surprise. Did you know that **CTRL+SHIFT+C** will copy the formatting from a piece of text and **CTRL+SHIFT+V** will paste it? Yes, just like the format painter.

Maybe you need to select all of your text before applying (or removing) a particular bit of formatting. **CTRL+A** is your shortcut for that.

Want to increase the font size of your text? **CTRL+SHIFT+>** is the answer (that's a "greater than" sign, probably on the same button with the period on your keyboard). **CTRL+SHIFT+<** reduces the font size of the selected text. The increments are the same as the increments in the font size drop down (12, 14, 16 . . . 28, 36, 48 . . .). Or you can go point by point . . . **CTRL+]** increases the font size by 1 point while **CTRL+[** reduces it by 1 point.

In Chapter 4, we talked about how there is direct and indirect formatting. There may be times when you want to strip the direct formatting off of a paragraph in an effort to clean it up or troubleshoot an issue. To reset the formatting to the underlying style, just select the affected paragraph and press **CTRL+Spacebar** to remove the character formatting. **CTRL+Q** removes any paragraph formatting. **CTRL+SHIFT+N** returns the current selection back to the Normal style.

Sometimes when I'm typing I create a section title but forget to capitalize the first letter of each word. Or, maybe I was typing too fast to notice that I accidentally activated my CAPS LOCK key for the last sentence. Either way I may want to quickly change the case of my text. To do so I need only select the text, then press **SHIFT+F3** in order to toggle between the different case settings in word.

While I'm creating that section title, I usually want to assign a heading style to it. **CTRL+ALT+1** will assign Heading 1 style. **CTRL+ALT+2** will assign Heading 2 and so forth. If I want to adjust after I've assigned the heading style, then **CTRL+SHIFT+Left Arrow** and **CTRL+Shift+Right Arrow** will promote or demote through the heading styles.

Summary

Fast typists often find the keyboard to be preferable to the mouse. Taking your hands off the keyboard to use the mouse can slow you down and break your train of thought. Learn the keyboard shortcuts for the five or 10 most common commands you use and you may find that you save quite a bit of time over the course of your day. Not to mention the value of a regular CTRL+S. There, I just pressed it again myself!

Index

Note: Page numbers followed by an *f* indicate figures.

Activating Microsoft Office, 173
Add-ins, configuring, 169, 169*f*
Add-ins, troubleshooting, 178–179
Advanced word options, 158–167
Alignment, 67–68, 68*f*, 82
Anchor points, text alignment, 67
Arrange all, windows group, 38
Arrange group, 23–24, 24*f*
Authorities, table of, 26
Auto Text Feature. *See* Building
    Blocks
AutoCorrect, 53, 53*f*, 143–144, 144*f*,
    201
AutoFit, tables, 72
AutoFormat as you type, options,
    155–156, 155*f*
AutoHotKey, 145
Automating Word, 137–138
    auto correct feature, 143–144
    building blocks, 138–141
    macros, 141–143
    suggestions for using, 147–148
AutoRecover information, 157

Background printing, configuring, 165
Background saving, configuring, 166
Backgrounds, pages, 22–23
Backup copy, creating option, 165
Backups, document management and
    deleting, 116–117
Backups, restoring, 165

Balloons, 31*f*, 32, 104, 104*f*, 153
Bar tab, 70, 70*f*
Barcodes, envelopes, 129
Bibliography, 25–26, 94–95
Blank document, troubleshooting,
    179–180
Blank page button, 12, 12*f*
Blogging, 209–210, 209*f*, 210*f*
Blue lines, 159
Bookmarks, 15–16, 15*f*
Borders, formatting, 23, 66–67
Brackets, text in, troubleshooting,
    185
Breaks command, 20–22, 22*f*
Bring to front, text, 24
Building blocks, 138–141
    creating a block, 138–141
    determining use of, tips for, 147–
        148
    editing text, 140
    insertion, configuring, 139–140
    organizer, 18, 140, 140*f*
    sharing, 139
    troubleshooting, 185
Bulleted lists, 87–93
Buttons, adding to, 6–7

Calculate feature, 211
Capitalization, changing, 9–10, 154
Captions, 26
Cassette tape icon, 142
CEIP. *See* Customer Experience Im-
    provement Program
Center justification, 63

The Lawyer's Guide to Collaboration Tools and Technologies: Smart Ways to Work Together
By Dennis Kennedy and Tom Mighell
This first-of-its-kind guide for the legal profession shows you how to use standard technology you already have and the latest "Web 2.0" resources and other tech tools, like Google Docs, Microsoft Office and Share-Point, and Adobe Acrobat, to work more effectively on projects with colleagues, clients, co-counsel and even opposing counsel. In *The Lawyer's Guide to Collaboration Tools and Technologies: Smart Ways to Work Together*, well-known legal technology authorities Dennis Kennedy and Tom Mighell provides a wealth of information useful to lawyers who are just beginning to try these tools, as well as tips and techniques for those lawyers with intermediate and advanced collaboration experience.

The Lawyer's Guide to Marketing on the Internet, Third Edition
By Gregory H. Siskind, Deborah McMurray, and Richard P. Klau
In today's competitive environment, it is critical to have a comprehensive online marketing strategy that uses all the tools possible to differentiate your firm and gain new clients. The Lawyer's Guide to Marketing on the Internet, in a completely updated and revised third edition, showcases practical online strategies and the latest innovations so that you can immediately participate in decisions about your firm's Web marketing effort. With advice that can be implemented by established and young practices alike, this comprehensive guide will be a crucial component to streamlining your marketing efforts.

The Lawyer's Guide to Adobe Acrobat, Third Edition
By David L. Masters
This book was written to help lawyers increase productivity, decrease costs, and improve client services by moving from paper-based files to digital records. This updated and revised edition focuses on the ways lawyers can benefit from using the most current software, Adobe® Acrobat 8, to create Portable Document Format (PDF) files.

PDF files are reliable, easy-to-use, electronic files for sharing, reviewing, filing, and archiving documents across diverse applications, business processes, and platforms. The format is so reliable that the federal courts' Case Management/Electronic Case Files (CM/ECF) program and state courts that use Lexis-Nexis File & Serve have settled on PDF as the standard.

You'll learn how to:

- Create PDF files from a number of programs, including Microsoft Office
- Use PDF files the smart way
- Markup text and add comments
- Digitally, and securely, sign documents
- Extract content from PDF files
- Create electronic briefs and forms

The Electronic Evidence and Discovery Handbook: Forms, Checklists, and Guidelines
By Sharon D. Nelson, Bruce A. Olson, and John W. Simek
The use of electronic evidence has increased dramatically over the past few years, but many lawyers still struggle with the complexities of electronic discovery. This substantial book provides lawyers with the templates they need to frame their discovery requests and provides helpful advice on what they can subpoena. In addition to the ready-made forms, the authors also supply explanations to bring you up to speed on the electronic discovery field. The accompanying CD-ROM features over 70 forms, including, Motions for Protective Orders, Preservation and Spoliation Documents, Motions to Compel, Electronic Evidence Protocol Agreements, Requests for Production, Internet Services Agreements, and more. Also included is a full electronic evidence case digest with over 300 cases detailed!

The 2009 Solo and Small Firm Legal Technology Guide
By Sharon D. Nelson, Esq., John W. Simek, and Michael C. Maschke
This annual guide is the only one of its kind written to help solo and small firm lawyers find the best technology for their dollar. You'll find the most current information and recommendations on computers, servers, networking equipment, legal software, printers, security products, smart phones, and anything else a law office might need. It's written in clear, easily understandable language to make implementation easier if you choose to do it yourself, or you can use it in conjunction with your IT consultant. Either way, you'll learn how to make technology work for you.

The Law Firm Associate's Guide to Personal Marketing and Selling Skills
By Catherine Alman MacDonagh and Beth Marie Cuzzone
This is the first volume in ABA's new groundbreaking Law Firm Associates Development Series, created to teach important skills that associates and other lawyers need to succeed at their firms, but that they may have not learned in law school. This volume focuses on personal marketing and sales skills. It covers creating a personal marketing plan, finding people within your target market, preparing for client meetings, "asking" for business, realizing marketing opportunities, keeping your clients, staying in touch with your network inside and outside the firm, and more. An accompanying trainer's manual illustrating how to best structure the sessions and use the book is available to firms to facilitate group training sessions.

Many law firms expect their new associates to hit the ground running when they are hired on. Although firms often take the time to bring these associates up to speed on client matters, they can be reluctant to invest the time needed to train them how to improve personal skills such as marketing. This book will serve as a brief, easy-to-digest primer for associates on how to develop and use marketing and selling techniques.

/BA LawPracticeManagementSection
MARKETING • MANAGEMENT • TECHNOLOGY • FINANCE

The Lawyer's Guide to Concordance
By Liz M. Weiman

In this age, when trial outcomes depend on the organization of electronic data discovery, *The Lawyer's Guide to Concordance* reveals how attorneys and staff can make Concordance the most powerful tool in their litigation arsenal. Using this easy-to-read hands-on reference guide, individuals who are new to Concordance can get up-to-speed quickly, by following its step-by-step instructions, exercises, and time-saving shortcuts. For those already working with Concordance, this comprehensive resource provides methods, strategies, and technical information to further their knowledge and success using this robust program.

Inside The Lawyer's Guide to Concordance readers will also find:
- Techniques to effectively search database records, create tags for the results, customize printed reports, redline and redact images, create production sets
- Strategies to create and work with transcript, e-document, and e-mail databases, load files from vendors, manage images, troubleshoot, and more
- Real-world case studies from law firms in the United States and England describing Concordance features that have improved case management

The Lawyer's Guide to Increasing Revenue: Unlocking the Profit Potential in Your Firm
By Arthur G. Greene

Are you ready to look beyond cost-cutting and toward new revenue opportunities? Learn how you can achieve growth using the resources you already have at your firm. Discover the factors that affect your law firm's revenue production, how to evaluate them, and how to take specific action steps designed to increase your returns. You'll learn how to best improve performance and profitability in each of the key areas of your law firm, such as billable hours and rates, client relations and intake, collections and accounts receivable, technology, marketing, and others. Included with the book is a CD-ROM featuring sample policies, worksheets, plans, and documents designed to aid implementation of the ideas presented in the book. Let this resource guide you toward a profitable and sustainable future!

The Lawyer's Guide to Strategic Planning: Defining, Setting, and Achieving Your Firm's Goals
By Thomas C. Grella and Michael L. Hudkins

This practice-building resource is your guide to planning dynamic strategic plans and implementing them at your firm. You'll learn about the actual planning process and how to establish goals in key planning areas such as law firm governance, competition, opening a new office, financial management, technology, marketing and competitive intelligence, client development and retention, and more. The accompanying CD-ROM contains a wealth of policies, statements, and other sample documents. If you're serious about improving the way your firm works, increasing productivity, making better decisions, and setting your firm on the right course, this book is the resource you need.

The Lawyer's Guide to Microsoft Excel 2007
By John C. Tredennick

Did you know Excel can help you analyze and present your cases more effectively or help you better understand and manage complex business transactions? Designed as a hands-on manual for beginners as well as longtime spreadsheet users, you'll learn how to build spreadsheets from scratch, use them to analyze issues, and to create graphics presentation. Key lessons include:

- Spreadsheets 101: How to get started for beginners
- Advanced Spreadsheets: How to use formulas to calculate values for settlement offers, and damages, business deals
- Simple Graphics and Charts: How to make sophisticated charts for the court or to impress your clients
- Sorting and filtering data and more

How to Start and Build a Law Practice, Platinum Fifth Edition
By Jay G. Foonberg

This classic ABA bestseller has been used by tens of thousands of lawyers as the comprehensive guide to planning, launching, and growing a successful practice. It's packed with over 600 pages of guidance on identifying the right location, finding clients, setting fees, managing your office, maintaining an ethical and responsible practice, maximizing available resources, upholding your standards, and much more. You'll find the information you need to successfully launch your practice, run it at maximum efficiency, and avoid potential pitfalls along the way. If you're committed to starting—and growing—your own practice, this one book will give you the expert advice you need to make it succeed for years to come.

The Lawyer's Guide to Microsoft Outlook 2007
By Ben M. Schorr

Outlook is the most used application in Microsoft Office, but are you using it to your greatest advantage? *The Lawyer's Guide to Microsoft Outlook 2007* is the only guide written specifically for lawyers to help you be more productive, more efficient and more successful. More than just email, Outlook is also a powerful task, contact, and scheduling manager that will improve your practice. From helping you log and track phone calls, meetings, and correspondence to archiving closed case material in one easy-to-store location, this book unlocks the secrets of "underappreciated" features that you will use every day. Written in plain language by a twenty-year veteran of law office technology and ABA member, you'll find:

- Tips and tricks to effectively transfer information between all components of the software
- The eight new features in Outlook 2007 that lawyers will love
- A tour of major product features and how lawyers can best use them
- Mistakes lawyers should avoid when using Outlook
- What to do when you're away from the office

30-Day Risk-Free Order Form
Call Today! 1-800-285-2221
Monday–Friday, 7:30 AM – 5:30 PM, Central Time

Qty	Title	LPM Price	Regular Price	Total
_____	The Lawyer's Guide to Collaboration Tools and Technologies: Smart Ways to Work Together (5110589)	$59.95	$ 89.95	$_____
_____	The Lawyer's Guide to Marketing on the Internet, Third Edition (5110585)	74.95	84.95	$_____
_____	The Lawyer's Guide to Adobe Acrobat, Third Edition (5110588)	49.95	79.95	$_____
_____	The Electronic Evidence and Discovery Handbook: Forms, Checklists, and Guidelines (5110569)	99.95	129.95	$_____
_____	The 2009 Solo and Small Firm Legal Technology Guide (5110658)	54.95	84.95	$_____
_____	The Law Firm Associate's Guide to Personal Marketing and Selling Skills (5110582)	39.95	49.95	$_____
_____	Trainer's Manual for the Law Firm Associate's Guide to Personal Marketing and Selling Skills (5110581)	49.95	59.95	$_____
_____	The Lawyer's Guide to Concordance (5110666)	49.95	69.95	$_____
_____	The Lawyer's Guide to Increasing Revenue (5110521)	59.95	79.95	$_____
_____	The Lawyer's Guide to Strategic Planning (5110520)	59.95	79.95	$_____
_____	The Lawyer's Guide to Microsoft Excel 2007 (5110665)	49.95	69.95	$_____
_____	How to Start and Build a Law Practice, Platinum Fifth Edition (5110508)	57.95	69.95	$_____
_____	The Lawyer's Guide to Microsoft Outlook 2007 (5110661)	49.99	69.99	$_____

*Postage and Handling	
$10.00 to $24.99	$5.95
$25.00 to $49.99	$9.95
$50.00 to $99.99	$12.95
$100.00 to $349.99	$17.95
$350 to $499.99	$24.95

**Tax
DC residents add 5.75%
IL residents add 9.00%

*Postage and Handling	$_____
**Tax	$_____
TOTAL	$_____

PAYMENT

❑ Check enclosed (to the ABA)

❑ Visa   ❑ MasterCard   ❑ American Express

_____
Account Number   Exp. Date   Signature

Name _____ Firm _____

Address _____

City _____ State _____ Zip _____

Phone Number _____ E-Mail Address _____

Guarantee

If—for any reason—you are not satisfied with your purchase, you may return it within 30 days of receipt for a complete refund of the price of the book(s). No questions asked!

Mail: ABA Publication Orders, P.O. Box 10892, Chicago, Illinois 60610-0892
♦ **Phone: 1-800-285-2221** ♦ **FAX: 312-988-5568**

E-Mail: abasvctr@abanet.org ♦ **Internet: http://www.lawpractice.org/catalog**